Understanding Advanced Second-Language Reading

What distinguishes this book is its broad, yet thorough, view of theory, process, and research on adult second-language reading. Offering extensive discussions of upper-register second-language texts (both expository and narrative) that advanced second-language readers encounter daily across the globe, it also presents an assessment schema for second-language text comprehension as well as for the assessment of teaching.

Understanding Advanced Second-Language Reading:

- includes languages other than English in the discussion of second-language reading
- is firmly anchored in a theory of second-language reading—the concept of compensatory processing
- emphasizes the multi-dimensionality and dynamic nature of L2 reading development
- focuses on comprehension of upper-register texts
- balances theory and instructional practices.

Filling the need for a coherent, theoretically consistent, and research-based portrait of how literate adolescents and adults comprehend, and *learn to* comprehend, at greater levels of sophistication and whether that ability can be enhanced by instruction, this is a must-have resource for reading and second-language researchers, students, and teachers.

Elizabeth B. Bernhardt is Professor of German Studies; John Roberts Hale Director of the Language Center; and The W. Warren Shelden University Fellow in Undergraduate Education at Stanford University.

Understanding Advanced Second-Language Reading

Elizabeth B. Bernhardt
Stanford University

Routledge
Taylor & Francis Group

NEW YORK AND LONDON

First published 2011
by Routledge
711 Third Avenue, New York, NY 10017

Simultaneously published in the UK
by Routledge
2 Park Square, Milton Park, Abingdon, Oxon OX14 4RN

Routledge is an imprint of the Taylor & Francis Group, an informa business

© 2011 Taylor and Francis

Typeset in Minion and Gill Sans by Swales & Willis Ltd, Exeter, Devon

Library of Congress Cataloging-in-Publication Data
Bernhardt, Elizabeth Buchter.
  Understanding advanced second-language reading / Elizabeth B. Bernhardt.
    p. cm.
  1. English language—Study and teaching—Foreign speakers—Evaluation.
  2. Reading (Higher education)—Ability testing.
  3. Second language acquisition—Research—Methodology. I. Title.
  PE1128.A2B4577 2010
  418.0071—dc22
  2010004771

ISBN 13: 978-0-415-87909-5 (hbk)
ISBN 13: 978-0-415-87910-1 (pbk)
ISBN 13: 978-0-203-85240-8 (ebk)

Contents

Preface

Toward the end of the writing of the penultimate draft of this book in Fall, 2008, Michael Kamil and I were commissioned by the International Reading Association to write the introduction to the 100th anniversary edition of *The Psychology and Pedagogy of Reading* (1908) by Edmund Burke Huey. Even though I had read Huey as a graduate student and had often cited him for his commitment to understanding reading by taking the perspective of second-language reading, the real import of Huey struck me only in my 21st-century re-reading of the book. Beyond the sheer content of Huey's work that establishes the framework for reading research in the 20th century lies Huey's moral imperative: "We are all working toward daylight in the matter, and many of the discrepancies of facts and theories are more apparent than real" (p. 102). He couples this sentiment with the assurance that "the slightest improvement [in reading performance] ... means the rendering of a great service to the human race" (p. 421). His words shape the ethic for this volume: first, that educational research is about building clarification, not about destroying the arguments of others; and second, that understanding the reading process and rendering it more approachable for readers is fundamentally a research-based service endeavor rather than merely an academic one.

Re-reading Huey also provided grounding in how to approach a task that tries to capture what is known about an academic field in a reasonable, responsible, and engaging manner. Huey maintained an academic stance throughout his book, but he also made clear to the reader that he was *one* person with *a* view; not the final or even the exclusive view on the topic. I hope that I have done the same, by referring to my previous volume on the topic and by reverting to first-person now and again throughout the text. I have also tried to be as concrete as possible, offering examples in a variety of languages across an array of contemporary topics. I have also speculated in a way that one cannot speculate in the context of a research article but only in the context of a personal treatment of a topic. Again, I took guidance from Huey who reminds us that:

> Of course no two authors would select the same material for such a work upon reading. I have endeavored to present the most meaningful facts, and

those researches in which more or less definite results have been reached. Completeness of treatment and of reference is out of the question in a subject having such various and intricate ramifications. (p. x)

Understanding Advanced Second-Language Reading is a follow-up to *Reading Development in a Second Language* (1991) as well as an expansion and theoretical extension. Since the writing and publication of *Reading Development in a Second-Language* almost two decades ago both research about the area and perspectives on it have become more sophisticated, more elaborate, more precise, and more politicized. Fundamentally, since its publication, an acknowledgment of the complexities of second-language reading moved into the mainstream of American education. Even though many second-language researchers had attempted over the years to bring visibility to the area by connections to mainstream reading researchers, it took the discovery by these mainstream researchers themselves to accept second-language reading research as a viable, self-sustainable entity. There are several reasons for this epiphany that have come to the surface over the past decade. First of all, ignoring the enormous increase of second-language readers at every dimension and level of education was no longer possible. Federal demands for improved education and access for all mandated an understanding of children, adolescents, and adults needing to learn in a language they often do not speak well or know in any substantive or concrete way. Major comprehensive, privately or federally-funded syntheses such as the *RAND Reading Study Group Report* (2002), *Report of the National Reading Panel: Teaching Children to Read* (NICHD, 2000), *The Report of the National Literacy Panel on Language-Minority Children and Youth* (August & Shanahan, 2006), and *Effective Literacy and English Language Instruction for English Learners in the Elementary Grades* (Gersten et al., 2007) among others, all offered the critical recognition that a research-based understanding of second-language reading needed to become an important component of national education policy. A second but no less compelling reason is that the decade and a half since the publication of *Reading Development in a Second Language* was marked, too, by a significant increase in the American and British presence around the globe prompted principally by war, but also by natural disaster in areas in which languages other than English dominate. The need for English speakers to become users and comprehenders of languages other than English, in short order, and to levels well beyond survival, tourist expressions was equally critical. Time for translation was no longer available; time had also run out for a simplistic view of cross-cultural understanding held by some and needed to be replaced by sophisticated, experienced, and hypersensitive users of an array of global languages. A third reason for the public awakening to the reading of second languages is rooted in the technology revolution. *Reading Development in a Second Language*, written in 1989–1990 and published in 1991, was written before the internet revolution and well before mass public access to cable programming across the globe. The virtually universal access to technology and, hence, to an expansive array of cost-free authentic materials, both written and aural, enabled a new kind of mass literacy in which all persons could look at a primary source and, with appropriate knowledge, understand it without an interpretive intermediary. Technology did for the need for cross-cultural understanding what no amount of rational argument from academics could.

There are significant ironies at play here. Arguably, second-language reading is the dominant global literacy. Millions across the globe routinely access expository information from the internet written in English—a second language for the overwhelming majority. Further, millions conduct academic work and exchange information via a lingua franca—English—again, a non-native tongue for the overwhelming majority. This academic work is not centered on the how-to's of getting to the train station and or of how to read a theater time schedule, but on advances in pharmacology, on up-to-the-minute information on meteorology; about current news and events; on the analysis of literary text; or on a thousand other areas that characterize the contemporary world. Yet we know very little about how high-level, rapid and sophisticated processing occurs and the extent to which it matches native-speaker processing given equivalent interest and background levels. More significant, however, is that we know even less about how to bring readers to sophisticated, advanced uses of literacy in a second language. Indeed, many learners achieve such sophistication, but the overwhelming majority appears not to. Further, little published evidence exists about the learners who do reach fluency in the reading and processing of sophisticated text. Meeting the challenges set forth by these new circumstances is absolutely critical for the research community.

A second significant irony is the relationship between reading development in a second language and general second-language development. Little documented cross-over in the research fields exists. Data in second-language acquisition have remained confined principally to evidence about speaking or writing. There are some obvious reasons: both speaking and writing are productive and are, therefore, visible. Reading comprehension, much in contrast, is relatively invisible and can only be inferred, never directly accountable for processes in the way that one can hear or see that a particular linguistic form has been integrated or not. Perhaps most importantly is that reading has not been included in second-language acquisition (SLA) theory. A theory failing to acknowledge the powerful role that literacy plays in all human learning and interaction in the 21st century is wanting indeed. In fact, in many SLA theories, input is a major variable in theories of acquisition. Failing to consider the importance of how much language surrounds an individual learner in writing and how that kind of input does or does not have an impact on linguistic form acquisition is clearly an arena to be researched, discussed, and acknowledged. Researching learners in technologized societies without giving consideration to the amount and quality of print environment is a significant shortcoming in a field as critical as SLA. An important sign on this horizon, however, is Han and D'Angelo (2009) who have written on the complexities of reading for comprehension and reading for acquisition.

Understanding Advanced Second-Language Reading casts a contemporary light on these issues, synthesizing new data, explicating new theory, and directing its discussion toward learning to read in the upper reaches of complicated text, or what is called in the contemporary argot, the reading of superior-level, upper-register, advanced texts, referring to texts with low frequency and highly nuanced vocabulary, or texts that have more unstated thought than articulated words encased in a syntax far beyond that which appears in oral speech. *Understanding Advanced Second-Language Reading* also concentrates on instruction and assessment. Ultimately, instruction (for lack of a better word at the moment) will take place within academic contexts that are not labeled "language courses" but, rather, courses in which specific content learning must take place from text characterized by genre-specific elements. Whether instructors sense the extent to which they have responsibility to teach how to glean information from text is a serious issue. Moreover, whether instructors have strategies for doing so, and which mechanisms exist to tell both instructor and reader/learner whether text interpretation is accurate, remain areas that must be understood. In the precise and significant arena of using second-language texts to make decisions; to establish policy; or to guide courses of action in the modern world a critical skill is capturing accurately and interpreting appropriately the content and intention of texts written by persons from other backgrounds; other world views; other linguistic systems.

Understanding Advanced Second-Language Reading does not, of course, pretend to hold an exclusive answer to these dilemmas; rather, it tries to guide researchers, teachers, and learners through the fascinating cognitive, social, and procedural labyrinth of adult second-language text processing. Indeed, a number of important volumes, such as Grabe and Stoller (2002), Grabe (2009), Han and Anderson (2009), Hedgecock and Ferris (2009), Hudson (2007), Koda (2005), and Swaffar and Arens (2006) have appeared over the years on the subject and I have contemplated, wrestled with, and been influenced by, their insights. Yet, none of these volumes provides a theory to accommodate the many complexities of second-language reading research which, by rights, must include a theory of instruction. The volumes tend to do one (research synthesis) or the other (instruction) but rarely both. Ironically, then, in spite of the growth of interest in the area of second-language reading, no coherent, theoretically consistent, and research-based portrait of how literate adolescents and adults comprehend and, better said, *learn to* comprehend at greater levels of sophistication, and whether that ability can be enhanced by instruction, has yet appeared. *Understanding Advanced Second-Language Reading* is meant to fill this gap. It addresses the following questions: What evidence has reading research produced since 1991 to help explicate the development of adolescents and adults in understanding second-language texts? How do these findings reconcile with the most current model of second-language reading? Do these findings mandate a revision or an adaptation of that model or do they call for a back-to-the-drawing board effort? What do these findings say specifically about learning to understand very complicated, upper-register texts such as literary and interpretive essay texts? How should we approach the teaching of upper-register texts? How should we assess both the teaching and the learning of comprehension in a second language? Which research lines should we pursue?

Understanding Advanced Second-Language Reading, like *Reading Development in a Second Language*, is a personal statement regarding reading in a second language. Beyond getting older and (I hope) wiser, the book is still touched by the spirit of Dust Bowl empiricism that my mentors at the University of Minnesota inspired me with. I have never rejected the need to examine learners in their learning and comprehending of second-language texts. I have often tried to conduct these examinations as naturalistically as possible, but I have just as often observed within the context of interventions and deliberately and consciously designed experiments. In contrast to the previous volume, which was built more on research and less on experience, this volume provides a more balanced perspective—a greater level of first-hand instructional experience coupled with research. The volume also represents a continued yet renewed ethical commitment to understanding and assisting users of second-language literacy. The volume reflects the belief espoused in my commentary in *Reading Research Quarterly* (2003):

> As the world becomes both more and less complicated and as English continues to grow in dominance on the world stage, risks become greater of peoples actually becoming more separate from each other than closer. As English and English-speaking values grow in influence and machine translation deceives us into complacency about the need for second languages, the danger becomes one of losing culturally-authentic interpretive knowledge and abilities. It is through text and through text analysis in many languages that these abilities will be sustained and knowledge of interpretation will grow. The cost of monolingualism and monoliteracy is great. A world in which expression is exclusively on the terms of and within the perspectives of the English-speaking world is indeed a dangerous place. (p. 115)

Understanding Advanced Second-Language Reading intends to serve as a reminder of the importance of diversity and as a caution that globalization is, at its root, culturally superficial.

As a personal statement, the book is based in the multiple iterations of the model of second-language reading originally posited in *Reading Development in a Second Language*. Over the years, the model has been revised on the basis of a growing, reliable data base. The current model (Bernhardt, 2005), used as a backdrop as well as an organizing principle for this volume, is influenced by and dependent upon the concept of compensatory processing (Stanovich, 1980). Compensatory processing refers to how various knowledge sources that come to the aid of a reader and how these knowledge sources influence and assist each other during comprehension. Key knowledge sources reiterated repeatedly in this volume are *first-language literacy, second-language grammatical knowledge,* and *other.* In contrast to the model posited in 1991, the compensatory model does not view reading in a second language as an additive two-dimensional process, but one that is multidimensional and dynamic. It argues that development is more about interaction in multiple spaces than it is about iteration. The metaphor used repeatedly in the volume is one akin to model construction rather than one similar to recurrent loops in a computer program. Compensatory theory is at the heart of each of the following chapters.

A similar, yet not identical, organization to *Reading Development in a Second Language* characterizes *Understanding Advanced Second-Language Reading.* *Reading Development in a Second Language* was organized inductively. It laid out a set of data. Data generated for the volume as well as a complete review of the published data base were discussed and then a generalized conclusion was formulated and vivified by the developmental model provided. The book then focused on instruction and assessment. This organizational pattern was meant to follow logically from the order in which effective teacher development takes place: a conceptualization; a period of learning what is known about a particular learning process; then concepts of instruction and assessment directed toward the particular phenomenon. The contrast with the present volume lies in its deductive nature. *Understanding Advanced Second-language Reading* takes as its premise a compensatory model of reading and analyzes research and instruction from that premise.

Specifically, Chapter 1, 'Exploring the Complexities of Second-Language Reading', renews and revitalizes the discussion of what a second language is and who its readers are. It also re-poses the question *What is reading?* again refocusing on social dimensions; cognitive dimensions; and sociocognitive dimensions and adding a compensatory dimension. Indeed, significant new, as well as modified perspectives, have emerged over the past decade, including those from the National Assessment of Educational Progress (NAEP) and from the Programme for International Student Assessment (PISA). *Understanding Advanced Second-Language Reading* attempts to capture these additions and modifications within a second-language framework. Chapter 1 also introduces perspectives on research and theory brought by views of particular text types. While *Reading Development in a Second Language* focused almost exclusively on expository text, *Understanding Advanced Second-Language Reading* recognizes the criticality of literary and other upper-register, advanced text types such as commentaries and essays, arguing that the reading and interpretation of these types of highly nuanced texts are, indeed, some of the more challenging of all second-language tasks and are, therefore, worthy of particular attention. *Reading Development in a Second Language* asserted the importance of literary text; *Understanding Advanced Second-Language Reading* expands the discussion to include other kinds of nuanced text. This chapter also examines reading as a part of proficiency-oriented language teaching. It discusses reading acquisition qua reading acquisition, but also reading in its role to enhance and buttress the other language skills; i.e., the relationships between and among reading, writing, speaking, and listening and how these relationships play out in classrooms.

Chapter 2, 'A Compensatory Theory of Second-Language Reading', focuses on models of second-language reading developed since *Reading Development in a Second Language.* In contrast to the model posited in *Reading Development in a Second Language,* constructed on the basis of qualitative data principally generated by means of recall performances, the model set forward in this volume captures the most critical finding of the last decade: the huge import of first-language literacy on the processing and comprehending of the second. Fundamentally, this acknowledgment of L1/L2 relationships accommodates a sociocognitive view at the macro level, but not at the microlevel—the individual reader level. Adapting Stanovich's 1980 framework and view of interaction as compensation for knowledge gaps, deficiencies, and misconceptualizations, this chapter alludes to unstated and unexplained variables, such as the role of motivation and affect in the second-language reading process. Chapter 2 also highlights the critical research shortages in a number of significant areas in second-language processing, most especially vocabulary acquisition in the context of comprehension and syntax. In contrast to *Reading Development in a Second Language,* which took a more descriptive approach to learning and instruction, *Understanding Advanced Second-Language Reading* is guided specifically by the model posited in this chapter. In other words, *Understanding Advanced Second-Language Reading* is more inductive in nature. It establishes a theory and then discusses instruction and assessment and the evaluation of instruction and learning in light of that particular theory.

Reading Development in a Second Language contained a lengthy discussion of individual research studies and their perspectives. Since its 1991 publication more than 200 additional research studies on adolescent and adult readers of second languages have appeared. These new studies appear in Chapter 3, 'Sketching the Landscape of Second-Language Reading Research', in a tabular form along with discussion of their implications. The discussion on certain topics is slightly abbreviated given the publication of a thorough research review in the *Handbook of Reading Research, Volume III* (Kamil, Mosenthal, Pearson, & Barr, 2000) and the greater emphasis is given to studies published since 1998. *Understanding Advanced Second-Language Reading* also reviews the research areas that were substantial in *Reading Development in a Second Language* (such as word recognition and phonological dimensions of text processing) and those that became more significant in light of new data (such as first language/second language relationships). *Understanding Advanced Second-Language Reading* also explicates particular phenomena regarding second-language text processing, such as automatic word recognition; the role of phonology; and affect and motivation.

An interesting phenomenon to note is that lines that were relatively easy to draw in 1991 in *Reading Development in a Second Language,* such as what was considered to be a 'study of background knowledge' or a 'study of oral versus silent reading' are, a decade and a half later, almost impossible to draw. Given greater research-based understandings and more sophisticated research designs, studies do not easily fall into specific categories because researchers have come to acknowledge and account for multiple variables involved in the second-language reading process. In many cases I have tried to examine each study for its contributions to an array of variables. Hence, the reader will encounter in *Understanding Advanced Second-Language Reading* an alphabetized list of second-language studies with the tables, rather than one that is categorized as in *Reading Development in a Second Language.*

The review of the studies tabulated is a *critical* review in the best sense of the word. It examines studies in light of their meeting of certain research standards also set over the past years. Questions posed within the context of each study are whether more than one text was employed in the data collection; whether subjects are differentiated according to native language background; and whether a first-language literacy level and a second-language grammatical knowledge level were established. *Understanding Advanced Second-Language Reading* argues that, without a set of fundamental research standards being met, the difficulty of comparing and contrasting findings in second-language reading research will remain and their synthesis will be elusive, if not impossible.

Chapters 4 and 5 focus specifically on sophisticated and nuanced upper-register text and its impact on learning, comprehension, and teaching. Chapter 4, 'Compensatory Theory in Second-Language Reading Instruction', takes as its point of departure the concept of teaching method and how scholars have suggested an approach to the teaching of second-language reading. While these approaches are important as guidelines within basic instructional settings, the chapter will argue that the approaches are fundamentally procedural and non-organic; in other words, they tend to focus on techniques rather than on comprehension processes. Perhaps more critically, they tend to ignore the first-language literacy knowledge that most second-language readers bring to the act of reading. The chapter offers an instructional procedure that takes first-language literacy into consideration and which intends to lead the individual reader toward independence. The chapter also highlights the growing importance of low-frequency vocabulary words in the reading of upper-register texts and provides some suggestions about using technology to buttress the learning of such words.

Chapter 5, 'Second-Language Readers and Literary Text', discusses the use of literary text for the learning of second-language reading. At the most obvious level, the chapter examines the kind of knowledge that one must have and/or (for second-language learners) must actually acquire, in order for comprehension to occur specifically regarding literary texts. At another level, though, this chapter tries to provide insights into the educational character of using literary texts as primary tools for literacy and language learning.

The chapter places literary reading within three major facets of the second-language comprehension process. First, the reader's current knowledge base—meaning the first language knowledge base—is a major contributing factor to the reconstruction of a second language text. This contribution ranges from: the linguistic level in which the more literate one is in the first language, the higher a given second-language performance is; to being able to retrieve the information from a second-language story that is compatible with first-language cultural patterns, but not retrieving incompatible information; and to conceptual issues. The chapter then acknowledges the manner and degree to which the L1 knowledge base interacts compensatorily with second-language linguistic abilities. The interaction takes the form of knowledge being able to override linguistic deficiencies (meaning that readers with low-level second-language skills can, in some contexts, exhibit high-level comprehension abilities) but also the form of being able to denigrate or negate actual language skills (meaning that readers with high-level language skills can doubt their own abilities when the text does not match their knowledge base). In parallel to *Reading Development in a Second Language*, which presented new data focused on knowledge sources for expository texts, *Understanding Advanced Second-Language Reading* also offers a new study—a longitudinal study of readers interacting with literary text against the backdrop of their prior knowledge. The new data also address the nature of the teaching context and the curriculum, as well as the more subtle question of language learning qua language learning and probes the relationship between the enhancement of the knowledge base and the development of the linguistic/language base. In other words, the chapter interrogates whether by aligning the knowledge base more closely or, said another way, by providing more compensatory power through cultural background knowledge, positive growth in the second-language linguistic base can actually be stimulated for advanced language learners.

Chapter 6, 'Assessing the Learning and Teaching of Comprehension in a Second Language', returns to one of the more controversial features advanced in *Reading Development in a Second Language*—the use of immediate recall for assessment purposes. This alternative in second-language reading contexts portrays the use of recall as a measure that is both quantitative and qualitative. With little, if any, test-development necessary, practitioners and researchers, for that matter, are able to ask students or subjects to read an array of passages and to provide extensive responses to those passages through immediate or even delayed recall. Practitioners are able to examine the recall patterns within the context of individual language structures as well as within the context of passage topic. Being able to examine student performance carefully enables teachers and researchers, as well as students and subjects, to diagnose grammatical and vocabulary abilities at an extremely sophisticated level. The problem with this alternative is that while it provides lots of "items" across many passages, it is relatively time-consuming to score. This dilemma frequently leaves practitioners with a "bad choice"; i.e., stuck, because of the constraints of resources, with a superficial score that is not terribly useful. *Understanding Advanced Second-Language Reading* continues to advocate for the use of recall. It demonstrates the development of a scoring matrix and how to import such a matrix into a spreadsheet. Lastly, the chapter provides an alternative method to the scoring of recall protocols, namely holistic rating on a 4-point scale. The opportunity-costs of rating versus scoring recall protocols are discussed as well as factors that appear to contribute to particular ratings vis à vis scorings.

Chapter 6 also examines teacher performance within the context of analyzing student learning and engagement and, therefore, effective teaching. By taking a learning rather than a performance perspective, the chapter offers suggestions for gauging student learning and for examining how teaching performances are evaluated. If instructors proceed in their teaching according to the principles outlined in the previous chapters about the process of reading in a second language, lessons will include dimensions that enable instructors to uncover the conceptual representations of text that readers construct; that enable instructors to realign the representations when they are inappropriate; that assist instructors in locating and diagnosing misunderstandings arising from cultural misconstructions, linguistic deficiencies, and from the conflation of the two; and that empower instructors to proceed with instruction in terms of sociocultural knowledge, in terms of linguistic knowledge, and in terms of analytic skills. The basic discussion in this chapter is the call to bring about programs that are consistent with the research base and that bring students to higher levels of linguistic proficiency and cultural appreciation, and to assess effective teaching accordingly.

'Continuing to Research Second-Language Reading', Chapter 7, reviews the research program set forth in *Reading Development in a Second Language,* examining the extent to which that program was fulfilled. It then argues for studies in the areas of technology support and innovation that include evaluations of computer software packages that currently exist for the development of comprehension, as well as technologies for word learning and translation. The chapter also urges the profession to conduct studies investigating effective teaching strategies as well as effective conceptualizations for teacher preparation for language learning courses that focus on texts in the upper registers. A subset of these studies must include questions of effective literature instruction. Clearly, the instruction of literature is linked to interpretive processes that are unique in comprehension. Finally, the chapter focuses on the development of research into the compensatory model. Far more precise specifications of variables in the current model should be determined as well as studies attempting to falsify various dimensions of the model. Only through scientific rigor can the model be strengthened and developed.

Reading is an interactive process; writing a book about reading is even more interactive. Over the years, I have been privileged to receive attention about reading in a second language from multiple sources—from my own students, colleagues in the reading and applied linguistics fields, and from secondary and postsecondary teachers. I have been influenced by their reactions and commentary—both positive and negative. On the positive side, this book tries to expand upon features that were acclaimed in *Reading Development in a Second Language*, such as the extensive literature review and the conceptual framework that was at once cognitive and social. There were times, however, in which I felt no one ever read beyond the literature review and the model posited. In *Reading Development in a Second Language*, I tried very hard to provide an instructional model as well as a discussion of the importance of different types of texts, but that portion was ignored. I accept as a personal failure my inability to communicate effectively and will try with many of the same concepts again. The work in *Reading Development in a Second Language*, on the other hand, was also often criticized for its reliance on recall as a measure of comprehension and as a gauge for interpretation. Issues of validity continue to be raised. I remain as unconvinced of the invalid nature of recall as my critics do of its validity. Hence, the reader will find a continued use of recall as *a* tool used to provide insight and understanding in the second-language comprehension process. Of course, criticism is better than no response at all. *Reading Development in a Second Language* was often ignored because of its references to languages other than English and because of its insistence on permitting second-language readers to express their understandings in their dominant language. The book was often dismissed as *foreign language* in emphasis. Yet I will contend even more forcefully now that most language learners across the globe, admittedly learners of English, are *foreign* language learners. They are in contexts in which the dominant language environment (Chinese, Russian, Ukrainian, and so forth and so on) is not the one they are studying. To pretend otherwise is simply foolish. For teachers not to be able to use the strengths that learners bring with them is wrong and for researchers to simply ignore this fact is irresponsible. Of several additional volumes published in the past years I could find little evidence of a consideration of languages other than English. Indeed, studies might be cited that employed readers from an array of language backgrounds, but any significant discussion of language background and its influence on learning and teaching is absent. This volume returns to this particular point several times in the chapters that follow.

I have been blessed over the past decade to get to know elementary school teachers and researchers and to observe first-hand the challenges of teaching young children to read in a second language. I am neither so arrogant nor so unwise as to make claims within the context of this book about how children and their teachers go about this process. I urge readers seeking information about how children cope with and learn two literacies (and sometimes one literacy that is not a home literacy) to turn to experts in that field. While I examine some of the issues surrounding children and second-language literacy in Chapter 1, I go no further. I write this not with pride, but with admiration for those who have the sensitivity and knowledge to work in this critical area. There is a continued need for programmatic research with young children and their teachers. Without research-based knowledge generated in elementary schools with young children, there can never be a fully developed theory of second-language reading. Perhaps even more critical in this area is the need to quell some of the palpable phobia that exists among many classroom teachers of children who speak languages other than English *about* languages other than English. The cultural dimensions of bilingualism (often derisively referred to as *food, folks, and fun*) are intuitively appealing and easy to work into classroom procedures. Who doesn't want to participate in folk festivals and, thereby, display *respect* for other cultures? But getting beyond this superficiality and into the heads of children, probing how much literacy they come to school with; the nature of literacy in the child's background culture; and, perhaps most importantly the linguistic structure of the language children arrive at school with is a significant challenge for teachers who have been given few practical or conceptual tools and who are more often than not monolingual. We must all acknowledge and accept the genuine responsibility that teachers have to children at the cognitive level. This responsibility implies that a teacher should try to understand some of the linguistic substance that individual children bring to school.

Another gap for others to fill is technology. In 1991 when *Reading Development in a Second Language* was first published, the question of how email was composed and read and how email would accommodate different character sets were areas of concern. More than a decade later, those areas of concern, while never actually researched in a second language, have become trivialities much like exploring the difference between a pen and a pencil. In the present context, key questions that need to be probed concern the nature of electronic text for second-language readers; how the processing of hypertext affects these readers; how the knowledge sources that second-language readers bring to using hypertext are activated and how these influence the navigation process. Parallel to research with children, the interactions of second-language text variables with electronic text need to be fully explored. That exploration will require researchers who are technically literate, knowledgeable about second-language reading, and cognizant of the first-language literacy research. Translation software and self-help conveniences such as electronic dictionaries attached to electronic text and independent, handheld technologies providing definitions, translations, parts of speech and other information also need to be researched thoroughly. The extent to which such devices can improve comprehension in the short term and whether there are any long-term benefits are important areas to consider. Ultimately, a question to pursue is whether live, teacher-based instruction can be effectively replaced by electronic means.

I noted in *Reading Development in a Second Language* that writing a book is both arrogant and humbling. It is arrogant because a one-person view is really not possible. To develop a view or a theory is to build on the work and insights of many others. And writing a book is humbling because one realizes how complex processes are and how many excellent thinkers are involved in trying to make sense of these complexities. Another bit of arrogance for which an apology is due is the excessive US-orientation of the present volume. On the one hand, the academic area of *reading* is very much a Western-oriented, English-speaking industry made up principally by scholars across North America, Australia, Great

Britain, and Israel. The research base, in other words, is by and large English-speaking (admittedly with some important contributions from Northern Europe, particularly The Netherlands). Yet, just because the bulk of published research appears to be English-speaking, it does not necessarily follow that these are the only scholars across the globe who think deeply about second-language reading. The dominance of English and English-based publishing outlets is perhaps far more the cause of this appearance. For my own ignorance of other lines of thought that exist in many other languages I apologize. Finally, I apologize for the overreliance on German as a foreign language in this volume. Although I have tried to provide examples in Spanish, French, Japanese, Arabic, Tagalog, Indonesian, and Urdu, I fully acknowledge these examples are not balanced. My excuses are two: German is the language in which I work and, given that German and English are Germanic languages, I am hoping that the reader can rely on his/her English-language knowledge to cope with some of the German examples. I have also tried to provide translations wherever necessary.

The task that the book sets for itself is providing a relatively exhaustive treatment of research and theory about second-language reading and how that theory predicts the performance of second-language readers across the globe; how readers can become proficient at comprehending nuanced upper-level texts and how they can maintain that proficiency independent of instruction; and directions for further thought, research, and theory development. *Understanding Advanced Second-Language Reading* is written in the hope that its research synthesis; its theory based on compensatory processing; and the applications of research and theory to learning and teaching will represent a tipping point for more useful and sophisticated analysis to assist second-language users in their comprehension and interpretation of texts. This is a tall order, but it is one that I put forth in the hope of honoring fine traditions in reading research. Huey (1908) reminded us long ago of both the importance of second-language reading and of the criticality of looking at the big picture of comprehension processes, from eye movement to interpretation. I have tried to stay true to Huey's challenge. Reflecting on the 19th century when he would have begun his career, Huey comments at the beginning of the 20th century:

> There yet remain to be written many most interesting chapters on the psycho-physiological phases of reading, which will be made possible as investigation proceeds further. The work that has already been done by many hands and in many lands illustrates well how the federated science of the world is making solid progress with specific problems, and bears promise of a day when education shall rest on foundations better grounded than were the individual unverified opinions about "Reading," for instance, even twenty-five years ago. (p. 184)

The 21st century has begun with the efforts toward the conduct of large research syntheses in reading. These syntheses have challenged the field and helped to enhance teacher education and, concomitantly, the reading abilities of many. This press has provided untold insight and motivation.

This volume has had many titles. Options were *Second-Language Reading as a Language and Literacy Process*; *Reading Research and Practice in a Second Language*; *Language and Literacy Processes in Second-Language Reading*; *Second-Language Reading as a Compensatory Literacy and Language Process*; *Second-Language Reading as a Compensatory Process*; as well as *Second-Language Reading as a Trialogic Bakhtinian Process* all of which had postmodern subtitles of one sort or another. Upon submission, the book was entitled *Understanding Second-Language Reading*. Reviewers were quick to point out that even this simple title needed a subtitle and to note moreover that there was a major emphasis in the volume on upper-register texts read by adults. This led to a further suggested title of *Understanding Adult Second-Language Reading* to which I responded negatively because of ambiguities inserted by the word adult. I wanted to make sure that teachers of younger learners did not feel excluded and that they would be invited to view the entire developmental process of learning to read in a second language. I also wanted to make sure that no matter the age of the reader, success in reading second languages would ultimately bring them to upper-level, complicated, advanced texts. Even the final compromise title, *Understanding Advanced Second-Language Reading*, brings forth potential ambiguities with which I am uncomfortable. *Advanced* in the context of this volume refers to *upper-register* or *complicated* authentic text. It does *not* refer to the conceptualization of *Advanced* as a point on a scale in the proficiency-based use of the word *advanced* embodied in the ACTFL-FSI framework or in the Common European Framework. The title emphasizes text potentially and may not bring forward process explicitly. So be it. Obviously, the thought in this book represents the hard work of many persons, or as Huey noted "by many hands in many lands." The flaws in any interpretations set forth in this volume are clearly mine. I write in the hope that the volume provides a platform for significant progress in all dimensions of second-language reading.

Acknowledgments

I want to acknowledge my most important research legacy—my PhD students: Yoshiko Saito, Michael Everson, Leslie Schrier, Diep Nguyen, Diane Tedick, Mary Therese Berry, Mary Crerand, Vicky Berkemeyer, Mahdu Parashar, Salem Aweiss, Salim Khaldieh, Roger Minert, Michelline Chalhoub-Deville, Judith Brisbois, Frank Gahren, Peter Heinz, Kim Griffin, JoAnn Hammadou, Thomas Destino, Jean LeLoup, Tona Dickerson, Marjorie Demel, John Angell, Ellen Cowley, Carolyn Mendez, and Per Urlaub. While many of them did pursue investigations of second-language reading and others did not, they all enhanced my life and sharpened my analytic skills and I am very grateful to have been blessed by my interaction with such wonderful intellects.

Many thanks to Alys George, to Helen Kim Chou, and to Kate McQueen who diligently worked with me to fact check, to comb journals and books for important citations, and who painstakingly corrected my incessant bibliographic sloppiness. Their patience and interest in the book were heartening. Alys' added gracious cheerleading and tough-minded cross-checking were particularly helpful when I could see no light at the end of this very long tunnel. Thanks also to Eve Guianan who exhibited infinite patience in working with me on the artwork for this book. And much appreciation to my co-workers and native informants Patricia de Castries, Monica Brillantes, Silfia Asningtias, Ramzi Salti, Yoshiko Matsumoto, and Shahzad Bashir, as well as colleagues David Red and Shabbir Gilani, for their willingness to help me find and understand examples of texts. And special thanks to Karin Crawford who collaborated with me on the data gathering for the assessment chapter. She did much of the qualitative analysis in that section. Finally, I want to acknowledge Joan Molitoris who would stop her own work to help me think through points particularly about upper-register texts and literary analysis. I appreciate her wisdom and good judgment.

I also want to express my appreciation to John Hennessy, President of Stanford University, who has been a great cheerleader and instrumental in acquiring the Endowment for the Directorship of the Stanford Language Center. The Endowment was bestowed by Bruce and Elizabeth Dunlevie and named in honor of their close friend, John Hale, professor of classics and director of the liberal studies program at the University of Louisville. The support of this endowment from the Dunlevies has made *Understanding Advanced Second-Language Reading* possible. The following authors and publishers graciously granted permission to reprint figures from their publications: Figure 2.3 from Barbara Wing, *Listening, Reading, Writing: Analysis and Application*, Northeast Conference; Figure 2.5 from Michael Kamil, Peter Mosenthal, David Pearson, and Rebecca Barr, *Handbook of Reading Research, Volume III*, Erlbaum and Routledge; Figure 2.6 from Mary McGroarty, *Annual Review of Applied Linguistics*, Cambridge University Press; and Figure 4.1 from Elfrieda Hiebert, *Reading More, Reading Better*, Guilford Press.

I appreciate the hard work and good cheer of Rachel Hutchings for her careful copy-editing. A special note of thanks to Dr. Richard Willis, Production Manager, Swales & Willis Ltd, and to Sara Stone, Production Editor at Routledge, for their careful attention to this book and for their patience. Finally, I am especially grateful to Naomi Silverman, Acquisitions Editor at Taylor & Francis, for believing in me and in this project.

Clearly, being married to Michael Kamil, a person who embodies the highest standards of scholarship, hard work, "big picture-ness," and concern for all to learn to read and comprehend has been a dramatic influence and inspiration in the completion of this volume. I am eternally grateful for his support, harsh and targeted criticism, and unwavering assistance.

Chapter 1

Exploring the Complexities of Second-Language Reading

Reading in a second language has led an interestingly schizophrenic existence over the centuries as both universe and as subset. For example, European and American history underline that reading was at one time the *only* purpose for learning a foreign language. Howatt (1991) reminds us that reading in 19th-century Europe was "a more practical and useful objective than learning to speak" (p. 154). The same view held in American education circles in the early 20th century when the National Education Association's Committee of Ten declared that "foreign language instruction in American schools should be for reading only" (Bernhardt, 1998, p. 48) and that only the most gifted students should pursue it and pursue it to the level of "approximating reading in the mother tongue" (Coleman & Fife, 1949, p. 167). This declaration was not merely reflective of what educators felt was important in the American school curriculum; it also underlined the social status linked to being able to read another language. Huey (1908), in fact, refers to reading in another language as the "acme of scholarship" (p. 4), underlining what I referred to as the "stigma of elitism" with which American foreign language instruction still struggles (Bernhardt, 1998, p. 49). After the Second World War, when the oral approach to language learning was seen to be of value, reading then became a subset of the language learning curriculum, a supporting character in the project. In that role, it buttressed language learning dimensions, in particular the learning of grammatical form. *Reading Development in a Second Language* noted the importance of reading within the field of language teaching because of the durability of reading skills as juxtaposed to speaking skills that attrite rapidly. Unquestionably, reading affords the second-language learner the luxury of time that is inconceivable with online spoken discourse and it provides an arena for linguistic explorations that cannot be approached through aural channels. With time, learners accompanied by grammars and dictionaries can, in theory, "decode" a passage; in speaking or in listening there is no time available to use ancillaries. Given the time factor, reading is often used in instructional settings as practice material. In fact, texts are often used to illustrate particular grammatical features that learners are meant to acquire. Or texts are written "around" particular semantic fields to ease the learners' vocabulary burden. In fact, much of beginning language instruction focuses on the instrumentality of written texts for language learning purposes or as material for "translation practice, grammatical analysis, vocabulary study and, finally, test questions" (Bergethon & Braun, 1963, p. ix). Any exploration of second-language reading should surely acknowledge the multiplicity of variables and conceptualizations at play in any discussion of it in order to provide credible insight into the process. This has rarely been the case within the research area of second-language reading.

Confused Concepts of Language and Culture

When *Reading Development in a Second Language* was written in the late 1980s and published in the early 1990s, reading in a second language was essentially a subfield of foreign language education and applied linguistics. While professional conferences on literacy lent program space occasionally to second-language research, the field of second-language reading was considered to be derivative, relying on first-language beliefs, models, and research designs (Weber, 1991). As the years passed, and second-language learners essentially grew up in schools, it became clearer that the concerns should not be, and could not be, exclusively on English-as-a-Second-Language learning (ESL) but, rather, needed to focus on higher-level literacy skills. The model of learning language within two years of instruction producing new Americans fluent in school English was simply not viable. Consequently, the area of second-language reading broadened to become a concern for all educators. Further, as language backgrounds became more complex, it became clearer that empty slogans such as "Provide students with a rich language environment" and "value the home language of the child" were helping neither learners nor their teachers through the second-language literacy learning process. While the mantra *Every teacher a second-language teacher* became a truism in a huge number of countries across the globe, there was little if any acknowledgment of this complexity within the literacy community. That community was stymied by the notion of literacy learning for children who *did not* have a command of the language of schooling—a language that was very different from their school-age peers who *did* have a spoken command of school language. In fact, in a review conducted on materials for literacy teachers (namely, textbooks and journals focused on professional development), few if any research-based materials were available (Bernhardt, 1994a) for teachers at any grade-level for enhancing the reading development of second-language learners across the globe.

At some level, this is not a surprising development, given that culture and language became concepts which, by the end of the 20th century, were increasingly popularized. Arguably, they were so broadened in conception that they came to mean almost anything to almost anyone. The standard definition of *culture*, a consistent pattern of behavior known to members of communities, had come out of the sociology literature and into popular speech. Indeed, the end of the 20th century saw the use of terms such as "corporate culture"; a "culture of consumerism"; and the "culture of the classroom" used as commonplace terms, denoting expected patterns of behavior and connoting in-groups and out-groups. Phrases such as "it's not part of the culture here," referring to how individuals should (or should not) behave in particular professional or local community settings, became a part of everyday language. In like manner, *language* began to be used as a term referring to utterances unique to particular settings. In other words, a *language of business* referred to words and phrases used primarily in corporate settings and the *language of the classroom* referred to words and phrases used to accomplish classroom goals and procedures—words and phrases not generally used in other settings. Academics began referring to means of speaking that learners had to acquire in order to become part of academic cultures as languages. Science was at the forefront of this use of *language*. Science educators argued that students of science need to learn the cultural rules of scientific procedures as well as the words and phrases that scientists in particular areas use. Knowing how to conduct experiments properly and to write those experiments up using words appropriate to the setting (*hypothesis* rather than *guess*; *research* rather than *find out*; *experiment* rather than *test*; and the like) meant learning and using the *language of science* (Lemke, 1990).

The profound monolingualism of Americans might be at the heart of this set of beliefs. If one has only one perspective and one language and no experience with anything else, there is little wonder that the focus has been on English (in the ESL acronym) as the synonym for *language* and on English-speaking culture and its subcultures as the synonym for *culture*. This array of beliefs sets forth an incredibly narrow perspective—one that does not provide appropriate grounding for understanding the complexities of reading and learning to read in a second language. To underline the point: learning to speak or to write *I hypothesized that my research would yield the following data* while already knowing how to speak or write *I guessed that what I was looking at would help me find information* is a substantially different process from learning to compose *Es wurde von der Annahme ausgegangen, daß die Untersuchung die folgenden Daten hervorbringt* [I hypothesized that my research would yield the following data] after knowing how to utter *Ich mache ein Experiment* because when a learner moves from a first-language into a second, a set of linguistic features complexifies the already complex content environment, in this case, science and, specifically, the scientific method. At the culture level, learning the social rules of whether one brings a cup of coffee to a business meeting, or whether one may drive a better, faster, bigger car than one's boss, or the conditions under which a pupil may interrupt her teacher are vastly different from social rules within culturally complex discourse environments such as whether and how long one may hold the floor and how to relinquish it to an "unequal" interlocutor.

In *Reading Development in a Second Language* the distinction between *language* and *language as a linguistic system*, as well as the distinction between *culture* and *subculture* were made; to make these distinctions in the early years of the 21st century is even more crucial. The field seems to have lost, or perhaps never had, the notion of linguistic difference between and among languages, yet the research and theory to be explicated in further pages of this book make it eminently clear that these linguistic differences are critical toward understanding text processing. Access to literacy when one is essentially shifting social registers (as in the example above from an everyday expression to a more appropriate expression; i.e., everyday language to technical language) is very different from shifting between everyday language in Swahili, for example, to technical language in English. There are additional levels, both cognitive and social, in that process that the learner learning a new social register will rarely encounter. Examining culture in the same framework is equally critical. Switching behavioral norms within an overarching familiar cultural framework (such as moving from one corporation to another or from an urban school to a suburban school) can, indeed, be somewhat disorienting for a period of time. This disorientation is, however, of a different kind and quality from what one would encounter in moving from a single-gender elementary school in Saudi Arabia to Oak Park Elementary School in Westerville, Texas. Inhabitants do not look the same and they do not speak a language that is remotely related to the pupil's home language. Even the chairs and blackboards are different, and notions of equality and collaboration might be poles apart. To deposit all of these experiences under the term *culture* and then to treat them as equivalent experiences is to denigrate and profoundly misunderstand the processes.

A corollary phenomenon exists in the reading/literacy field. The term "reading" has become rather dull, meaning that somehow in the eyes of some academics it is too commonplace, too restricting. *Literacy* is the more fashionable notion. It is the term that in the early 1990s referenced reading and writing connections and which, in a current iteration, refers to the ability to navigate semiotically through the world. In other words, all objects that one encounters are "read and understood"—not just printed matter. This principle, while interesting enough on the surface, leads to a void that is so unbounded as to become practically meaningless. Working with printed material and learning to contribute to the print world are important and critical skills. A major difference between the beginning and the end of the last decade of the 20th century in the conceptualization of reading is the general admission that reading is a sociocognitive process. Around 1990, a very real distinction existed between research that was cognitively oriented and research that was socially oriented. Each of these perspectives, on its own, consistently fell short in providing either explanations for, or adequate predictions of, second-language reading performance. Only a wedding of the perspectives—that reading is both cognitive and social; that one does not follow the other, but co-occurs—pushed the field forward.

Perspectives on the *Who, Why,* and *What* of Second-Language Reading

When *Reading Development in a Second Language* was written, the question of *who* second-language readers actually were, was a question to be explored and answered. The answer that *Reading Development in a Second Language* offered was one very much within the North American context. The first group referenced was children who were placed in schools that used a language other than the mother tongue who needed "school" reading. The second group referenced was adults. That group was further categorized into immigrant groups, temporary graduate student groups, and foreign language learners all of whom were seeking second-language skills for their education, job enhancement, or for interest. This bifurcation between children and adults, focused exclusively on educational settings (education in the academic sense), presents an interesting and relatively naive picture in the 21st century. One explanation for this naiveté is that, in fact, *Reading Development in a Second Language* was written before the internet: and the internet changed second-language reading in much the same way that it changed everything else in our world. The internet increased the number of second-language readers dramatically in that it made the availability of second-language materials (admittedly, written principally in English) immediate, plentiful, easy to access, and cost-free. It enabled readers (many of whom are non-native readers of English across the globe) to find materials on their own without mediation from some kind of academic institution that made choices for the reader. This kind of unfettered access to materials meant that anyone with an internet connection and a translation feature could have access to materials written in essentially any language. The breadth, then, of what it means to be a second-language reader and who could be characterized as such could never have been predicted in 1991. More importantly, and most assuredly, the implications of the breadth have yet to be fully explored.

An accompanying question is *why* anyone would read in a second language. An obvious early 20th-century answer, based in aesthetics, is that literary works written in the original can only be fully appreciated in the original. If this were the only answer to the question, then second-language reading would be little more than an academic exercise for an elite few. The aesthetic answer does not account for the millions of second-language readers across the globe who regularly read in second languages. A more compelling answer lies in the desire to gain unfiltered information in its convenient and overwhelming availability. While the very act of reading implies a filtering process, the act of reading "in the original" actually refers to a primary layer in the act of communication. Many readers are hungry for the ability to relate directly to a source rather than indirectly through translations and adaptations. In a world broken by misunderstanding that leads to unbelievable trauma and bloodshed, the ability to try to understand as directly as possible, rather than through multiple levels of intermediaries, is desired. A final answer lies in globalization itself. High-quality information is not the purview of just one language or culture. Understanding how to predict tsunamis, for example, given that significant research is conducted in distinct parts of the globe, means that even when researchers might publish in a *lingua franca* such as English, they might discuss the same phenomenon in their native language— and that discussion often takes place, again, on the internet. Globalization has not meant the *esperanto-ization* of global discussion. It has meant a recursive process of reading, speaking, and writing in multiple languages on the same topic. During the drafting of this chapter, for example, issues of mine safety are at the forefront globally. In the US State of Utah, a mine tragedy captured the hearts and minds of many as six miners were lost and unrecoverable. At the same time, the world focused on China, with the most significant mine safety issues in the world, when 137 miners were killed due to a lack of proper safety procedures—and this after a so-called major improvement in mine safety in China. Chinese and Americans interested in mine safety and all that surrounds mines, including the psychological health of miners and their families, might wish both information and solace from others and each other experienced in mine safety hundreds of miles, languages, and cultures away. Again, the recursive process of using technology able to accommodate a number of languages, as well as knowledge about psychological effects, was at play on the global stage. None of this information was housed exclusively in a single language and, most assuredly, was not discussed in a single language.

The question of *what* second language readers actually do and how they manage to do it has remained open for debate throughout the years that have passed since *Reading Development in a Second Language*. Many believe that those needing to read a second language simply *do* the same thing that they *do* in their first. Yet anyone who has ever tried to learn to read a second language recognizes immediately that the existence of the first language and literacy makes the processing different. Second-language reading is tantamount to operating in stereo—the first language is the *clear* channel. The clear channel is there in the first language, providing phonology (that is *never* identical to the phonology of the input or second language). It also provides processing strategies (such as "do not bother looking at function words because they are not all that useful," an English-based processing strategy that will impede comprehension in German). Word recognition strategies (such as "where does the word begin and end in this Thai text?") are also included on the list as is a concept of fluency—*pared* [*wall* in Spanish] ("looks like *parade;* I don't have time to stop, I'll go with *parade*"); and so forth. But perhaps most importantly, it is the reader's clear channel of first-language culture and first-language literacy that guides the development of the conceptual model on which understanding is based; it is this model that provides the anticipatory strategies discussed in *Reading Development in a Second Language*. It is the model developer—that clear channel—that is *not* rooted in the target language and culture but rather in the first layer of literacy—the first language and culture—that renders the process so absolutely different. Admittedly, reading involves a text; an ability to perceive that text is language written down; and the use of strategies that are helpful in understanding the text. The analogy stops there. The existence of two channels—a clear channel from first-language knowledge and a degraded channel from second-language knowledge—which operate simultaneously, sometimes deliberately and sometimes incidentally, sometimes facilitating and sometimes distorting—makes for a unique conflation of factors for anyone who tries to comprehend in a second language.

As mentioned above, anyone who has ever tried to comprehend in a second language would interpret the above as self-evident. Yet, the misconception of "it's all the same" has undermined research progress in the area, belittled the challenge of reading in a second language, and has impeded assistance to teachers. Believers in the misconception seem to be unable to get past the notion that all reading involves a text and a set of strategies and, therefore, they are incapable of getting past anything but the most superficial concept of the process. Perhaps a medical example might be helpful. A corollary might be Type I and Type II diabetes. While Type I and Type II diabetes are both diseases related to the production of insulin, they are radically different in how they are treated and which mechanism is involved. One involves an inability to *produce* insulin, the other an inability to *use* insulin. Those are two very different processes—much like a native speaker who can produce language fluently and the second language speaker who must learn to use that language. A musical example might also be helpful. There are genuine and profound differences between playing the piano and playing a pipe organ; a guitar and a banjo. On the surface, these instruments might appear to be "the same," but the learning processes, the approaches, and the output abilities are all different. While there might be keys, and strings, and sheet music, and scales and so forth involved, the actual ability to use the instrument is different. And very critical in the use of these examples is that higher levels of proficiency bring about greater distinctions rather than fewer. At the earliest level, one might be able to play a basic tune on the organ if one can play the piano but with greater proficiency and more complicated "texts," the differences become more and more apparent.

Processing Perspectives

Reading Development in a Second Language provided the dictionary definition of *reading* as an act of "taking in"; as one of "understanding"; and as one of interpretation. The definition is consistent with that of the RAND Reading Study Group Report (2002):

> We define reading comprehension as the process of simultaneously extracting and constructing meaning through interaction and involvement with written language. We use the words *extracting* and *constructing* to emphasize both the importance and the insufficiency of the text as a determinant of reading comprehension. (p. x)

The Study Group adds that this extracting and constructing process is within a sociocultural context. Even so, the tentative and tenuous nature of the definition is clear; yet, the act of reading for the context of this chapter continues to refer to how written text is processed in the brain by a reader and how that processing brings about a conceptualization of what is written. There can be no doubt that the nature of the input language is critical; that the nature of the reader's processor or brain, i.e., how it accepts the input, is crucial; and how the mixture of both input language and reader processor brings about an understanding. In fact, *Reading Development in a Second Language* provided its readers with the perception of a reader as being hardwired (the image of a computer in the head was offered as in Figure 1.1) and that the software in the computer operated on the input data and led to output/understanding. There is still much to be gained in understanding reading in a second language from this perspective. Although this view is often criticized within sociocultural theory, it, nevertheless, underlines the importance of the cognitive activity of the reader on input data. The figure also emphasizes that input data and output data are two different entities. The input data provided in Figure 1.1 is a sentence from the

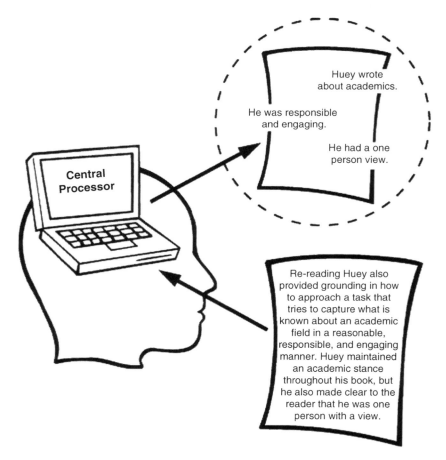

Figure 1.1 A reader's reconstruction in first-language reading

introduction to this book. The reader's output is illustrated by the key points that the reader chooses to process.

The nature of a reader's cognitive operations continues to be of primary importance in understanding reading in a second language. Figure 1.2 tries to capture the essential differences in the cognitive operations in first language and second language. A principal difference is that the input text and the software in the central processor are only partially compatible—like trying to input Roman numerals into an Excel spreadsheet. The central reading processor will tend to have a complete set of first-language rules (here illustrated by "English: Complete Edition") and most assuredly an incomplete or degraded set of second-language rules (illustrated in the figure by "Indonesian: Limited Edition"). The processor will tend to use the program in which it has the most confidence (or the most lines of programming)—the complete set of first-language rules—in order to

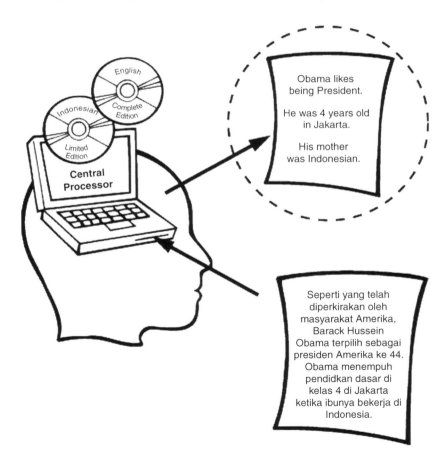

Figure 1.2 A reader's reconstruction in second-language reading

operate on the second or in this case the input language. Output will indeed be a reconstruction of the text, in parallel to first-language processing (Figure 1.1), but that conceptual output will be characterized within a first-language framework. In other words, the first language provides a cocoon that wraps around the interpretation of the second-language text. Another key point within second-language contexts is that the output, while reasonable, may be totally inaccurate based on the content of the input text as is the case in Figure 1.2.

Reading Development in a Second Language was also quick to acknowledge social dimensions to reading. It first illustrated the interpersonal dimension of reading (Figure 1.3), referring to the notion that even two readers from the same culture can, and often do, develop different understandings or interpretations of the same text. If this were not true, then the whole field of literary criticism would be out of business. The text used in the figure is a line referring to compensatory theory used in Chapter 2 of this book.

Each reader grasps the notion of "seriality"; yet Reader 1 focuses on reading models and Reader 2 on poor readers. When inserted into the second-language context, the interpersonal dimension becomes complexified (Figure 1.4). In this instance, the two readers are processing text written in Spanish. Reader 1, as an L2 reader, has an incomplete and at times inaccurate processing program ("Spanish: Limited Edition"). The conceptualization of the text is dependent

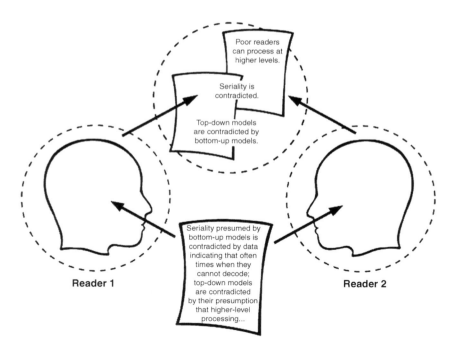

Figure 1.3 The text reconstruction of two first-language readers

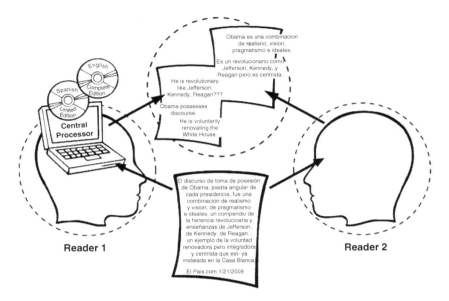

Figure 1.4 The text reconstruction of a first- and of a second-language reader

upon the strength and accuracy of the processing program, and the output con-ceptualization, compared with the native speaker, may produce a conceptual model with little overlap between the two readers. Reader 1 questions her pro-cessing, relies heavily on cognates, and willingly conceptualizes some of the text in an illogical fashion. Reader 2 (with a "Spanish: Complete Edition") is able to read the passage and distill key elements. The lack of overlap illustrated in Figure 1.4 between the first-language and second-language reader is often at the core of the difficulty in upper-register language instruction when the fluent native or quasi-native chastises the L2 reader for sloppy or off-target readings, ignoring the complexities introduced by the processing steps the L2 reader must encoun-ter in making an interpretation.

Reading Development in a Second Language also acknowledged the intraper-sonal view of reading; i.e., that readers are fluid in their understanding and inter-pretive processes (Figure 1.5). Readers can take different points of view; change intentions toward the text; and they can deliberately seek alternative conceptu-alizations. The same reader interacting with the same text focuses in Context 1 on materiality and refers back to Gutenberg. In Context 2, the reader focuses on the implications for the public. The intrapersonal view acknowledges that when readers change perspectives their interpretation and processing changes alongside the perspective. This change, of course, can happen whether a reader is reading Thomas Mann's *The Magic Mountain* or the set-up manual for the Bluetooth-compatible ear hook for a mobile phone. No matter the text, the

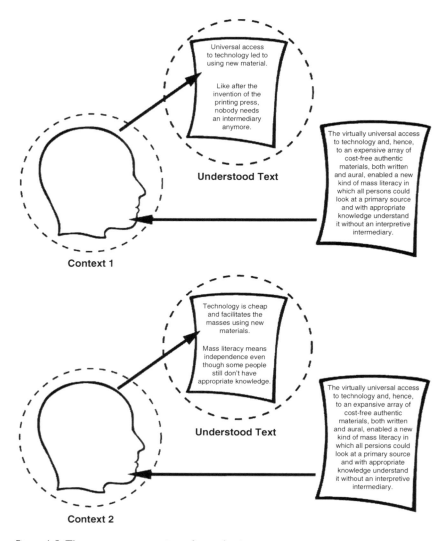

Figure 1.5 The text reconstruction of a reader in two contexts

reader's purpose, the intention of the author, the place of the text in society, what the text *says* about social hierarchy, and so forth, all come into play and guide the interpretation of the text. For the second language reader, the difference becomes one of experience and knowledge. To remain with the computer metaphor, the second-language experience is about writing more lines of program, more *if then* statements that are linked to an enhanced knowledge of the linguistic forms of the language as well as their semiotics. In other words, the more enhanced the input processor becomes, the greater the likelihood of multiple interpretations or the increased capacity to cope with ambiguity and to resolve it. A key feature, however, is that interpretation continues to be made against the backdrop of another program running in the background that influences interpretation. For the first-language reader, the issue is using different parts of the same program; for the second-language user, the issue is using different parts of two programs one of which is dominant in the early stages of fluency and never entirely disappears; the second of which becomes more pronounced over time and learning, but rarely becomes dominant.

Perspectives from the National Reading Panel

Some additional insight and complexity is introduced into the discussion by the report of the National Reading Panel (NICHD, 2000). That particular US report drove significant legislation and policy directions in the United States and most certainly was influential internationally. While the report acknowledges that it did not focus on second-language concerns, the findings of the report were so influential that they spilled over into second-language issues. Volumes such as Grabe (2009) and Han and Anderson (2009) refer to this influence. Indeed, the report's findings help to capture and vivify some of the differences between first- and second-language reading.

The report argues from a research base that all instruction should include at least five components for effective reading instruction. The first is that all learners should have *phonemic awareness.* Phonemic awareness is the ability to manipulate sounds in oral language such as being able to perceive a rhyme and concomitantly construct one such as *cat* and *hat* or perceive initial sounds (*fish* and *fan*) and final sounds (*sin* and *can*). It appears that readers in their first language will have difficulty with the concept of literacy if they cannot conceive of these kinds of relationships between and among sounds in their native language. The question in a second-language context is whether a reader only needs to be able to do this in his/her *first* language (*Hut* and *Mut*, in German, for example) or must also be able to perceive these distinctions in the second language. Important here are issues of foreign accent and the extent to which the first-language phonemic awareness is necessary or sufficient. A second point underlined by research is a reader's knowledge of *phonics* or the ability to understand a set of rules that translate text into oral speech. Again, the question lurks of whether the reader's first-language ability in this regard is necessary and/or sufficient. The German reader above would understand in German that the misspellings *Hud* and *Mud* have the same phonology as *Hut* and *Mut.* The question remains the extent to which that same reader has to acquire a set of phonics for the second language. *Reading Development in a Second Language* provided the example in French of Kes ke sest? for *Qu'est-ce que c'est?* Does the second-language reader really need accurate phonetic rules and if so *how* accurate? Given that there are many competent readers of foreign languages who maintain non-native accents, most assuredly the answer is that perfect or even native-like accuracy is not required.

Three additional components cited in the National Reading Panel Report are *fluency*, *vocabulary*, and *comprehension*. Where do second-language readers stand vis-à-vis these particular research findings from the National Reading Panel? Fluency is the rapid processing of words. Does the L2 reader have to be able to translate print into sound rapidly, and how accurate does that sound have to be? Can the second-language reader have a fluency based in first-language phonology and will that fluency be sufficient or will it stifle comprehension? In traditional second-language pedagogy, learners are often asked to read passages aloud—ostensibly to improve their reading comprehension, but in reality to improve their pronunciation. In my first published study (1983), I provided evidence that the practice of reading aloud focused second-language readers so much on pronunciation that it indeed impeded their ability to comprehend. Koda (2005) continues to probe this question. Finally, according to the National Reading Panel, vocabulary and comprehension instruction are critical to learning to read. Undoubtedly, the two are inextricably intertwined and form the core interest of the present volume. In any discussion of comparisons between first- and second-language reading, vocabulary and comprehension are the areas of reading that make the distinction between L1 and L2 perhaps most vivid. All reading begins with an oral/aural vocabulary; for first-language readers, the process is one of recognizing words already in the oral/aural lexicon and then in enhancing the lexicon by adding more and more words. In great part, the placing of new words into that lexicon implies a learning of word and concept. In contrast, second-language readers do not have necessarily an oral/aural vocabulary that vaguely represents the second-language or the language of interest. Yet, very importantly, they often *do* have a concept for a particular word as well as that word in their L1 oral/aural vocabulary. The process for many second-language readers then is to attach a new oral/aural representation to a concept that already exists; for many other second-language readers, the process is to learn both concept and new oral/aural word in both their second language and possibly, though not necessarily, in their first. Finally, the act of comprehension itself that entails all of the former makes for a profound complexity for all readers, but it places second-language readers into double jeopardy. Not only do second-language readers have to control linguistic forms, and do so automatically, they must tackle cultural differences that are not different, but commonplace, for readers from the first-language group. As *Reading Development in a Second Language* made clear, while there are subcultural differences in all cultures such as what a Southern accent "signals" in the American psyche, the second-language learner has no direct access to these subcultural differences. Comprehension is far more layered in a second language than in a first. And because the layers are inconsistent with the expectations or the "layers" that a first-language group possesses, the interaction between and among layers of knowledge is not necessarily supportive and may actually impede comprehension.

Expanded Perspectives

All of these views and insights, even with their enhancements, taken individually, fall short. They are, as Kramsch (1998) would argue, reflective of "the ever growing encroachment, in all walks of life, of an information-processing view of language and language use. This view, which values the transmission, retrieval, and exchange of information, is not always compatible with [...] critical analysis and interpretation" (p. 29). The criticism is fair: thus far, reading has been characterized by both cognitive and social dimensions and hence as a sociocognitive process, yet one firmly rooted in transmission and information exchange. *Reading Development in a Second Language* illustrated the process as shown in Figure 1.6. While the image admits to an interaction of text and a fluid (i.e., non-static) reader, it assumes that it is the reader who has the direct influence on the selection of features for processing. A continued exploration of the extent to which this assumption may or may not be true is important, a view affirmed by Hedgcock and Ferris (2009). Figure 1.6 also posits that the relationship between the reader and the reconstructed text is unidirectional. Whether this conceptualization is compatible with the compensatory processing theory offered in future pages of this book—a theory whereby the text signals back to the reader that some other knowledge source must come into play in order to buttress another lagging knowledge source—will also be interrogated and problematized in later chapters. Perhaps more critically, though, is whether this view is helpful toward conceptualizing and understanding the process of reading highly nuanced upper-register texts. Complexity lies in the processing of intricate, complicated and, often, obscure linguistic and cultural features *accurately* while trying to comprehend content and while remaining distant from it in order to assess the content's value and accuracy.

In future pages I try to explore in a more sophisticated manner what *text* actually means. Surely, contemporary literacy theory and, particularly, critical theory would posit that before there is a *text* there is a motivation to attend to that text. Critical theorists often speculate in depth about how that motivation is built by external societal forces (in other words, part of the *socio* in sociocognitive) and that those motivations, determined in large part by outside, reader-external

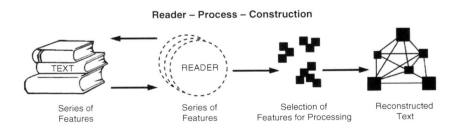

Reader – Process – Construction

| Series of Features | Series of Features | Selection of Features for Processing | Reconstructed Text |

Figure 1.6 Information transmission throughout the reading process

forces, drive the reader to engage with the material. The above mention of a user's guide to a Bluetooth-enabled ear piece for a cellular telephone is an excellent example of how society itself guides what is read. Given that a Bluetooth-enabled ear piece is not critical to the use of a telephone, but does have legal implications for hands-free phone use laws, it is its convenience and its status symbol quality that drive reading the "user's guide," not the inherent value of the text.

This argument becomes more nuanced with the reading of information text versus fiction, an issue that has received more attention and generates controversy in a manner different from previous decades and yet renewed from 19th-century controversies. At the heart of the matter is a set of humanities-based educational beliefs versus a more "practically" oriented approach to education. It would be foolhardy to embark upon an attempt to reconcile these two very different approaches from a philosophical point of view. Indeed, it is important to know and to read stories and most assuredly the aesthetic value of literarily rooted stories is a critical dimension to learnedness. In pre-industrial times, the whole of learnedness was, indeed, based in the ability to read, comprehend, and discuss the great literary legacies. Up to the present moment, there are many who still hold to this position, arguing that real learnedness and cultural sympathy are tied up in the tradition of literary reading and that the function of learning other languages is to be in greater touch with, and sympathetic to, an array of cultures. Yet, there is another version of this same story, driven indeed by the industrial revolution and its aftermath but also by research. This is the story of the role of reading information text, text that conveys a message that is verifiably factual and that applies *beyond itself*. It is the story of the application of reading as a knowledge in service to other procedures and knowledge and is bound up with the notion of practicality, of learning in order to be able to *do* something, and in the notion of linguistic integration.

Linguistic integration means that language skills cannot and should not be separated, but rather learned and used in support of each other. In its organic sense, communicative language teaching reminds that all modes of communication are worthy; modern perspectives on linguistics remind that word-based and sentence-based grammars are wholly inadequate descriptions of language; learning theory reminds that exploring learning through different modalities enhances learning; and globalization reminds that communication regularly takes both oral and written forms. The current era demands that the field expand its notion of the role that reading plays in modern language learning and the role that comprehension plays in general in the development of the ability to cope with demanding and complicated text. Hence, an expanded definition of reading is also in order. The definition provided by PISA (Organisation for Economic Co-operation and Development [OECD], 2006) is particularly helpful in this context:

> *Reading literacy* is understanding, using and reflecting on written texts, in order to achieve one's goals, to develop one's knowledge and potential and

to participate in society. This definition goes beyond the notion of *reading literacy* as decoding and literal comprehension: it implies that *reading literacy* involves understanding, using and reflecting on written information for a variety of purposes. It thus takes into account the active and interactive role of the reader in gaining meaning from written texts. The definition also recognises the full scope of situations in which *reading literacy* plays a role for young adults, from private to public, from school to work, from active citizenship to lifelong learning. It spells out the idea that literacy enables the fulfilment of individual aspirations—from defined aspirations such as gaining an educational qualification or obtaining a job to those less immediate goals which enrich and extend one's personal life. Literacy also provides the reader with a set of linguistic tools that are increasingly important for meeting the demands of modern societies with their formal institutions, large bureaucracies and complex legal systems.

The importance of the PISA definition lies in its recognition that reading does involve intricate linguistic tools for gaining information *and* that the act of understanding has a role well beyond transmission; it includes notions of citizenship and effective and meaningful social participation.

But what could any of this mean in the concrete? A fascinating example of the functioning of upper-level second-language reading skills was provided by the events surrounding the inauguration of Barack Obama as 44th President of the United States. It is rare that one event captivates a global audience of all social strata and all cultural and political perspectives and that might be taken as an instance of world citizenship. The event was reported in this manner by the Associated Press:

> Before a jubilant crowd of more than a million, Barack Hussein Obama claimed his place in history as America's first black president, summoning a dispirited nation to unite in hope against the "gathering clouds and raging storms" of war and economic woe. (*Associated Press*, 2009)

A lower proficiency second-language reader might struggle with *jubilant* and *dispirited* as well as with the *-ing* forms of both *summoning* and *gathering*. But what of the higher-proficiency reader? That reader is able to make headway through words and a grammatically complicated sentence, but should also be able to glean and provide evidence for the political perspective of the writer who has provided a picture of a forward thinking public utterly unhappy with the status of war and financial despair. At an even deeper level, whether the second-language reader would recognize the allusion to George Washington and Valley Forge would be a genuine hallmark of very refined and specific cultural knowledge. That reader would be able to hypothesize about the function of evoking an iconic American image.

A German reader would have encountered a similar description on the

Frankfurter Allgemeine Zeitung website, *FAZ.net* ("Barack Obama als Präsident vereidigt"), on the same day:

> Barack Obama ist am Dienstag als 44. Präsident der Vereinigten Staaten vereidigt worden. Als erster schwarzer Präsident in der amerikanischen Geschichte legte er seinen Amtseid um 12 Uhr mittags auf den Stufen des Kapitols ab. In seiner Rede vor Hunderttausenden Menschen auf der Washington Mall setzte Obama den „aufziehenden Wolken und tosenden Stürmen" der Krise, in der Amerika sich gegenwärtig befinde, eine Botschaft der Zuversicht entgegen: „Die Herausforderungen, mit denen wir konfrontiert sind, sind real. Sie sind ernst, und sie sind zahlreich. Sie werden nicht leicht oder kurzfristig gemeistert. Aber wisse, Amerika, sie werden gemeistert."

The native reader of German is provided a very similar picture with parallel emphases. But what is interesting for the upper-level yet non-native reader is the delicate differences—that Germans read of a crisis in America and that Obama used confrontational language to meet the crisis. The performative use of *wisse* in particular underlines the confrontational nature or, as William Safire put it, "the imperious, lecturing pointer phrase ... that get-this tone" (Safire, 2009). And, of course, whether the German writer of the piece, or Germans themselves, capture the flavor of the iconic George Washington image without a mention of George Washington is fascinating. These two paragraphs, one in English and one in German, underline the import of conducting fine-grained cultural analysis through literacy. Trying to grapple with a question such as *what perceptions do Germans have regarding the American political situation?* requires a sensitivity to language and culture in order to provide a well-documented answer that is not well understood.

A look at January 21, 2009 headlines of websites from Spain such as El País. com or elmundo.es provide a different perspective. In contrast to the German language report's exclusive use of crisis and confrontation is an emphasis in these Spanish sites on service "moral al servicio" (Caño, 2009), responsibility "una nueva era de responsabilidad," and humility "humildad" (González, 2009). While the cognates are easy to perceive for a native reader of English reading Spanish, the larger question is, of course, why a culture would choose these arenas to emphasize rather than nuclear war, the economy, or racial politics. Arguably, allusions to service, responsibility, and humility would resonate with the predominantly Catholic population in Spain. A further analysis of the text in relation to their lead-ins might or might not confirm this hypothesis. But most assuredly, a detailed analysis in the second-language context requires a sensitivity to specific words that evoke particular images or cultural identities. Careful reading and comprehension go well beyond "knowing the meaning of" *servicio*, *responsabilidad*, or *humildad*.

Two final examples are provided by Tagalog and Arabic. Abante.com.ph,

January 22, 2009, a website published in the Philippines led with the headline "Peace, security isusulong ni Obama." And explains in the lead paragraph:

> Kapayapaan at seguridad ang binigyang diin ni US President Barack Hussein Obama na tatahakin ng kaniyang administrasyon, kung saan layunin nitong magkaroon ng mahusay na relasyon sa mga Muslim at pagsawata sa banta ng nukleyar.

Likewise, aljazeera.net on January 21, published a parallel perspective on the Obama inauguration entitled *Khitab al-tansib*:

وقد لاقى خطاب التنصيب ترحيبا واسعا في عدد من العواصم العالمية التي رأت في كلام الرئيس أوباما لهجة جديدة غابت كليا عن مفردات الإدارة الأميركية السابقة في عهد الرئيس السابق **جورج بوش**.

فقد توجه إلى العالم الإسلامي بعبارات أكد فيها عزمه تحسين العلاقات و"البحث عن طريق جديد نحو الأمام.. يقوم على المصالح المشتركة والاحترام المتبادل"، مشددا على التمسك بالقيم الديمقراطية التي قامت عليها الولايات المتحدة ."

وفي عبارة لافتة شدد فيها على أهمية القيم وليس القوة، حث أوباما مواطنيه على عدم التخلي عن المثل الأميركية بقوله "نرفض أن نخير بين أمننا ومبادئنا.. ما زالت المثل الأميركية تضيء في العالم.. لذا أقول لجميع الشعوب والحكومات التي تتطلع لنا اليوم: أميركا صديقة كل أمة وكل رجل وكل امرأة وكل طفل يبحث عن مستقبله في سلام وكرامة."

كما أكد عزمه التعاون مع حلفاء الولايات المتحدة لمواجهة المشكلات العالمية واعتماد الدبلوماسية طريقا مفضلا للسياسة الخارجية

Each article centers on the relationship between the regions of the Arabic- and Tagalog-speaking world and the United States, not on particular characteristics of Obama per se or of the impending financial crisis.

The point in this exercise of examining limited amounts of text in German, Spanish, Tagalog, Arabic, and English on the same topic is to refine and solidify the definition of upper-register reading that I provided above. I noted earlier that *complexity lies in the processing of intricate, complicated and, often, obscure linguistic and cultural features accurately while trying to comprehend content and while remaining distant from it in order to assess the content's value and accuracy*. To expand on the point, learning to read in the upper registers of a second language entails being able to process the minutiae of word and grammatical nuance *while* constructing a message and *simultaneously* remaining aloof from that construction in order to assess its content and intention. *Understanding Advanced Second-Language Reading* tries to bring compensatory theory to bear on explaining the complexity of second-language reading. While most of the research and theory that currently exist could be criticized for focusing exclusively on the "minutiae of word and grammatical nuance" with a bit of added focus on the message-construction process, how a reader learns to bring the array of knowledge sources necessary to assess content and intention and thereby to learn from upper-level second-language discourse remains unexplored territory. Future chapters of this book hope to provide insight and direction for further analysis.

Chapter 2

A Compensatory Theory of Second-Language Reading

Theory is important. A good theory, so I was told at the University of Minnesota, is one that synthesizes the past, explains the present, and predicts the future. In other words, a good theory accounts for previous and present findings from data collections and predicts or projects what future findings will be. Good theories are explanatory and hypothesis-generating. They are also efficient. Extensive numbers of parameters and dependencies indicate that the theory either is not stated sufficiently directly or is not nuanced adequately to enable it to account for the majority of observations of whatever phenomenon. There are many theories of first-language reading. Grabe (2009) and Hudson (2007) rehearse most of these L1 theories in their volumes. Yet, these volumes never draw direct links between the assumptions made in the theories, the growing second-language reading data base, and second-language reading theory development. In order to make progress in the field, rehearsal of old theories and recapitulations of studies without reference to a theory render little service. This chapter, in contrast to other writings on L2 reading, poses questions about whether the assumptions made in certain theories actually fit or describe the second-language reading process and/or whether a theory based in a first-language process can ever adequately capture the second. Interestingly, Hudson fails to refer to any theory of second-language reading while Grabe dismisses what exists: "In L2 reading only one general descriptive model of reading has been proposed (Bernhardt, 1991; 2000) and it is somewhat vague in its specifications of component abilities and implications for reading development" (Grabe, 2009, p. 104). In contrast, Hedgcock and Ferris (2009) describe the situation differently by referring to the "complex factors" (p. 35) outlined in Bernhardt's (2005) compensatory model.

With these intellectual positions in the background, this chapter traces the roots of theory development regarding second-language reading and examines how each theory of second-language reading development, in its own idiosyncratic way, accounted for, and provided direction for, future investigations about second-language reading. The theory extrapolated in this volume was, undeniably, influenced by all of the thought put forward over many years by many generations of scholars, most of whom were interested in first-language reading questions. To ignore these influences would be utterly dishonest and disrespectful of the countless data collections and interpretations of those data collections offered in an array of scholarly outlets by researchers across the globe.

Second-language reading has been of theoretical interest since well before there was any attention placed on the importance of second-language reading as a concrete process. In fact, the contemporary Anglo-centric world (and particularly that part of the world centered in North America) would probably fail to recognize the role that languages other than English have played in the development of theories of human psychology and learning. Since the inception of the research field known as *psychology* (developed out of *philosophy*) researchers have used non-native languages as case studies, that is, as interesting instances of variables to be controlled in order to observe learning and comprehension processes. This situation is particularly visible within the context of reading in second languages. How readers already literate in one language approach another was used as a research focus at the end of the 19th century (Cattell, 1885; Javal, 1879) and in the early 20th century (Huey, 1908) in order to probe what the act of language understanding seemed to be about. This is an important point not only for its historic significance but also to remind us that there are many human questions that can, and still should, be asked within the context of second languages. As platforms for posing research questions, second languages permit researchers to view readers who have already mastered concepts of literacy and who have an arsenal of strategies to understand language. This configuration enables researchers to view how *language*—in particular the *second* language— functions in contrast to contexts in which dimensions of language and literacy are conflated such as when observing younger learners who have completed neither *language* nor *literacy* learning.

Interestingly, scholars at the end of the 19th century understood what scholars throughout most of the 20th century ignored and even shunned: examining second-language instructional contexts. Even though the oldest known work on scientific reading—Huey (1908)—acknowledged the utility of probing second-language reading, the field of reading was by and large oblivious to it. And even throughout the development of intelligence testing (as a response to massive immigration) and linguistic developments (as a response to military needs), second-language reading research remained relatively dormant. The field was re-awakened by Goodman (1968) who recognized the dilemmas of reading encountered by increasing numbers of minority-language children entering the United States. With the mid-1960s' patterns of massive immigration and the need for schooling for children and adults in a language other than their native one, an urgency to re-open the questions surrounding second-language reading arose.

Goodman and the Psycholinguistic Perspective

Reading in the 21st century would not be the field that it is without the work and influence of Kenneth Goodman. At some level, he popularized reading research;

at another level, he rejected the concept of reading research. Regardless of perspective and the manner in which history will interpret his legacy, Goodman's recognition of the uniqueness of the second-language phenomenon was a critical catalyst in the development of the research area of second-language reading. What made Goodman's work special? A simple answer is that he *listened* carefully to readers and he let them *read* connected text. Like an excellent music teacher who can hear tones and nuances that others do not know even exist and who works with students as they play their instruments, Goodman took readers for what they were and tried to understand their processes within the context of authentic pieces of text; there were no mistakes, only failures to appropriately put a piece of text together. This view of reading was incredibly influential. This intensive kind of observation led Goodman (1968) to work within what he termed a psycholinguistic framework: a framework that posits that a comprehender is actively engaged in relating experience (*psycho*) with words (*linguistic*) on the page.

In order to get a sense of readers' engagement or how they were using their experience coupled with the knowledge of the language, readers (mainly young readers) were asked to read aloud and their renderings were analyzed using a technique called miscue analysis. Miscues refer to mistakes that readers make while reading orally, including ones based in self-correction, words that look similar, substituting one word for another, or changing grammatical category. If, for example, the reader read the previous sentence orally, it might come out as:

> *Miscues mean miscues that readers make while reading aurally, orally, including ones found in personal correction, words/works that look the same, or that alter grammaticality.*

In spite of the deliberate exaggeration here for effect, the italicized sentence illustrates what Goodman was discovering: that readers put their own meaning into the text while comprehending and that what they understand can alter what they "see." The more readers are involved in comprehending, the higher the probability of increased miscues. This is a classic depiction of "top-down" reading—that "hypothesize[s] that reading becomes more conceptually driven as fluency develops" (Stanovich, 1980, p. 47). *Reading Development in a Second Language* documented that, as of the turn of the century, Goodman's conceptualization—even though it was developed on the basis of first-language literacy—was the most frequently invoked theory of reading in the entire data base on second-language reading. At the time, an extremely useful collection of studies was produced by the Center for Applied Linguistics and edited by Sarah Hudelson—*Learning to Read in Different Languages* (1981). That collection remains one of the first set of data-based studies regarding reading in a second language. As noted in *Reading Development in a Second Language*, the collection's greatest strength was also its greatest weakness. It relied exclusively on miscue analysis which (within a second-language context) never was able to distinguish, nor did it ever try to distinguish, between a miscue and a mispronunciation.

Around the same time, another extremely influential set of writings had been published, *Reading in a Second Language: Hypotheses, Organization, and Practice* (MacKay, Barkman, & Jordan, 1979). Within the collection, also unified by a psycholinguistic perspective, Coady (1979) synthesized Goodman's sentiments into what he termed was a "psycholinguistic model of the ESL reader." In his work, Coady argued that second-language reading consisted of three interactive elements: conceptual abilities, background knowledge, and process strategies. He argued that when the three sets of sources interacted, the result was comprehension. He elaborated that the "process strategies," ranging from concrete strategies such as word and syllable identification to contextual and lexical meaning, would change in relation to each other as proficiency increased. On page 11, Coady prophetically uses the word "compensate" and allows that "a weakness in one area can be overcome by strength in another." Coady never provided any evidence to support his perspective, which nonetheless provided a critical starting point in thinking about second-language reading. While intuitively appealing, Coady's synthesis, conceptualized as a serial process, without a definite starting point, does not rate as a scientific model because it was never tested (Figure 2.1). Ironically, or perhaps not, given the top-down nature of the perspective, Coady's model does not include *language* in any of its dimensions as an important variable for discussion. As a model of "ESL" reading, one might conclude that English is the language of focus; yet, as future research would document, the nature of the first language involved in the second-language reading process would render the exclusive English focus virtually irrelevant. Further, a notion of text genre, another feature that would come into play in later research, was ignored.

A Focus on Language

The foreign language field (a deliberate distinction from ESL teaching) has always been focused on a multiplicity of languages. The great structural linguists who came before the current generation left an important set of reminders

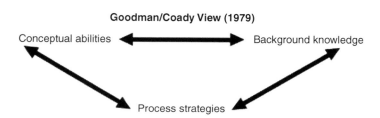

Goodman/Coady View (1979)

Conceptual abilities ⟷ Background knowledge

Process strategies

Figure 2.1 Goodman/Coady view of reading (1979)

about language form. Anyone who has ever tried to learn a language that inflects extensively or that has multiple cases or that uses an orthographic system different from that of a mother tongue has obsessed at one time or another about contrastive form and what those contrasts actually mean for learning and understanding. But observing language processing in action is difficult. The methodology discussed above, miscue, enabled researchers to infer language processing from what they heard. Another methodology for the observation of language processing is by means of eye movement; in other words, rather than listening to readers, one watches readers. This is, in fact, the methodology that Cattell (1885) originally used—observing readers read a newspaper through a pinhole in that newspaper. Such observations led Cattell to document that the eye was stationary much of the time during reading. By the end of the twentieth century, technology was well beyond pinholes and human observation, and computerized tracking for data collection and analysis became common. An eye movement methodology requires a computer set-up attached to a camera that tracks the movement of the eye across a page. These movements indicate where the eye stops (fixation), how long it stops (fixation duration), and in what sequence it stops (chronology of fixation). Well beyond applications in reading, the methodology enabled researchers to examine how engaged readers/see-ers are in visual displays, ranging anywhere from efficient cockpit arrays to the effective commercial arrangement of cereal boxes on supermarket shelves.

Important research programs at the University of Minnesota, the University of Illinois, and at Carnegie-Mellon University (LaBerge & Samuels, 1974; McKonkie & Rayner, 1975; Carpenter & Just, 1977) contributed significant understandings to the reading process. Findings such as the visual span, the role of shape and length in word recognition, or how many letters could be captured within a fixation (7 +/− 2), the average length of a fixation (100 milliseconds), and whether readers skip around the text (no, they tend to read in a linear fashion, fixating about 80% of the content words and about 20% of the function words) solidified the notions of the physicality of reading. Generally speaking, these findings were produced from "bottom-up" theories of reading that examined lower levels of processing (such as word recognition) before higher levels and that posited that comprehension processes could, or would, begin after cycling through lower levels of processing.

But, of course, theory needed to come into play or else these findings were nothing more than "facts" about the nature of eye movement in reading. What about the relationship between these facts about reading and comprehension during reading? The programmatic work of Carpenter and Just (1977) condensed the relationship between eye movement and comprehension into the "eye-mind assumption," meaning that it is comprehension itself that guides the movements: the eye stops to pick up key information; it stops at different durations depending upon the nature of the information, and it retraces its movements if meaning is inconsistent. Contradicting the assertions about reading made within the psycholinguistic framework, Carpenter and Just documented that readers do not lightly sample from text; in fact, readers densely sample from text. Their work along with that of Stanovich (1980), Rumelhart (1977), Kintsch (1974), and van Dijk (1979) brought reading theory into a multidimensional view. Stanovich (1980) articulates that "a third class of theories is formed by those models that posit neither a strictly bottom-up nor strictly top-down processing, but instead assume that a pattern is synthesized based on information provided simultaneously from several knowledge sources (e.g., feature extraction, orthographic knowledge, lexical knowledge, syntactic knowledge, semantic knowledge)." He further notes that within interactive models "each level of processing is not merely a data source for higher levels, but instead seeks to synthesize the stimulus based on its own analysis and the constraints imposed by both higher and lower-level processes" (p. 35).

Interactive models and their implications for second-language reading were discussed at length in *Reading Development in a Second Language*. The theory and research apparatus used within the Carpenter and Just framework, for example, enabled a vivification of a broad research question such as *Do native, non-native yet fluent, and non-native non-fluent readers of German "see" things differently when reading?* into a narrower one, something akin to the following: *When native readers of English read in German—a language known for its flexibility in word order—do these non-native readers scan the text to put it into English syntax for ease of comprehension?* Findings indicated that the answer was "yes and no." Native Germans read in a relatively linear fashion; non-native, non-fluent readers put German into their own syntactic rules for word placement; and non-native yet fluent readers were somewhere in the middle—not mentally rearranging German words, but certainly spending more time in areas of the text that both natives and the non-fluents were simply skimming (Bernhardt, 1987). Native readers of German also directly fixated endings of words, emphasizing the importance of inflection in meaning construction. In contrast, readers of English moved from content word to content word indeed seeing function words, but rarely spending more than 100 milliseconds on them (Carpenter & Just, 1977), underlining the importance of syntax to English-language comprehension.

These findings underline the significance of grammatical manifestations of the *second* language vis-à-vis the *first* language in the second-language reading process. While Coady never even mentions language, a view of the second-language reading process housed in eye movement emphasizes the micro-level differences in the manner in which forms are processed. While English readers rely heavily on the SVO nature of English and exhibit a word-order strategy for garnering meaning, readers of German and developing readers of German have to use morphological elements to establish meaning through understandings of case markings. Within the context of this particular research paradigm a reasonable conclusion is that the acquisition of reading in a second language means the acquisition of native-like behaviors; i.e., acquiring the automatic ability to process areas of the text that are critical for meaning.

At some level, an eye movement methodology was the reverse side of miscue analysis. The former looked at readers; the latter listened to readers. Both remain research methods that can isolate sections of the text in which readers falter, (mis)interpret, concentrate, and so on and so forth. Both provide insights into the physicality of reading; i.e., the outward manifestations of the reading process. It is important to add, of course, that both of these methodologies *reflect* how comprehension must be occurring, but do not provide direct evidence of how readers extract and reconstruct meaning from text.

Seeing Readers Through a Different Lens—Recall

Any decent research study, of course, needs to include a measure of comprehension. Traditional methods of assessing comprehension have been multiple-choice questions or cloze. Multiple-choice questioning is always problematic because second-language readers tend to play a matching game with the words in the question and the words in the text (Wolf, 1993) as in:

> *Juan es estudiante y vive en la residencia estudiantil que se llama 'Central West.' Muchos estudiantes viven allá también pero algunos viven en apartamentos en la ciudad.*
> *Dónde vive Juan?*
> *A. en la ciudad*
> *B. en la residencia estudiantil*
> *C. allá.*

And cloze testing was essentially debunked as a local-level grammar measure rather than as a global measure because readers could receive passages in random form and still successfully complete a cloze passage (Shanahan, Kamil, & Tobin, 1982). In other words, readers could take a cloze test based on the above passage as in:

> *Any decent research study of _____ needs to include a measure _____ comprehension. Traditional methods of assessing _____ have been multiple choice questions _____ cloze. Multiple-choice questioning is _____ problematic because second-language readers _____ to play a matching game _____ the words in the question _____ the words in the text.*

or in the following manner:

> *Multiple-choice questioning is always _____ because second-language readers tend _____ play a matching game with _____ words in the question and _____ words in the text. Traditional _____ of assessing comprehension have been _____ choice questions or cloze. Any _____ research study, of course, needs _____ include a measure of comprehension.*

and receive essentially the same score. Comprehension ability is not as critical as grammatical sensitivity in order to succeed on the cloze completion task.

Free recall was seen as a reasonable alternative to these kinds of direct items. Although not without its critics, recall with foreign-language readers enables a teacher/researcher to examine the manner in which readers put the text together (or reconstruct it). Briefly, in using free recall the following steps are employed. First a passage of around 200–250 words is chosen. Next, readers are told they can read the text as often as they like and that when they are finished they will be asked to write down everything they remember *in the language in which they feel most comfortable*. Then readers read (without any ancillary materials). After reading, they put the passage out of sight and write down what they remember, tending to write in their dominant, i.e., native language. Writing in their dominant language means that the readers do not focus on their own ability to produce the foreign language grammar. In other words, an assessment through recall remains a reading test and does not turn into a writing test or another reading test, but reveals how readers interact with any particular text they are asked to read.

As an example, take a passage in German that concerns a scientific experiment that probes money perceptions by poor and affluent children. The words *Größe* (a cognate with English) and *Geldstück* (partial cognates) are of particular interest. *Größe* was reconstructed by the subjects in the following ways: "size," "more important," "sum," "various denominations," and "value." This result is apparently anomalous because *Größe* is a high-frequency cognate meaning *big* or *size*. The explanation appears to be conceptual in nature. The physical size of money conflicts with the basic representation of US currency. American currency is thought of in terms of amount and denomination and, generally, not in terms of physical size. Paper notes are of the same size and the size of coins is not meaningful (nickels are larger than dimes; dimes are smaller than pennies). Hence, when the so-called dictionary or first-level meaning of the word *Größe* conflicted with the readers' cultural beliefs, they reconciled a new meaning for a word they already knew. A second example is the reconstruction of the word *Geldstück*— literally *money piece* or *coin*. This was reconstructed by English-speaking readers of German as a second language as *stack of money*. *Stack* probably comes from the use of phonemic and visual cues (Stück as *stack*) and is also consistent with the notion of *quantity of money* rather than size.

Another example is provided in Japanese (Figure 2.2). Native English speakers learning Japanese were asked to read and recall the passage.

One Japanese learner reconstructed the text in the following manner:

> *Your local Yomiuri distributor will soon be beginning a program to aid in crime prevention. A newspaper deliverer encounters lots of crime, being that they deliver early in the morning, and will begin training it's employees to be aware of these crimes, and what to do about them. Nearly 4665 branches will be participating in this activity. There were editorials in the paper detailing the many dangers involved in local communities.*

読売新聞の販売店は安全・安心な町づくりを応援します
　あなたの町の読売新聞の販売店（YC）が、身近な防犯活動に取り組んでいるのをご
存知ですか。多発する路上犯罪や子供を狙った痛ましい事件を少しでも防ぎ、安全で
安心な町づくりに貢献しようと、全国4665のYCが「全国読売防犯協力会」を結成。地
域を熟知したYCスタッフが朝夕の新聞配達の合間に不審者に目を光らせるなど地道
な活動を続けています。ひったくり犯を取り押さえたり、ひき逃げ事件を通報したりといっ
た成果も着実に上がっています。こうした活動の輪をさらに広げるため、身近な犯罪
を題材にした作品を公募する「読売防犯川柳コンテスト」も18日、全国一斉にスタート
しました。
　地域に愛され、信頼される存在でありたい――。読売新聞社とYCの願いです。（2005
年4月18日）

Figure 2.2 Japanese newspaper text

Another learner in this fashion:

> *Your towns yomiuri newspaper wants to encourage safety. We want to ward of criminal activity such as guns being fired and violence against children. For the sake of the safe country please contribute to the yomiuri anticrime group. We have staff who work day and night to inform people. We would like to report about stopped criminal activities and reports on on crimes. In order to gather appeal we will hold a nation wide comical haiku contest on the 18th.*
>
> *We want to promote trust and confidence in all the regions of Japan. Contact to yomiuri newspaper.*

One can perceive in the reconstructions of the two Japanese learners, a process similar to that exemplified in the German instance above. Learners reading Japanese try to make sense of an entire text by inserting lexical items they clearly understand but that do not actually reflect the text's contents. Examples are how the concepts of crime are used in each recall. The genesis of "guns being fired" can only arise from a reader's perception of crime or how "morning to night" becomes "in the morning" and "day and night" in the mind of the reader from concepts of the natural world rather than from the actual text.

Analyses such as these across multiple languages, principally German, French, and Spanish, enabled an extended metaphor (Figure 2.3) based on Coady's original. It was expanded to include phonemic/graphemic features, prior knowledge, metacognition, syntactic feature recognition, word recognition, and intratextual perceptions (Bernhardt, 1986). The elaborated interactive metaphor attempted to vivify the multidimensional nature of reading versus the two-dimensional, serial nature conceptualized by Coady. The attempt was to acknowledge the evidence that any one of the variables that had been isolated could interact with any other variable. Figure 2.3 explicitly denotes syntax as a key element and acknowledges that perceptions created throughout a text would be influential in the comprehension process.

Recall Protocal Analyses (1986)

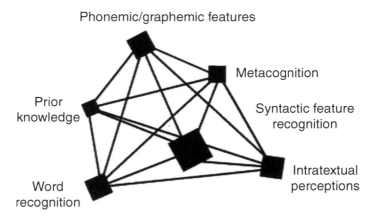

Figure 2.3 A model of second-language reading generated through recall protocol analysis (1986)

Reading research in the 1980s was influenced by, indeed, was essentially dominated by, the US federally-funded, Center for the Study of Reading, at the University of Illinois, Urbana-Champagne. The Center deliberately took as its challenge producing an interdisciplinary view of reading that included an emphasis on psychology, philosophy, discourse analysis, literary theory, and visual literacy among other areas. The notion of an active reader, one who was engaged in a "top-down fashion" and who brought significant background to the reading process was integrated with notions of text complexity, texts being far more than oral language being written down. Synthesizing these perspectives pointed toward background knowledge as a powerful force in driving readers' text reconstructions. The above text about the perception of money is an example. In that context, it is what the reader already knows about a topic that drives the comprehension process. Background knowledge is also at play in the reconstructions of the Japanese text. The fact that "crime" almost inevitably involves guns is an American stereotype, not a Japanese one. As *Reading Development in a Second Language* documented, a significant number of second-language studies focused on background knowledge by manipulating background knowledge often through visual means to observe its impact on reader comprehension. *Reading Development in a Second Language* was no exception to the influence of the background knowledge paradigm. In fact, a central focus of *Reading Development in a Second Language* was on background knowledge. *Reading Development in a Second Language* included a study in which background knowledge was deliberately controlled across an array of topics. Readers self-reported their level of knowledge regarding a number of topic areas that ranged from Latin American politics, to the US space program, to viticulture. Their depth of background knowledge was rated according to a scale developed by Hare (1982). Readers were then given texts in Spanish spanning the topics mentioned. In spite of the design improvements provided by the insertion of rating depth of background knowledge with the Hare scale, the level of readers' background knowledge did not yield data that explained proficient performance. In fact, some readers used background knowledge effectively; others did not. Some had knowledge and used it; some had knowledge and did not use it.

Findings such as these, based on almost 200 recall protocols, coupled with hundreds of additional recall protocols generated from previous studies, provided an extensive data base from which to categorize reader behaviors over texts (expository and narrative), languages, and time spent learning. This categorization process led to the development of the model in Figure 2.4. The model predicts that as readers develop their reading proficiency, they seem to experience a rapid growth in vocabulary and word recognition and that fewer and fewer errors are attributable to inaccuracies based on words. It also posits that background knowledge does not follow levels of proficiency but is, rather, a variable linked to personal idiosyncrasy. In other words, in order to model that readers sometimes used background knowledge and sometimes did not, a relatively flat line was employed within the model to illustrate the phenomenon across years of

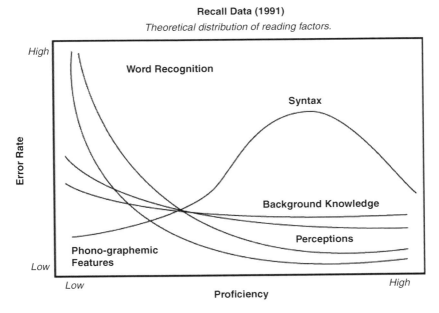

Recall Data (1991)
Theoretical distribution of reading factors.

Figure 2.4 A theoretical distribution of factors involved in second-language reading (1991)

instruction. Further, the model hypothesizes that errors based in syntax, rather than decreasing in frequency, increase in frequency as the reader becomes more proficient, a phenomenon not unlike the U-shaped phenomenon observed in other second-language learning contexts (Kellerman, 1985). In this case, as readers become more confident, they seem to be more confident at taking risks. These risks surface as molding messages from an array of words that take on a syntactic life of their own. An illustration of this phenomenon from *Reading Development in a Second Language* is the assignment of syntax. German sentences such as *Ich vergaß, mir seine Adresse aufzuschreiben (I forgot to write down his address)* have been recalled as "I have forgotten your address" or "I am asking for your address when you write" or "I forgot, my address is given." Yet, beyond such evidence and all previous attempts at modeling second-language reading, this particular model left open questions of whether the model was applicable to all languages and language families; how to define error rate within the context of comprehension; and how to articulate proficiency over time. In other words, *language* remained a mystery variable as, too, did *comprehension*.

Back to the Drawing Board

The background knowledge era of understanding reading in a second language led to the logical conclusion that some texts were either going to be comprehended or not and that comprehension depended upon a reader's internally determined knowledge base. This conclusion essentially entailed the inference that *new* learning from text would be difficult if not impossible. The tautological nature of the view stymied research progress. Re-examining all of the variables that had been considered re-focused attention on a reader-internal variable that had never been fully explored—the impact of the reader's ability to read in his/her first language on the second language. Indeed, the importance of the thought on the interdependency of languages conducted in bilingual and immersion contexts is undeniable. Cummins (1979; 1991) asserted repeatedly that language processes shared common underlying mechanisms. Yet beyond developing an intuitively appealing and ultimately influential metaphor for the bilingual linguistic experience, data were never generated to clarify its nature.

The 1990s witnessed the formulation of the question of shared underlying competence in second-language reading as L2 reading was focused on as a *language* problem or as a *reading* problem. While the question had been posed earlier in an important volume by Alderson and Urquhart (1984) it was not earnestly investigated until a set of studies in the mid-1990s. Researchers acknowledged that in order to explore the question as posed, the first or primary reading ability or literacy level of readers had to be assessed and, simultaneously, readers' second-language ability had to be assessed so that the two variables could be included in any analysis of second-language comprehension. Both measurements had to be included in order to capture the level and degree of their mutual interdependency. Within studies, "literacy" ability tended to be defined, somewhat tautologically, as accomplishment on a standardized test of literacy in the first language. Bossers (1991), Lee and Shallert (1997), Carrell (1991), Brisbois (1995), and Bernhardt and Kamil (1995) all asked the question of different readers (children, adolescents, and adults) across different languages (Spanish, French, English, Turkish, Dutch) and noted similar findings: first-language literacy ability was a significant contributor to explaining second-language proficiency—upwards of 20% of any given performance in a second language could be explained on the basis of first-language ability. The studies also indicated that raw grammatical knowledge seemed to explain 30% of the reading proficiency performances generated. The good news was that 50% of the second-language reading process seemed to be accounted for; the bad news was that only 50% of the second-language reading process could be accounted for. Another important finding was that the 30% of the variance explained by grammatical knowledge seemed to be principally *vocabulary* (Brisbois, 1995). All of these studies, however, were not conducted over a significantly long term but mainly among learners who had upwards of 300 hours of instruction or time on task. Yet, an important key was the statistical method employed in each study—regression. The investigators were able to highlight how much of each variable (language or literacy) simultaneously contributed to the process. These findings put to rest for many the either/or notion of language threshold versus linguistic interdependence. In spite of continued misreadings of many of the studies (see Alderson, 2000; Hedgcock & Ferris, 2009; Grabe, 2009), the appropriate concluding synthesis is that language proficiency was involved in the process as well as literacy processes (Bernhardt & Kamil, 1995). One process did not precede or dominate the other. While one, language knowledge, was more contributory, it was insufficient to account for the observed second-language reading performances. Indeed, first-language performance had to be acknowledged for its critical contribution to explaining second-language reading performances. The need was for a model of second-language reading that accounted for both processes as contributions.

The findings were synthesized into a model (Figure 2.5) that tried to capture time in learning and/or instruction on the *x*-axis and comprehension ability along the *y*-axis. Rather than plotting error rate as in the model shown in Figure 2.4, this model posited a proactive trajectory over time. It also excluded children beginning the literacy-acquisition process by positing that learners with one literacy would never begin the second-language literacy process from a "0" origin, but would always begin the L2 learning process from a position of "some knowledge." The model also conceptualized "an unknown territory" of variables that had not been explained and an "unexplained variance" of time in learning well beyond the 300 hours of standard instructional time generally captured in research studies.

Three troubling features of the model remained. First, the model still appeared to conceptualize the second-language reading process as "additive." In

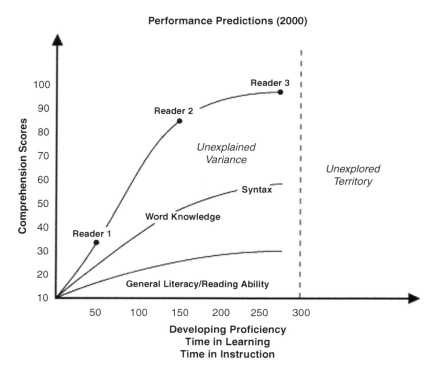

Figure 2.5 A model of second-language reading performance developed over time (2000)

other words, the model portrayed second-language reading as the addition of first-language literacy knowledge to second-language grammatical knowledge equaling a major portion of the explanation of second-language literacy. Second, the model conceptualized "first-language literacy" and second-language grammatical knowledge as monolithic entities. It did not specify the components of either, other than recognizing that vocabulary was a significant portion of second-language knowledge. Third, the model did not have a fully developed conceptualization of what might be entailed in the remaining 50% of the unexplained variance in the second-language reading process. While the model in Figure 2.5 acknowledged that this unexplained variance might be attributed to reader variables such as gender, age, engagement with the topic, motivation, knowledge, and to variables that remained unexplored, it did not attempt to speculate or predict how those variables might influence each other.

An elaborated configuration (Figure 2.6) tried to capture all of the variables that have been investigated in the second-language reading literature (Bernhardt, 2005). First-language literacy is a complex of variables that includes how a reader's first language realizes phonemics, how texts are structured, the purposes for reading, beliefs about reading, knowledge of how words and sentences are configured, and so forth. The model conceptualizes second-language knowledge as consisting of grammatical form, vocabulary knowledge, the impact of cognates, the distance between first language and second language, the value system attached to literacy, and so forth. And unexplained variance as noted in the pages above implicates the interaction of individual reader variables with the universe of texts and topics. How these predictions change against the context of different languages and orthographies and ages is posed in the model as a compensatory process. How did the notion of compensation re-emerge?

First, it was important to step back to reconsider the L1/L2 relationship. The studies reviewed above on that topic and their synthesis naturally led to two discomfiting conclusions. First, Bernhardt and Kamil (1995) noted: "The proportion of variance accounted for by L1 reading knowledge and second-language linguistic knowledge casts a shadow over the findings of many other studies that did not account for these variables. Any main effect found in previous

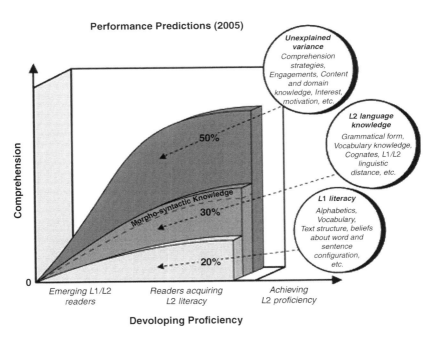

Figure 2.6 A compensatory model of second-language reading (2005)

studies could be potentially overwhelmed by considering these two variables" (p. 31). In other words, main effects from previous studies could be unwarranted in that observations and treatments might well have re-measured first-language literacy, calling it second-language reading ability. Second, these same studies might have also underestimated or overestimated second-language reading ability by failing to account for language knowledge. If these variables might override other variables, they might also play a positive role, namely, balancing their impact throughout reading. This multidimensional speculation was reminiscent of the argumentation behind Stanovich's (1980) interactive-compensatory hypothesis "where knowledge sources at all levels contribute simultaneously to pattern synthesis and where a lower-level deficit may result in a greater contribution from higher-level knowledge sources" (p. 47).

Third, it was also important to re-examine and re-evaluate theories that had been discussed throughout the years in detail. *Reading Development in a Second Language* thoroughly reviewed the theories on which the data base in second-language reading was perched. Studies were overwhelmingly top-down, conceptually oriented. Models such as Goodman (1968) and Smith (1971) were referenced in 65% of published studies. Interactive models such as that posited by Stanovich (1980) were referenced only 15 times. And yet Stanovich seemed to foreshadow an outline of the generation of second-language reading theory because qualitative analysis was indicating that conceptual processing aided *and* impeded lower-level processes such as word recognition. Further, that word recognition as a second-language feature was often irrelevant if a reader's first literacy was an orthographic match with the second. Stanovich (1980) reviewed both theory and research in outlining an interactive compensatory model and began by reminding the reader of assumptions set forth in bottom-up and top-down models of the reading process. Bottom-up models, referred to as data driven, presume that reading proceeds from lower-level processes such as recognizing words, up through conceptual-level processes. Bottom-up views tend to be either serial in nature, arguing that lower-level processes must be completed before higher-level ones can be engaged, or parallel in concept, noting that several lower-level processes can co-occur before moving to higher-level ones. The converse of bottom-up is top-down, which presumes that good reading is always conceptually driven, and that lower-level processes are important only in so far as they might signal or point toward conceptual features. Stanovich points out that neither view provides a sufficient explanation of reading: "Serial-stage models of reading run into difficulty because they usually contain no mechanism whereby higher-level processes can affect lower levels" (p. 34), and top-down or "hypothesis-testing models" are criticized "because they require implausible assumptions about the relative speeds of the processes involved" (p. 34). Seriality presumed by bottom-up models is contradicted by data indicating that often poor readers process at higher levels when they cannot decode; top-down models are contradicted by their presumption that higher level processing may override lower-level processing when the total amount of time for conceptual processing would have to exceed the total amount of time necessary for word recognition.

> The dominance of the top-down perspective has been such that it is widely assumed that the ability to use context to facilitate word recognition is a major determinant of individual differences in reading ability . . . to the contrary, [. . .] poor readers make use of prior context just as much, if not more, than good readers. Thus, it may be that good readers use context more effectively to monitor comprehension, whereas poor readers use it to aid word recognition. (p. 59)

Stanovich continued his review by noting that information-processing perspectives brought about a notion of interactivity—i.e., that lower-level and conceptually driven processing co-occur. And yet, in spite of co-occurrence these models presume that higher-level processes will always overtake lower-level ones. In other words, even interactive models are hierarchical in nature with lower-level processes feeding high-level ones and higher-level ones assisting in the processing of lower-level processes. He concludes:

> In order to make the compensatory assumption, we must first agree on the invalidity of bottom-up models of reading. That is, we must assume that it is not necessarily the case that the initiation of a higher-level process must await the completion of all lower ones. Once we have dispensed with bottom-up models, we are free to assume that a process at any level can compensate for deficiencies at any other level. This is the essence of the compensatory hypothesis. (p. 36)

Stanovich provides a complete literature review examining both word-level and sentence-level contextual processing in native English-language reading and contends that the interactive view in its hierarchical nature cannot explain readers' performances at both levels. Instead, he puts forward the notion of compensatory processing, a view indicating that "a deficit in any knowledge source results in a heavier reliance on other knowledge sources, regardless of their level in the processing hierarchy" (p. 63).

The theory set forth in this volume is that as literate individuals process their second language in reading they rely on multiple information sources not a priori determining what is an "important" source but, rather, bringing whichever source to bear at an appropriate moment of indecision or insecurity. This view seems to account for a greater number of observations and hence should be considered a superior theory for description and prediction. This volume also modifies the 2005 model by reimagining the concept of compensation with greater flexibility and porosity. The model consists of arrays of variables but tries to communicate that any component in an array can buttress any other component in a different array. The model also continues to posit that knowledge sources grow over time and become more available as proficiency increases.

Toward Re-examining the Data Base

The following chapter examines the data base in second-language reading with an eye toward isolating studies that specifically provide evidence of first-language literacy knowledge and/or second-language grammatical ability as contributions to the second-language reading process. If the hypotheses generated by the model posited in Figure 2.7 are credible, then there should be evidence of L1 literacy/L2 grammatical knowledge in all studies regardless of the actual research variables focused on in a particular study. Perhaps more significantly, if these variables are *not* in evidence, how do their findings change the configuration of the model in Figure 2.7? Further, is there any direct evidence of how readers compensate in the L2 reading with the first-language literacy and second-language knowledge bases? And how does compensatory behavior derive from components in the unknown variance helping researchers to make them known?

Second language research has little value unless it can be applied. Research has brought multiple variables into focus. The literacy level of readers has a profound impact on what they can accomplish. Readers who struggle in their first language will probably also struggle in their second. Readers who have an array of strategies in their arsenal do not need to be re-taught those strategies.

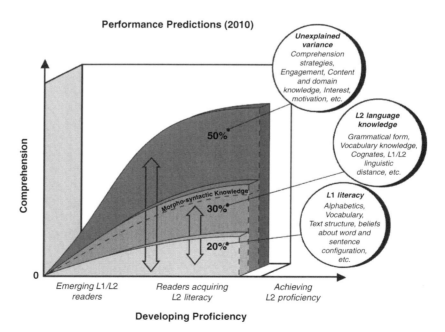

Figure 2.7 A compensatory model of second-language reading (revised)

Therefore, instructional sensitivity to readers' literacy level is critical. That grammatical knowledge counts in second-language reading might appear to be rather obvious. Yet the field needs to recognize both the constituents of that knowledge and that it seems to account maximally for 30% of the reading process. Spending 100% of instructional time for reading on 30% of the process helps to explain why readers perhaps do not make the progress they should make. Research also underlines the importance of idiosyncratic variables in reading. Building a culturally compatible knowledge base that enables readers to read in their areas of interest and expertise could enhance their reading proficiency by enabling them to use their L1 literacy capacity to the fullest.

The variables that have been brought into focus have come to the field through research methodologies eminently practical for instructional purposes. Analyzing how readers understand and reconstruct text makes for efficient instruction. Isolating learners' efforts at understanding, and searching within those efforts for features that cause comprehension breakdown, are the keys to enhanced, effective instruction and, ultimately, to better and more sophisticated theory development.

Chapter 3

Sketching the Landscape of Second-Language Reading Research

Educational research often cites the late 20th century as "The Age of Handbooks." Educational handbooks of all sorts appeared, such as *The International Handbook of Educational Research* (Keeves & Watanabe, 2003); *The Handbook of Research on Multicultural Education* (Banks & Banks, 2001); *The Handbook of Research on Teaching* (Richardson, 2001); *The Handbook of Second Language Acquisition* (Doughty & Long, 2003); *The Handbook of Reading Research Volume, I* (Pearson, Barr, Kamil, & Mosenthal, 1984), *Volume II* (Barr, Kamil, Mosenthal, & Pearson, 1991), and *Volume III* (Kamil, Mosenthal, Pearson, & Barr, 2000). In 2003, Blackwell Publishing listed 17 handbooks in its catalogue alone. This ironic and fundamentally valid "Age of Handbooks" observation refers to an attempt to gather most of the key information generated by a field, placing it into a handy, affordable package so that access is convenient and available to many, not just a few. This description sounds a bit like an academic version of a Walmart—one-stop academic shopping for almost anything. Yet, to be less sardonic, a handbook is a tool and any good handbook permits the reader to reference pertinent and current knowledge, and, perhaps more importantly, to access information considered to be of value by the cognizant academic community. Coterminous with the Handbook Age was the Meta-analysis Era. The late 20th and early 21st centuries witnessed a trend in American education and elsewhere toward mammoth research reviews and syntheses. The most influential of these for *Understanding Advanced Second-Language Reading* was the *Report of the National Reading Panel (NRP)* (NICHD, 2000) that reviewed and synthesized thousands of research studies published on children and pre-adults learning to read. A related undertaking, the *Report of the National Literacy Panel* (August & Shanahan, 2006), which focused on language minority children and adolescents, also reviewed and analyzed studies. These important taxpayer-funded national panels were not charged with the development of a theory of reading or with capturing the cognitive and metacognitive essences of the reading process for children and adolescents in either first or second languages but, rather, were charged with screening the research literature on reading in order to seek best practices for instruction and teacher preparation. They, nevertheless, took center stage on establishing what work is important, which variables count, and how interpretations of work examined holistically should be constructed.

The editors of the *Handbook of Reading Research, Volume II* (Barr et al., 1991) raise a warning flag about any such endeavor and remind us that "to collect the essential knowledge of the field of reading is an unattainable goal. Those of us who participate in such an effort become parties to the myth that the goal can be attained" (p. vii). They remind us of the compromise that all writers and readers enter into when they try to represent or understand a phenomenon as complex as reading as:

> a static set of truths. ... this static image is only an illusion. And we make the compromise because we fully expect our partners in the communicative act to know that these chapters represent points of departure rather than final destinations ... the very act of reading any review should encourage readers to question the adequacy of the representation and to begin to contemplate better representations. Such is the nature of progress. (p. vii)

I hope that this chapter, in fact this entire book, represents *progress* such as that brought about by other research syntheses. Unquestionably, all of the important synthesis endeavors mentioned above provide the background against which to present this construction of the second-language reading research landscape. Of course, like any painted backdrop it colors and provides a contrasting perspective against which statements are made. This chapter tries to consolidate the research base in second-language reading since the end of the 20th century to make it both convenient and accessible. But, more importantly, it also tries to construct it in such a fashion that it vivifies a notion of compensatory processing.

Methodology for the Present Review

The National Reading Panel itself established a set of criteria under which a study could and could not be admitted into its data base. In order to be included, a study had to have appeared in English in a refereed journal. Studies appearing in edited volumes were not considered to have met the rigor of outside review. Other criteria to which studies were submitted for scrutiny included the age of subjects from pre-school through the end of secondary school and, perhaps most significantly, a study had to have used an experimental or quasi-experimental design with a control group. Indeed, such careful examination, as well as the strictures imposed, were influential. The panel's procedures generated significant criticism. The methodology tended to exclude all qualitative studies given that the concept of "control group" is, by and large, alien to the qualitative/observational paradigm. Further, excluding studies from edited volumes means that certain studies that might actually meet the remaining quality criteria set by the panel were never reviewed and obviously considered to be unimportant.

These are serious criticisms. Similarly, the National Literacy Panel maintained exclusiveness with regard to refereed publications. Yet, it was not as restrictive as the National Reading Panel because it admitted non-experimental and qualitative studies into its data base.

In many ways, the criteria established for admission into the present data base remained similar to those used in *Reading Development in a Second Language.* At the same time, the strict criteria set forth by the National Panels were instructive for *Understanding Advanced Second-Language Reading* and their influence is undeniable. Fundamentally, the criterion of having appeared in a refereed professional journal has been adopted. This criterion is different from that used in *Reading Development in a Second Language* which included any data-based study from any source. Using this criterion might unduly exclude some important study here or there; applying it, however, means that each study in the *Understanding Advanced Second-Language Reading* data base has been examined thoroughly by knowledgeable professionals. A criterion not maintained in this volume, and enforced in the national panels, is what counts as "data." In the context of this book, any data collection can be included whether data are collected on one subject or on many and whether an inferential statistical analysis is conducted or not. This procedure admits far more qualitative studies than under stricter criteria. A final key difference remains and that is located in the intention of this volume. It is my hope that *Understanding Advanced Second-Language Reading* pushes theory forward, helping us to understand the interactive, interdependent components in second-language reading. *Understanding Advanced Second-Language Reading* holds unabashedly to a theory of compensatory processing. Hence, every study listed in the data base was combed for hints of compensatory processing. This ethic makes for a literature review with an overtly stated agenda.

Studies included in *Understanding Advanced Second-Language Reading* involve late adolescent readers and beyond. Hence, an overlap with a small number of studies mentioned in the National Literacy Panel Report might exist. Further, to be included in the data base, subjects had to have read words or connected text and the researchers had to have stated the intention explicitly to examine the second-language reading process. Indeed, there are studies in which subjects might be reading, but the intention of the researcher is to investigate some other variable, as is the case in many vocabulary studies or studies investigating multiculturalism, as examples. Studies that did not meet all of these criteria were excluded. Beyond these basic criteria, the present chapter tries to stay true to a view I articulated in a special issue of *Reading in a Foreign Language* (2004):

> In my view, the field still needs a substantial handbook that delineates research design issues that meet the unique needs of conducting second-language reading research. The following three areas need specific attention. First, there needs to be some established expectations for research studies. All studies should meet, first, some fundamental criteria: 1) employing more than one text in order to insure that data are not essentially single subject

in nature; 2) delineating subject groups and native language backgrounds; and 3) specifying L1 literacy level. I urge members of the field to generate commentaries on these fundamental criteria and others. Second, work on vocabulary in relation to text understanding is critical. Studies inevitably focus on vocabulary outside of textual contexts and then imply how words are used in online processing. We need to solve the problem of how to conduct research to get at the crucial issue of vocabulary use and learning.

In order to develop the data base, the following journals from 1998–2008 were perused: *Modern Language Journal, Applied Linguistics, TESOL Quarterly, Foreign Language Annals, Language Learning, Reading Research Quarterly, Journal of Literacy Behavior, NABE Journal, Die Unterrichtspraxis, Hispania, French Review, ADFL Bulletin, CALICO Journal, AERJ, Journal of Research in Reading, Research and Reading Instruction, Reading and Writing, Studies in Second Language Acquisition, Second Language Research, Journal of Adolescent & Adult Literacy, Reading Teacher, Reading Improvement, RELC Journal, Reading in a Foreign Language,* and *The Reading Matrix.* More than 200 studies meeting the above criteria were included. After the compilation of the items in the data base, each study was examined for certain other criteria: namely, the researchers' explicitly stated theme (strategy use, vocabulary knowledge, phonological processing, as examples); the number and type of subjects; the number of texts read by the subjects; the first and second languages involved; and whether a measure of first-language literacy and/or second-language proficiency level was taken. These data are listed in an extensive appendix to this chapter (see pp. 137–191).

Examining the data base in its entirety indicates that in many ways the field of second-language reading has not changed significantly since the publication of *Reading Development in a Second Language.* More than half of the data base is focused on readers of English as a second language. Some of these studies still fail to differentiate their subject populations. In other words, the generic L2 reader from a sometimes unknown array of second languages still populates the data base. Around a third of the studies focus on non-Western orthographies, while the overwhelming majority of studies center on L1 readers of Western languages reading other Western languages.

Areas of Review

As mentioned earlier, the categorization of studies for *Understanding Advanced Second-Language Reading* was not as easy to do as it was for *Reading Development in a Second Language.* In large part, research study designs became more sophisticated, rendering single-variable categorization much more difficult. Hence, at the end of the chapter, the studies are listed alphabetically for the convenience of the reader and researcher. In the narrative that follows, familiar themes emerge with considerable overlap across themes and studies. These familiar themes already highlighted in *Reading Development in a Second Language* are background knowledge, technology and its use in reading, strategies, testing, intrapersonal variables, L1/L2 transfer, phonological processing/word recognition, instruction, vocabulary, morpho-syntax, and genre/text features. The intention here is to review the studies in order to see what it is that they might suggest about compensatory mechanisms that are involved in second-language text processing. Each area is fraught with inconsistencies, contradictions, and incomplete information. The question remains whether there is a way to view these studies beyond potentially superficial inconsistencies, finding their commonalities and/or developing and enhancing a theory that explains what appears to be contradictory.

Background Knowledge

Background knowledge remained an important focus for research studies. In three important studies with Israeli and Arab high school students, Abu-Rabia (1996; 1998a; and 1998b) found that comprehension is higher with texts that are culturally compatible. The finding itself is not at all surprising; many studies over the years have already indicated precisely the point (Steffensen, Joag-Dev, and Anderson (1979), for example). The key part of the findings from all of the Abu-Rabia studies, however, is actually the attitudinal data attached: that learners tend to be more instrumentally motivated than integratively. This finding, generated by reading comprehension data plus questionnaires, is within the tradition exemplified by the English/French Canadian work by Gardner and Lambert (1972). Within a compensatory framework, then, it is arguable that motivational factors might be able to outweigh or to buttress culturally incompatible factors in second-language comprehension. Barry and Lazarte (1998) offer a study of high school learners of Spanish in high-knowledge and low-knowledge conditions and found readers from high-knowledge backgrounds were able to comprehend text complexity better than low-knowledge readers. Critical though in this study, which employed three different texts of different syntactic complexity, is the missing piece regarding grammatical knowledge. A strict measure of grammatical knowledge might have revealed a compensatory aspect related to prior knowledge from the study's data. It is important to recall that *Reading Development in a Second Language* reported that across multiple domains, knowledge did not adequately predict performance. Again, without an adequate measure of grammatical knowledge and first-language reading ability, it is difficult to argue for or against the size of the impact of prior knowledge.

Taking a text-based perspective on prior knowledge, Brantmeier (2005b) re-examined questions raised by Hammadou (2000) regarding the use of analogy as a comprehension aid. Similar to Hammadou she was unable to find significant differences attributable to analogy, but did find differences in subject prior knowledge with scientific texts. These findings continue to lend authority to the impact of background knowledge on general second-language comprehension without substantive understanding of how it operates. Neither Brantmeier nor Hammadou took measures of first-language reading ability, assuming that readers naturally understand how to identify and use a text feature such as analogy to assist in comprehension. Carrell and Wise (1998) examined topic interest and concluded that it is a dimension of topic knowledge affecting males more than females. The finding might be consistent with Brantmeier's programmatic work on gender and yet, without a measure of language proficiency, it is unclear what portion of the variance relates to interest, topic knowledge, and gender. Likewise, Leeser (2007) targeted background knowledge and how the future tense was processed and suffers from the same issue of lacking a language proficiency measure. Kim (1995) found gaps in prior knowledge causing difficulties in recall protocols of Korean high school students. Pulido (2004a; 2004b; 2007) documented the impact of prior knowledge on vocabulary gain among learners of Spanish as well as the fact that prior knowledge can influence the type and quality of words learned from text. Most assuredly this effect was linked to the cognate load shared by Spanish and English among English-speaking university students and hence a measure of grammatical knowledge, as well as literacy knowledge, would be critical toward understanding the relationship of word learning to prior knowledge. Stott (2004) studied 20 Japanese learners of English, manipulating their knowledge of a text source. Stott found that believing the text was culturally authentic (i.e., from an English-speaking context) led to higher comprehension scores than another group, which was told that the passage was a translation of an L1 source, was able to achieve. Again, the difficulty here is basing claims on one text, yet one can adduce the potential impact of belief or motivation as a compensatory factor in text processing.

Chan (2003) also put prior knowledge to the test and found that language proficiency was a more powerful variable helping high-proficiency readers compensate for a lack of prior knowledge. This study provides some important external direct evidence of the impact of language proficiency and yet, without understanding the level of literacy knowledge of the subjects involved, a substantive conclusion remains elusive. Similarly, Uso-Juan (2006) analyzed background knowledge as an element in compensatory processing and found that raw grammatical knowledge overwhelmed content.

These studies as a group offer important suggestions about the process of second-language reading. Yet, examining these studies as a whole belies continued problems with using single texts rather than multiple texts for data collection; ignoring the level of first-language literacy; and failing to heed levels of language knowledge. These many inconsistencies in the context of many different versions of what prior knowledge actually means render a definitive conclusion impossible.

Technology

Technology became a newer area of investigation over the past decades for some obvious reasons and also illustrates the difficulty of categorizing second-language reading studies. Three dimensions define investigations of technology and second-language reading. First, computer display and presentation were examined; second, investigations of hypertext displays and their relation to reading comprehension in a second language are included; third, vocabulary became of special interest due to the easy availability of online assistance, particularly related to word meaning.

Al-Othman (2003) examined the rate of reading via screen versus paper and found that speed and comprehension are related, and cautioned that readers who read more slowly may be at a disadvantage in online assessment formats. Al-Seghayer (2005) provides evidence that second-language readers prefer hypertext layouts that are explicit rather than unpredictable. Anderson (2003) found that problem-solving strategies were reported as the most frequently used comprehension strategy among both EFL and ESL readers while reading computer-based text. Bell and LeBlanc (2000) examined Spanish-as-a-second-language students reading computer-delivered texts and found that the overwhelming majority of readers reported a high comfort level with computerized texts. The researchers also examined L1 and L2 glossing and found no relationship between the language of the gloss and comprehension. Gloss language was related to frequency of look-up. Rott and Williams (2003) and Ko (2005) similarly examined glosses, indicating that subjects expect glosses. This affective dimension to learners' text-processing is also found in a series of groundbreaking studies—Chun (2001), Chun and Payne (2004), and Chun and Plass (1996)—that focused on German learners interacting with technology-enhanced materials. Chun (2001) found that vocabulary glosses linked directly to texts were more useful to learners than online dictionaries even though highest comprehension resulted from reader access to both. Chun and Payne found L2 readers resorting to translations for words when software provided them with such translations. Readers with low phonological working memory were heavy users of the translation feature. Basing their investigations on studies of German learners, Chun and Plass found that multimedia annotations were particularly helpful in enhancing comprehension. Ercetin's (2003) findings among ESL students were similar to Chun's. Ercetin added that learners preferred word definitions to visual and audio information in multimedia presentations although they used visual information to assist at the topic level of the text. Hirvela's (2005) case study of two ESL Korean learners indicates that learners need collaborative assistance from content area specialists in learning how to read computer-presented texts. Kasper (2003) traced the comprehension ability of L2 readers who practiced reading either in the context of hypertext or traditional paper texts and found that computer-based readers became better comprehenders over time. Kasper argued that online readers spend more time reading and that this leads to higher comprehension scores. Knight (1994) examined intermediate-level Spanish students and documented the efficacy of computerized dictionaries for both high verbal ability and low verbal ability students. Kol and Schcolnik (2000) found that training in reading computer-based texts was no more effective in increasing reading comprehension for second-language learners of academic English than reading from conventional paper texts. Leffa's (1992) work indicates that electronic dictionaries are faster to use and more efficient than paper dictionaries, leading users to higher comprehension scores. Sakar and Ercetin (2005) in a potential contradiction to Ercetin's (2003) findings documented that learners like visual rather than verbal annotations in reading materials but also found that these visual annotations interfere with comprehension. Yet, subjects reported positive attitudes about reading in hypertext. Shang (2005) documented the positive impact of composing and sending email on the second-language reading comprehension process.

In parallel to the background knowledge studies reviewed above, these studies that investigated technology-based enhancements and their relationship to second-language text processing tend to suffer from univariate approaches to what are clearly multivariate concerns. Yet, perhaps more importantly, these studies often fail to mention what the actual comprehension measures employed were and, more often than not, have no measure of first-language literacy with the exception of Knight (1994). The measure of first-language literacy is absolutely critical with regard to technology, given that the investigations could simply be reflecting what learners do in their first-language literacy rather than bringing any insight into the second-language reading process. That said, 21st-century readers are clearly accustomed to computer-based reading. Technology-based reading does not seem to introduce extraneous variables into the reading process that negatively affect readers.

Strategies

Strategies have a long and important history of interest in second-language learning exemplified by the excellent work of Andrew Cohen, Rebecca Oxford, and others. Distinguishing between and among strategy qua strategy studies and reading strategy studies is not an easy or, perhaps, even a realistic task. Yet some researchers specifically refer to reading strategies. Allan (1992), for example, examined an instrument to assess test-taking strategies and offers recommendations about getting information on test takers as test takers. Auerbach and Paxton (1997) advise teaching learners about second-language research, having them translate those research strategies into comprehension strategies. The researchers found positive affect as well as increased comprehension awareness as a result of their treatment. Similarly, Block (1992) examined comprehension monitoring among second-language readers of English who were Chinese- and Spanish-speaking. She found that monitoring appeared to be correlated more with reading than with native language background, implying a strategy unique to second-language processing and distinct from first-language literacy. Chi (1995) taught readers strategies for relating texts to previously read texts and found that such strategy training produced more reflective responses to texts, although whether the strategy work actually enhanced comprehension remains murky. Jiménez, García, and Pearson (1996) found that good comprehenders effectively transferred knowledge back and forth between languages, accessing cognates as well as translating. Similarly, Kern (1994) found that translation is an important strategy used by second-language readers while Yang (2002) argues for comprehension monitoring as a top strategy for proficient L2 readers. Maeng (2005) who examined several high-proficiency Korean readers of English found a successful transfer of strategies across languages. Similarly, Parry (1996) examined reading strategies, but found that strategies were not generic but rather culture-bound, implying a specific L2 dimension. Phakiti (2003) compared the strategy use of men and women learning English in Thailand and found no difference in comprehension, with males reporting a slightly higher use of metacognitive strategies. No further argument regarding the relationship of gender, strategies, and their direct relationship to second-language processing is made. Saricoban (2002) examined and compared higher- and lower-comprehenders in pre-reading, reading, and post-reading conditions. Significant differences in strategy use among the subjects were found only in the reading and post-reading conditions. Saricoban emphasizes that readers do not automatically use their prior knowledge in text reading, a finding consistent with *Reading Development in a Second Language.* Taillefer and Pugh (1998) probed the reading strategies of professional students reading in English as a second language. Similar to previous studies, the readers transferred L1 comprehension strategies into the L2 reading and indicated that good L1 strategies can compensate for weaker L2 language proficiency, a finding consistent with a compensatory view of second-language reading comprehension. Stavans and Oded (1993) were unable to isolate strategies based on good and poor comprehenders. Each group seemed to use the same strategies, but poor comprehenders used them less flexibly. Again, this finding is possibly only interpretable in the context of the first-language literacy level of the subjects. The noted inflexibility might be related to an inability to use such strategies in a first-language context. The authors also cast doubt on their data interpretation by expressing skepticism about using multiple-choice formats for assessing comprehension. In a design similar to Saricoban (2002) with advanced-English level Turkish subjects, Yigiter, Saricoban, and Gürses (2005) found that good readers shift their strategy use depending on the reading purpose. Predicting, interpreting, and reflecting, among others, were just some of the strategies isolated as important and effective throughout the reading process. Mokhtari and Reichard (2004) showed that similar metacognitive comprehension strategies were employed by first- and second-language readers most specifically at higher levels of proficiency, implying that first- and second-language reading become more alike in the upper registers. These latter two studies each lend credence to the notion that the studies were designed in such a fashion that they might have merely re-measured or re-analyzed first-language literate behavior rather than revealing much about second-language text processing.

This important area needs to be reconsidered in light of first-language literacy capacity. The question of whether there are specific L2 strategies for comprehension or whether strategies are simply a part of the personal L1 arsenal is an important question to probe. If the former is correct, studies need to be conducted that compare and contrast L1/L2 strategy use in order to isolate the specific L2 strategies; if the latter hypothesis is correct, studies that assess the compensatory nature of L1 strategy use in L2 comprehension would shed light on the L2 processing. There is a line of thought that increasing amounts of classroom time should be devoted to strategy learning; there is another line of thought, arguing that strategy training is taking important instructional time away from background knowledge acquisition. This is an important issue to resolve and the present data base presents us with more contradictions than assistance.

Testing

Most of the contributions to the area of testing published since *Reading Development in a Second Language* relate to large-scale, high-stakes tests involving reading. Anderson, Bachman, Perkins, and Cohen (1991) examined the construct validity of an English-as-a-second-language reading comprehension test with 28 speakers of Spanish at three proficiency levels and discovered interactions based on item topics, test-taking strategies, and test performance. They argue for using both qualitative and quantitative data sources for conducting validation studies in reading. Given the limited sample size and its lack of diversity, conclusions other than the very broad ones outlined would be difficult at best to generate. Choi and Bachman (1992) examined students taking either of two different tests in order to probe Item Response Theory (IRT) versus Rasch modeling. The investigators argue for the usability of IRT models for assessing test items. Godev, Martinez-Gibson, and Toris (2002) re-investigated a topic examined over the years by Shohamy (1984), Gordon and Hannauer (1995), and Wolf (1993). These studies all indicate that comprehension products will be more accurate if assessments are taken in the strongest language available to the students, most likely their native language. Lumley (1993) investigated teacher judgments with respect to difficulty levels established through the results of Rasch-based item responses, finding that there was substantial agreement between these two data sources. Perkins, Gupta, and Tammana (1995) also examined item difficulty. They concluded that neural networks are an effective means of predicting item difficulty, indicating that reader background knowledge is a critical processing component. Riley and Lee (1996) investigated the comprehension products generated by recall protocols versus summaries. They found that the two tasks generate different performances and caution about how directions are given to subjects. Stavans and Oded (1993) essentially examined test-taking strategies, but also underlined their concerns about cultural conflicts with multiple-choice type items. Salmani-Nodoushan (2003) finds the impact of language proficiency more significant than factors such as background knowledge in reading and, therefore, casts doubt on the need for special purpose tests. This finding lends credence to the contention that if enough texts are used the prior knowledge variable drops out. Throughout the entire L2 reading data base a problem has always been that of examining only one content area and then making claims about all content areas or all reader knowledge bases.

Obviously, if compensatory processing helps to explain and predict performance in second-language reading then assessment strategies will need to account for compensatory behavior and take such strategies into consideration within the context of interpreting test data. The additions to the testing data base add little by and large to theory development and perhaps even less to a consideration of alternative assessment mechanisms. Large-scale testing retains a multiple-choice perspective and still has not reconciled itself to findings regarding language of assessment and comfort level. Chapter 6 returns to this particular concern.

Intrapersonal Variables

A synonym for intrapersonal variables is individual differences. Intrapersonal variables is a preferable concept because it underlines the internal complexity of the individual reader (gender, attitudes, interest) and focuses on internal (i.e., personal) rather than apparently shared processing operations that are both cognitive and social. Two studies verify the importance of a powerful working memory (a reader-internal variable) and high levels of second-language comprehension: Abu-Rabia (2003) working in Hebrew and Russian and Harrington and Sawyer (1992) working in Japanese. In programmatic research, Brantmeier (2003a; 2003b; 2003c; 2003d; 2004a) isolated gender variables in search of comprehension differences. Brantmeier finds gender differences in some instances in which passage topics are explicitly gender-related. Yet, isolating one variable, such as gender, while ignoring other powerful variables, casts a skeptical glow on the potential importance of gender as a variable. If subjects' general literacy knowledge had been assessed, thereby providing a level analytic field for further analysis, perhaps the gender variable per se could be exposed. Interestingly, Phakiti (2003) examined gender within the context of Thai-speaking learners of English and found no difference in comprehension abilities. Brantmeier (2005a), Saito, Garza, and Horwitz (1999), and Mills (2006) examined anxiety. All researchers discovered a level of anxiety related to reading: Brantmeier finds that reported anxiety levels were lower with literacy tasks than with oral tasks; Saito et al. find anxiety with literacy related to general anxiety levels about second-language tasks; and Mills indicates that positive affect is related to higher reading scores. Davis, Gorrell, Kline, and Hsieh (1992) probed student attitudes in relation to their literary study. They discovered positive attitudes toward such study that were related to recreational reading habits in the foreign language. Examining Arabic-speaking learners of English in a cooperative learning environment, Ghaith (2003) found that cooperative learning positively affected reading achievement and yet had no impact on self-esteem and attitudes toward schooling. Focusing on four subjects, Kamhi-Stein (2003) explored the impact of home-language attitudes toward reading in a second language. Kamhi-Stein found that viewing the home language as a positive resource led to significant translation behavior regardless of English language proficiency level. Such findings point toward the use of L1 literacy knowledge as a key knowledge source which in this case overrode language knowledge. In a similar vein, Suh (1999) focused on two subjects, and found that prior reading instruction had the greatest impact on attitudes toward second-language reading. Brantmeier (2006), Mori (2002), and Kondo-Brown (2006a) all isolated interest and motivation and their impact on comprehension. If their studies had included an analysis of first-language literacy their conclusions would have greater power and credibility. If readers already have a confidence in their ability to use literacy for understanding, it is not unreasonable to assume that they might have greater interest and motivation in gathering more knowledge through reading. If individuals are struggling with a cognitive process, it is likely that their motivation will be stifled and their interest low. This is a literacy issue not a second-language issue.

Transfer

Transfer, or the relationship between L1 and L2, is one of the older areas of second-language acquisition research. One might argue that the notion of the L1/L2 relationship was one of the first inquiries posed regarding second-language acquisition. Questions of overlap, or interference, and assistance have been with the field since its inception. Important statements have been written throughout the years, using work such as Odlin (1989) as powerful theoretical bases. The concept of the L1/L2 relationship has also been a significant guiding principle in second-language comprehension, addressed in the early years empirically by Clarke (1980) and others, reintroduced as a theoretical issue by Alderson and Urquhart (1984) in their critical volume, and then reopened both empirically and theoretically in the late 1990s by researchers in both North America and Europe. Bernhardt and Kamil (1995) examined English-speaking college students reading in both Spanish and English, finding that L1 literacy explained 20% of the variance in readers' performance and linguistic knowledge around 30%. Brisbois (1995) found that French learners exhibited a reliance on their first-language literacy for their second. Carrell (1991) found similarly, although learners in the English and the Spanish groups performed differently. Hacquebord (1999) examined native and non-native readers of Dutch within the context of the same test and documented the significant overlap in performance between first and second languages. These studies taken as a whole make clear that learners compensate back and forth between and among knowledge sources for deficiencies in both language and literacy knowledge, underlining the notion that the old belief in language proficiency *or* literacy knowledge needs to be replaced by both/and. There is an important first language/second language connection and the connection exists on multiple levels.

Koda (1993) argues that L1 strategies are used in the processing of L2 texts. Morrison (2004) finds that readers who successfully monitor comprehension processes also successfully employ the strategy in L2. Nakada, Fujii, and Kwee (2001), using an MRI technique, find that the same areas of the brain are used for first- and second-language text processing. Parel (2004) argues for a threshold of second-language vocabulary knowledge that activates syntactic analysis rather than relying on a model that views first-language strategies as activators for comprehension. Paribakht (2005) notes that readers rely on their first-language vocabulary in order to try to make sense of L2 vocabulary words. Data generated by Pichette, Segalowitz, and Connors (2003), using active versus non-active reading, support the threshold hypothesis. They contend that there is less evidence for the argument that L1 reading skills are important for L2 comprehension when readers are actively engaged. Saiegh-Haddad (2003) investigated oral reading fluency and found a significant impact from linguistic proficiency. Arabic readers were less influenced by oral reading fluency than Hebrew speaking subjects, reinforcing the notion that orthography might be the key variable in the study. Tian (1991), using literary texts, supports the concept of an L1/l2 relationship, expanding the notion of common underlying proficiency to include linguistic universals. Upton and Lee-Thompson (2001) probed the use of both L1 and L2 in L2 text processing. The investigators used qualitative techniques to generate evidence to conclude that L1 and L2 are constantly present in all L2 text processing, as did Morrison (2004). Seng and Hashim (2006) found in parallel. Van Gelderen et al. (2004) found that first-language literacy contributed significantly to L2 comprehension and that L2 vocabulary knowledge was also a contributing factor. Van Gelderen et al. (2003) verified through structural equation modeling that L1 and L2 reading proficiency rely on identical factors: language knowledge, speed, and metacognitive activity. Salataci and Akyel (2002) found, similarly, a two-way impact of L1 and L2 on readers of Turkish and English. Walter (2004) focused on the importance of working memory for second-language comprehension. Yamashita (2002a, 2002b) examined Japanese university students and provides evidence for the compensatory hypothesis. Proficiency in the second language was a stronger predictor than first-language literacy.

Based on the findings of these studies, it would be foolhardy to make the case that the first language or the first literacy do not influence second-language text processing. While the evidence is convoluted and shaky, it does exist. The studies outlined here have been undeniably influential in the present volume. The question is no longer one of *whether* there is influence. The question is one of *how*. *How does the existence of language knowledge and literacy knowledge operate in second-language text processing? How can learners be encouraged to draw on their knowledge sources to function and comprehend in second languages?* These remain absolutely key questions.

Phonological Processing/Word Recognition

Akamatsu (2003) documented that the first-language orthography (alphabetic versus non-alphabetic) influences L2 word recognition, validating Chikamatsu's

(1996) findings that the L1 primes readers for word recognition. Everson (1998) investigated English-speaking learners of Chinese and found evidence among college-level learners for the phonological processing of Chinese characters. Everson and Ke (1997) found evidence of the struggle with phonology encountered by English-speaking learners of Chinese as did Fraser (2007) who investigated reading rate. Flaherty (1998) found that readers able to handle abstract designs were more successful than others when learning to read Japanese, while Fender (2008) noted that spelling difficulties for non-native readers of English had a negative impact on comprehension. Fukkink, Hulstijn, and Simis (2005) attempted to increase learners' access to words by training them through the use of technology. Subjects were able to become faster at recognizing words, but it had no impact on their reading speed or on their ability to comprehend. Given the cognate/orthographic overlap between Dutch and English, the finding is unsurprising. Taguchi and Gorsuch (2002) and Taguchi, Takayasu-Maass, and Gorsuch (2004) also examined rapid word recognition by having subjects use a technique called repeated reading. In both instances the researchers noted that while it was possible to increase reading fluency in a second language, that increased fluency did not necessarily lead to increased comprehension. Hirai (1999) researched optimal reading rate and listening rate among Japanese users of English and found the two rates similar with a proficiency effect for lower-level learners in listening.

Koda (1998) compared phonemic awareness between Chinese and Korean learners of English and could find no significant difference even though Chinese is logographic and Korean alphabetic. In a similar study, Koda (1999) investigated orthographic awareness and found that learners from an alphabetic background were more aware of orthographic variations than those from a non-alphabetic first language. Investigating English-speaking learners of Japanese, Mori and Nagy (1999) found proficient readers using context to interpret unknown *kanji* and not using specific morphologies, while Kondo-Brown (2006b) found readers using their phonological knowledge. Nassaji (2003) examined readers of Farsi learning English. The investigation concluded that automatic word recognition skills are critical for comprehension to occur in second-language text processing, a finding consistent with first-language reading research based in young children acquiring literacy. Van Wijnendaele and Brysbaert (2002) examined Dutch and French learners as both L1 and L2 users. The researchers provide evidence that word recognition across languages is rooted in visual processing and embedded in phonology but that the phonology is not necessarily the target phonology. This empirically based comment is consistent with the speculation articulated in *Reading Development in a Second Language*. It provides important evidence about the potential need to acquire oral language for fluency attainment in second-language reading. Wade-Woolley and Geva (1999) found Russian first-language learners of Hebrew more morphologically sensitive, but less accurate at word recognition than English first-language learners of Hebrew. Wade-Woolley (1999) further indicates that L2 readers rely on both orthography and phonology to understand new words rather than giving priority to phonology, providing additional evidence of compensatory processing at multiple levels.

These studies provide evidence that fluency in word recognition is a necessary yet insufficient condition for second-language text processing. Yet, in this area too, many questions remain for the second-language context. Fluency for young first-language readers is related to building the relationship between aural vocabulary and print. For readers who already have a first literacy, the matching process is very different because there are many more potential matches. To draw on the studies noted above, while it is possible to increase fluency through repeated reading, repeated reading may well only focus on word form and perhaps pronunciation. Hence, there is little surprise that there is potentially no impact on comprehension. Pronunciation, in fact, remains a mystery within the second-language reading process. While researchers have provided evidence regarding fluency, it remains unclear how and whether that fluency maps on to an accurate phonological representation of words in foreign languages. Readers in several cases drew upon their morphological or phonological knowledge from L1 in order to process in the L2. Given this observation, *how much of that knowledge do second-language readers modify in order to process in the L2 or do they modify the L2 to fit their L1 knowledge base?* This particular group of studies provides evidence of compensatory processing in visual and phonological domains; the details of the compensation remain hidden.

Instruction

How one assists learners in becoming effective comprehenders is a critical area. The area focuses on outcomes rather than process. The studies cited below indicate that investigators have been focused on outcomes and have been influenced by the concept of extensive reading, by strategy instruction, and by the tasks that readers are asked to do in the comprehension process.

Bell (2001) documents the effectiveness of reading programs based on large volumes of text as does Hayashi (1999) examining Japanese college learners of English. In a similar spirit, Lai (1993) provides data on the effectiveness of recreational summer reading. Mason and Krashen (1997) also offer evidence of the effectiveness of programs based in large volumes of text. They also document the importance of having readers respond to texts in some way. In like manner, Maxim (2002) underlines the feasibility of having college students read large amounts of connected text and documents vocabulary gains. Renandya, Rajan, and Jacobs (1999) also documented the effectiveness of extensive reading. Horst (2005) finds that extensive reading is supportive of vocabulary growth and offers suggestions for assessing vocabulary growth. Other studies in this arena are Iwahori (2008), Nishino (2007), Takase (2007), Yamashita (2004), Hitosugi and Day (2004), Leung (2002), and Kweon and Kim (2008) all of which provide data in support of extensive reading. Problematic in the entire area of extensive reading is what an extensive reading program is actually measured against. Few of the studies make a comparison; Hitosugi and Day is a rare exception. Claiming that readers learned more vocabulary during an extensive reading program begs the question of more vocabulary than *in what other context*?

Gascoigne (2002) examined English-speaking learners of French in their earliest stages of French acquisition and concluded that exposure to second-language texts from the very beginning of L2 instruction is beneficial. Ghaith (2003) found that instruction based in cooperative learning was an effective tool for enhancing comprehension. Hudson (1991), focusing on science and technology learners, noted that an instructional focus on content led to higher comprehension scores than the absence of such instruction. Focusing on five readers, Jiménez (1997) found that special strategy instruction was effective for helping learners to make inferences. Rusciolelli (1995) surveyed students on their reading strategy instruction and found that they considered instruction in skimming and guessing word meanings from context most helpful. Kramsch and Nolden (1994) examined text reconstructions on the part of low intermediate-level German students and encourage, in their terms, "oppositional reading practice" to guide readers into culturally compatible text interpretations. In like manner, Scott and Huntington (2007) focused on interpretation and found L1 useful in teaching literary interpretation at very low levels of L2 proficiency. Oded and Walters (2001) examined the effectiveness of two types of reading assessments (text summary versus making a list) and found that those who wrote summaries presented higher comprehension scores than those who were asked to perform the more mundane task of listing. Pichette (2005) found that as readers advance in proficiency, the stronger the relationship between amount of reading and reading comprehension becomes. Sengupta (2002) practiced process-oriented rather than word-based reading with Chinese-speaking English learners. The learners were able to adopt the process approach within instruction but found it difficult to continue with it on their own. Hui-Tzu (2008) compared two different instructional treatments, one with vocabulary enhancement and one without, within set topics and indicated that direct vocabulary exercises were more helpful to readers than simply reading in a particular word field.

Clearly, studies that examine effective approaches within the context of control groups are critical in order to provide concrete credibility for instructional guidance. Moreover, finding effective instructional practices is necessary but, like other areas in this data base, insufficient. The key feature related to instruction is the extent to which teachers are prepared to offer second-language reading instruction. How do teachers learn to use some of the instructional techniques mentioned above? Bernhardt (1994a) documented, through an analysis of major literacy journals and textbooks for methods courses, that second-language issues are rarely mentioned, concluding that teacher candidates are underprepared for teaching an L2 population. Similarly, García, Montes, Janisch, Bouchereau, and Consalvi (1993) found insufficient material for preservice and inservice teachers to knowledgeably deal with second-language readers. Johnson (1992) in an

ESL setting and Graden (1996) in a French and Spanish secondary school setting examined teacher beliefs about reading and found that the beliefs about literacy in general guide their instruction. This finding could be characterized as the instructional corollary of compensatory processing. Teachers also rely on what they know and use that information even though it might not be directly appropriate in their instruction. In other words, first-language literacy knowledge buttresses or shores up a lack of direct knowledge about the second-language comprehension process.

Vocabulary

Examining vocabulary acquisition in the context of reading is problematic because of the difficulty of separating word learning from comprehension. In other words, a reader might learn a word but might not use that word to enhance comprehension. Simultaneously, there is little doubt that a reader must have a large word arsenal in order to read effectively and, hence, reading and vocabulary knowledge are always conjoined. Within the context of the Brisbois (1995) study which, as an example, indicated that vocabulary knowledge was the lion's share of what might be termed language knowledge, it is clear that what is discovered about vocabulary acquisition in the context of reading is absolutely key to understanding second-language text processing.

Bengeleil and Paribahkt (2004) examined vocabulary acquisition within the context of advanced and intermediate Arabic-speaking readers of English. Readers with advanced-level English were more able to successfully infer words. Both groups used similar inferencing processes, providing evidence of the transfer of L1 literacy to L2 literacy. DeBot, Paribahkt, and Wesche (1997) examined ten ESL learners to uncover how they acquire second-language vocabulary. Investigating learners from various language backgrounds, they found consistency in the manner in which learners used context to learn words. Fraser (1999) conducted a strategy training study to increase word retention and found several strategies to be useful. Hayati and Pour-Mohammadi (2005) found that the use of a bilingual dictionary is helpful for reading comprehension, but does not bring about word retention. Horst (2005) examined 21 adult learners from various first-language backgrounds and across different proficiency levels and argues that extensive reading is an effective means of vocabulary retention. Pigada and Schmitt (2006) found similarly. In a study probing the question of when readers look up words, Hulstijn (1993) found no relationship between readers' strategies for using context to understand words and looking them up. Khaldieh (2001) found vocabulary was a key variable in comprehension but that proficiency level was the main predictor of comprehension.

Pulido and Hambrick (2008) provide similar evidence of the importance of literacy knowledge for vocabulary acquisition. Kim (1995) found vocabulary difficulties as a key source of interference in comprehension. Kroll, Michael, Tokowicz, and Dufour (2002) found higher proficiency levels led to faster word recognition (i.e., evidence of the role of language knowledge) but that lower-proficiency subjects were less able to do the task even in their native language (i.e., evidence of the impact of literacy knowledge). Laufer and Hadar (1997) investigated native-speaking Hebrew high school and university learners of English, analyzing their dictionary-use habits. Their study recognizes that learners at different ability levels and objectives need different types of dictionaries. Prichard (2008) indicates that learners need instruction in actual dictionary use. Leffa (1992) examined college-level students with access to electronic glossaries. The investigator found electronic glosses efficient and their use led to higher comprehension scores on the five short passages used in the study. Luppescu and Day (1993) found dictionary use related to vocabulary test achievement but not to individual items on a comprehension assessment. Nassaji (2004) related prior knowledge and ability to inference the meaning of unknown words, providing evidence of a high-level literacy strategy. Paribakht and Wesche (1999) examined how reader knowledge guides the process of inferencing, another indication of compensatory processing. Parry (1991) argues for extensive reading in a qualitative analysis of vocabulary learning strategies. Examining university learners of Spanish, Pulido (2003, 2004b) conducted programmatic research and found, consistent with other studies, that prior knowledge influenced vocabulary acquisition and that the higher the second-language reading proficiency, the greater the probability of vocabulary gain. In Pulido (2004a), though, passage sight vocabulary—as a measure of prior knowledge and proficiency level—was not related to vocabulary gain. Rott (1999) examined the acquisition of passive and active vocabulary, finding that upwards of six encounters of a word led to retention, although long-term retention diminished over time. Rott and Williams (2003) found affective dimensions in glossing. In a later study, Rott (2007) found that words glossed at least four times were retained longer than those glossed less often. Wesche and Paribakht (2000) found that enhancing reading texts with vocabulary retention exercises led to vocabulary gains, while Waring and Takaki (2003) argue that word frequency in graded readers is critical for retention. Similarly, Zimmerman (1997) found direct vocabulary instruction led to student gains, another finding absolutely consistent with L1 vocabulary research. Alessi and Dwyer (2008) provide evidence that accessing vocabulary during reading is superior to pre-reading vocabulary instruction.

These studies are of critical importance, particularly for the design of instruction and learning materials. This area illustrates the difficulty, perhaps the inability and inappropriateness, of separating vocabulary from prior knowledge as well as separating vocabulary knowledge from strategic use.

Morpho-Syntax

A number of important studies examine specific grammatical variables such as morphological features or syntax. The area, at some level, is not unlike the research area of transfer, given that some researchers conduct their investigations against the backdrop of how a specific feature functions in L1 and L2. For example, Hoover and Dwividi (1998) investigated highly fluent English-speaking French readers, comparing them with native readers of French and found no processing differences but some slowing of processing around grammatical forms that exist in French but not English. Juffs (1998) found L1 language-based differences in how second-language readers from an array of language backgrounds disambiguate main, versus relative clause, verbs. Individual features were probed by Berkemeyer (1994), for example, who examined English-speaking readers of German and found significant correlations between their ability to isolate anaphoric references and their German-language text comprehension. Similarly, Degand and Sanders (2002) isolated connectives and signaling phrases and found such markers are important in reading comprehension. Lee (2007), working with the passive, found similarly. In contrast, Ozono and Harumi (2003) also researched connectors in texts, finding that high-proficiency readers were less dependent on explicit connectors than lower-proficiency readers. Lower-proficiency learners seemed to be able to understand some but not all connective devices in texts. Given the differences in languages and numbers of texts used (Berkemeyer employed only one text, Ozono and Harumi, six texts, Degand and Sanders, 18), coming to confident conclusions in this arena is difficult. Kitajima (1997), similar to Berkemeyer who used German as the language of focus, examined whether training in anaphora can have a positive impact on readers' comprehension of Japanese. Koda (1993) also found English-speaking learners of Japanese to have higher comprehension when they were aware of, and sensitive to, case-marking particles. Dussias (2003) examined the manner in which native and non-native speakers disambiguate certain syntactic patterns. The researcher found that both groups disambiguate in terms of words closer to each other rather than distant. Felser, Roberts, Marinis, and Gross (2003) revealed that learners disambiguate sentences more frequently with a lexical strategy than with grammatical rules, similar to Khaldieh's work in Arabic that established that vocabulary knowledge was more significant to comprehension than inflectional morphology. Marinis, Roberts, Felser, and Clahsen (2005) found second-language readers of English ignoring certain syntactic information using a distance-based strategy even when the L1 background should enable them to resolve the syntax. Ying (2004) examined *that*-clauses and again discovered a limited distance strategy but, after time, a preference for a relative clause strategy.

A set of studies examined grammatical complexities from different perspectives. Gascoigne (2005) found learners were not intimidated by texts with long, grammatically complex text and argued that a threshold level in grammatical understanding is unnecessary. Lee (2002) probed whether readers acquire particular grammatical forms, using future tense as the focus form, through reading. The study indicates that comprehension is dependent on form frequency, context clues, and reader attitude or the way readers approach the reading task.

Leow (2001) manipulated texts in order to highlight certain grammatical forms in Spanish. Text enhancements did not affect readers' processes, contradicting Lee (2007). Similarly, Leow, Ego, Neuvo, and Tsai (2003) found no positive effect for enhanced texts on the learning of grammatical forms. Lazarte and Barry (2008) also researched syntactic complexity, coming to similar conclusions. Stevenson, Schoonen, and de Glopper (2007) found readers able to compensate for their L2 grammatical deficiencies by trying to disambiguate while retaining a focus on comprehension.

Until the field adequately investigates how a second-language reader engages the language forms necessary for comprehension, huge lacunae will exist in the development of an understanding of second-language reading. The studies listed here have made interesting attempts to isolate particular features. By and large, however, they suffer from a lack of precision about how knowledgeable readers are regarding particular structures or if they have an active use of them. The studies often do not contain a thorough analysis of comparable features in readers' L1. Hence, capturing the intricacies of forms in the context of comprehension is lacking in these studies. The studies suggest that lexical processes often compensate for grammatical deficiencies or that readers ignore grammatical deficiencies by drawing on other knowledge sources, which supports the notion of compensation. Yet, as with other areas, *how* readers manage to make these systems function simultaneously remains unclear.

Genre/Text Features

Beyond describing the manner in which knowledge sources are at play in second-language reading, this volume focuses on reading in the upper registers and how the nature and types of higher-level texts are used for instruction and research with second-language readers. Hence, the research that centers on particular features of text as well as on individual genres is of critical importance. Questions of text simplification and text modification remain; in other words, while it might not be useful to simplify texts there could be ways of restructuring them (such as adding graphics or using familiar text structures) that might render texts more comprehensible and might enable readers to cross into the upper ranges of very complicated text. The genre question at present remains principally one of the use of literary text. How the reading of literary text contributes to reading development in a second language also remains prominent; it is, in fact, almost overwhelming on the landscape. Data collections on how commentaries, editorials, perspectives, cultural essays, and the like are processed and how meaning is constructed from very dense text fraught with deep cultural, social, and historical allusions are virtually non-existent.

Reading Development in a Second Language noted that text simplification did not seem to be a productive direction for second-language reading instruction. Over the past decade, though, researchers have continued to probe the impact of simplification. Oh (2001) examined several hundred Korean learners of English and found, consistent with previous studies, that text simplification had little benefit in comprehension and that, in actuality, more expansive texts assist readers in becoming more proficient. Wong (2003) examined reading comprehension and the acquisition of French-language forms. In support of previous studies, Wong indeed found that simplification assisted the recall of idea units but not overall comprehension or the learning of grammatical forms. Yano, Long, and Ross (1994) found positive effects for L1 literacy and L2 proficiency, but not for text simplification. Using a variety of scoring procedures, Young (1999) found that Spanish learners had generally higher comprehension scores on authentic texts in contrast to texts that had been supposedly simplified. Rott (2004), in parallel with many other studies, indicates that modifying texts actually disadvantages learners and that tasks that they are asked to perform with texts can also interfere with comprehension. Keshavarz, Atai, and Ahmadi (2007) provide further evidence that text simplification does not assist comprehension and that proficiency level is the largest predictor of comprehension. It appears that the level of language proficiency can compensate for the complications of upper-register text.

Another line of research examined particular features of text as well as investigating different modalities. Carrell and Connor (1991) compared reading and writing and found readers more able to read descriptive than argumentative, namely, persuasive styles. While this finding seems to be reasonable, 33 subjects spread across 12 different language backgrounds were included in the subject pool. The confounding of language factors and rhetorical style mandate some caution. Chu, Swaffar, and Charney (2002) examined Chinese speakers reading in English across texts that reflected text structure patterns reflective of English and Chinese. They found that the readers were, by and large, insensitive to the textual differences, generally unable to recognize or discern such rhetorical conventions. These differences did, however, have an impact on comprehension. Sengupta (1999) found that over time readers can raise their rhetorical consciousness. Camiciottoli (2003) examined metadiscourse and likewise found that the content itself was more responsible for comprehension level than was the manner in which the texts were structured. Ghahraki and Sharifian (2005) found reading proficiency to be the key link in distinguishing rhetorical features in Farsi-speaking English learners. In other words, the better overall readers were able to understand micro-features of text. Brantmeier's (2005b) quasi-replication of Hammadou (2000) probed the impact of structuring texts around analogy as a means of enhancing comprehension. Subject knowledge contributed more to reading comprehension than did text structure. Lund (1991) found reading comprehension higher than listening comprehension among English-speaking learners of German, with reading comprehension performances more precise and listening performances more elaborate. Park (2004), similar to Lund in examining the differences between listening and reading, found linguistic proficiency most significant with reading, and that prior knowledge played a significant role in listening among Korean learners of English. This is hardly surprising since in reading a reader can review the texts, but listening is time-bound. The study underlines that reading is "easier" than listening. In study after study, either literacy knowledge or language proficiency was a dominating variable in the research. All of these studies point to the significance of authenticity in the reading process and that research should be directed toward understanding second-language reading within the context of authentic texts that are neither manipulated nor overanalyzed.

A body of work examines the literary genre, specifically. Davis (1992) suggests through his investigation with university French learners that students be encouraged to use personal experiences to develop their understandings of literary texts. Davis, Gorell, Kline, and Hsieh (1992) surveyed university learners of French about their reading of literary texts, finding that they have positive attitudes toward such reading, coupled with a belief that literary reading will help them to understand French-speaking people better. Donin, Graves, and Goyette (2004) examined narrative and expository reading among adults using French as a second language. They found a significant language proficiency effect and greater detail recalled from the narrative texts. DuBravac and Dalle (2002) probed college-level learners of French, finding that narrative texts helped readers to generate more questions than the expository texts used. The researchers also found greater miscomprehension in the expository text. This finding is unsurprising given the assistance of background knowledge, its possible misuse in the reading of expository text, and the inherent ambiguity of literary text leading to multiple, often conflicting and rarely "correct," interpretations. Tang (1992) found differences in literal and metaphorical language understanding. Dykstra-Pruim (1998) used children's books to assist the reading of adult beginning German learners. The German learners praised the time they spent reading children's books and believed they benefited from such reading. No pre–post comprehension measures were taken. In an extensive study of literary reading at the college level, Fecteau (1999) used English (L1) and French (L2) texts. The researcher found that the ability to recall the English-language texts predicted the ability in the second-language texts. Fecteau found, however, no relationship between proficiency in the second language and reading the literary texts in the second language and reasonably argues that the ability to deal with literary texts is independent of the second language. Zyzik and Polio (2008) focused on the instructional dimension of literary text and found that when *language* comes into focus in the context of a literary text, it is *vocabulary* that is perceived as key. Hanauer (2001) examined poetry as a text genre. Parallel to Fecteau's findings, the study indicates that among Hebrew readers of English, literary beliefs are involved in the second-language understanding process and that poetry which is highly technical can enhance consciousness regarding cultural differences. Horiba (1996) found English-speaking learners of Japanese more attentive to lower-level text features than their first-language counterparts and relatively insensitive to the coherence of texts. In other words, foreign language readers were not able to perceive the "big picture" in the texts they were reading. Kim

(2004) found literature circles helped to enhance reading comprehension for second-language learners of English. Liu (2004) used comic strips to enhance the reading comprehension of learners of English from a variety of linguistic backgrounds. Enhancement was found within lower-proficiency students with no concomitant impact among higher-proficiency students. In other words, higher-proficiency students did not need the compensatory support offered by the comics.

A Reprise

The intention of this review, reiterating the admonition of the editors of the *Handbook of Reading Research, Volume II*, is to question representations and to develop better ones. In this chapter, I tried to depict a landscape for second-language reading in which the dominant features are first-language literacy skill and second-language grammatical knowledge. I deliberately looked for these features in each study I reviewed; admittedly, what one looks for, one usually finds. Whether this is the illusion to which Barr et al. were referring in their attempt at synthesis or whether it constitutes an adequate representation is only for other readers and researchers to decide. Whatever the case, having provided a representation and having it contemplated, discussed, and accepted or rejected is the "nature of progress" that we need in the field of second-language reading. Chapter 7 will take the areas raised in this review and cast them in the context of future research.

Chapter 4

Compensatory Theory in Second-Language Reading Instruction

The compensatory model illustrated in Chapter 2 is constructed, broadly speaking, around three key components that appear repeatedly in the studies of the second-language reading process outlined in Chapter 3. The task of this chapter is to present the case that these key components should be present, therefore, in the instruction of second-language reading and should provide an organizational basis for upper-register literacy learning as well as assessment. To reiterate, the component that seems to contribute the most to second-language readers' performances is *language knowledge*; the second largest research-based component is *first-language literacy*; the third component, about which far less is known is *other*, which must surely entail factors such as background knowledge and motivation. To understand the notion of compensation is to grasp the critical point that these factors are *not* independent of one another; in fact, they are even *more than dependent*, they are inextricably intertwined because they are used by readers simultaneously in a compensatory fashion. One factor does not operate without the other in second-language reading contexts. Given this state of affairs, this chapter embraces three tasks. First, it interrogates how scholars who write about the teaching and learning of second-language reading account for and/or acknowledge these factors. In that discussion, it questions how and, for that matter, whether teachers can be cognizant of the second-language reading process and teach the components, while not tearing them apart, and whether they can bring readers to understand how to engage their natural compensatory tendencies profitably. Second, the chapter probes how second-language readers employ the variables in a compensatory fashion and how they might learn to use these factors in a more sophisticated fashion as they reach toward independence. Finally, it offers illustrations of instructional sequences that use first-language literacy to help learners strive toward the upper reaches of comprehension.

Instructional questions, either within classroom contexts or directed toward individual learners, are important. As I noted in the introduction, this book was conceptualized within the philosophy that, and written with the ethic that, research into second-language comprehension possesses some scholarly, yet only minimal, merit *unless* it is accompanied by an instructional approach as well as some assessment strategies. In parallel to previous chapters, this chapter provides a retrospective on the teaching of second-language texts as discussed in *Reading Development in a Second Language*. It also examines current thought about the teaching of second-language reading, underlining the evolution of this thought. It then culminates in an instructional strategy for learning to comprehend advanced-level, upper-register texts. This chapter (Chapter 4) focuses principally on expository texts because the preponderance of second-language reading across the globe takes place within the expository context, measured by the content of internet-based texts. A subsequent chapter (Chapter 5) examines the unique case of the learning and teaching of literary texts. Ironically, within the US cultural context, most discussion of second-language reading takes place within the arena of literary reading. A further chapter (Chapter 6) then considers the assessment of learning and the teaching of upper-level texts, both expository and literary. As a first step, however, this chapter explores contemporary thought about second-language comprehension instruction set forward, principally, by authors of authoritative, book-length treatments.

A Retrospective

Reading Development in a Second Language reviewed the patterns of instruction for reading in a second language that were recommended at the time. Principally, as a "skill" in support of other language skills, reading instruction was seen as a process based on typical first-language instructional models: SQ3R, skimming and scanning, the use of pre-questions, oral reading, vocabulary study, and the like were all recommended techniques to be used (p. 180). Further, concepts of stages in reading (word, to phrase, to sentence, to paragraph) were discussed as well as the notion of simplified or structured materials. At the time, theory rarely invaded either classroom instruction or materials. *Reading Development in a Second Language* argued that the quick fill-in-the-blank kind of exercise, designed as or entitled a "reading exercise," did not actually require a reader to use any of the knowledge sources necessary for successful comprehension. In fact, such exercises were seen as actually enticing the reader into playing the usual guessing game of picking an answer because it "fits" grammatically rather than because it is a logical semantic choice—a point supported by Swaffar, Arens, and Byrnes (1991) who write of their conviction that materials can actually subvert what theory and research say about second-language reading. In the years since the publication of *Reading Development in a Second Language*, materials for reading instruction have changed. There are many more authentic selections, although the selections at least in the formal US instructional context are often narrative (not necessarily literary) and less often expository. Contemporary materials still contain pre-reading questions, comprehension questions, and writing activities related to the reading selection. A clear shift in materials also came about with a focus on learner strategies that urge readers to perceive the significance of print features such as size and bold face, or looking for key words. Materials have also been influenced by cooperative learning techniques that suggest pair work for discussing a topic in advance in order to engage background knowledge. These materials belie a sequence within the instructional model. A way to characterize the explicit and implicit recommendations made about the instruction of reading in a second language is to use the word "procedural" or "distanced." Recommendations tend to be focused on procedures to be practiced, outside of texts, that are then supposed to transfer to texts. To underline this contention, it is critical to note that authors rarely use the word comprehension. In other words, there tend to be suggestions that theoretically should lead to comprehension but taking on the concept of comprehension— *what* it means to understand and *how* that understanding develops and *whether* it is reasonable with the cultural context—is rarely addressed. Reading instruction is often conceptualized like music instruction in which learners practice scales and fingering, but rarely get to play a song.

Reading Development in a Second Language offered its own set of suggestions on how to assist learners in their comprehension processes. The instructional strategy offered, called the Recall Protocol Procedure, developed from the notions that readers were, indeed, reconstructing texts as they read in a second language and that these text reconstructions, generally invisible to instructors, both facilitated and masked comprehension processes. The procedure was designed as a teaching strategy that would reveal to instructors and learners where comprehension was being both facilitated and short-circuited in linguistic, conceptual, and cultural terms. In brief, the procedure suggested using a text of around 200 words. Readers are given the instructions to read the text as often as they like (within a fairly restricted time limit) and to surrender the text. They are asked to then write down *in the language in which they feel most comfortable* what they recall from the text. Subsequently, teachers are then urged to examine the readers' recalls and to develop lesson plans based on cultural, conceptual, and grammatical features that interfered with comprehension.

The procedure itself takes an individualized approach to readers' comprehension. Rather than approaching instruction in a generic fashion, the Recall Protocol Procedure acknowledges that readers come to texts with different knowledge sources and that instruction either needs to account for these sources and somehow *neutralize* them or *use* them in some way. Immediate recall requires that teachers probe individual conceptualizations and then construct lessons on the bases of the reconstructions. This procedure stands in sharp contrast to traditional approaches that anticipate learner difficulties rather than examining them as they are generated. It takes into account the variables of background knowledge and grammar but, like other approaches, does not directly address a crucial variable, text topic, as a key part of genre.

Since the publication of these suggestions for teaching reading comprehension in a second language, other book-length materials have appeared that provide alternative versions of how best to approach instruction in second-language reading contexts. Contemporaneous with *Reading Development in a Second*

Language, was the groundbreaking volume *Reading for Meaning* (Swaffar, Arens, & Byrnes, 1991) which argued that:

> reconsideration of native language use in reading and testing of reading is a fairly radical suggestion in today's communicatively-oriented classroom … the notion that maximal exposure to the second language fosters comprehension has dominated at least the theory if not always the practice in our discipline … Occasional use of L1 … may teach more L2 in the long run. (p. 69)

The volume challenged teachers with four tasks: "activate reader schemata"; "guide … an awareness of text structure"; "assist in strategy development"; and "promote relaxed interaction" (pp. 70–71). It also offered extensive discussions on the sequencing of reading tasks, particularly focused on discourse structure, suggesting six instructional stages, ranging from the rapid review of a reading text in order to establish its general topic, through exercises focused on the propositional nature of texts, to readers' reconstructions of the text in the foreign language. Importantly, Swaffar, Arens, and Byrnes (1991) reflect on grammar and reconceptualize it as a critical component in facilitating the construction of meaning. They contend that grammar in reading must be considered within the framework of a given text; in other words, it is often the text itself that determines the grammaticality of particular word sequences—not the word sequences in isolation. They also provide helpful matrices for testing.

Wallace (1992) whose previous volume was entitled *Learning to Read in a Multicultural Society* (1986) is theoretically consistent with other volumes written in the 1990s. She places her work against the backdrop of reading as a social process, acknowledging that any written genre actually evokes a social setting or process—the newspaper advertisement is addressed to a particular client with a particular set of needs or desires and socioeconomic status; the regional newspaper is focused on the social context of a limited geographic space with its needs and concerns, and so forth. She also acknowledges that second-language readers have different levels of first-language literacy and that this set of circumstances has an impact on what can and does happen in second-language classrooms. She offers some helpful suggestions for text selection. Wallace comments about authenticity, text simplification, and so forth and offers a set of "pre-reading activities" (p. 88) designed to orient the reader not only to content but also to highlight critical vocabulary for that content. She poses helpful questions such as what readers would anticipate in certain kinds of texts or how topics themselves would contribute to the nature of the text structure. She also lists tasks to do while reading, such as answering inserted questions that readers should pose while reading. In addition, she provides activities for speaking and writing based on texts read. Wallace uses highly charged phrases such as *hypocritical* versus *insincere* or *corrupt* versus *shady* to illustrate how readers must learn to interpret text within the context of the social valence attached to words and phrases. This is an absolutely critical notion found in few publications on second-language literacy. In sum, Wallace offers an integrative approach to the role of reading both for support of other language skills and for integrating information into the reader's knowledge store. Such an approach is consistent with the social context of literacy in which readers use literacy to operate on the world, to achieve their desires and goals, and to be influenced by it.

Silberstein (1994) begins the pedagogy section of her volume *Techniques and Resources in Teaching Reading* with the unique concept of non-prose reading (p. 19). Non-prose reading is essentially the reading of signs or messages in isolated, non-connected discourse and includes how students, even at a low-proficiency level, can read such texts with a critical eye—what is believable, what is useful about such texts. She argues that this is the beginning for very low-proficiency students and she provides a wealth of ideas about using charts and tables to introduce reading—in order to have students working with concepts at the early stage of literacy learning when they might be potentially overloaded with a density of print. Silberstein then articulates an instructional sequence around expository text and places important emphases on pre-reading, "predictive" (p. 48) processes that then lead readers naturally into fruit-ful discussion and evaluation based on the texts they read. In a plan consistent with Swaffar, Arens, and Byrnes (1991) and others she pays careful attention to the teaching of rhetorical structures and devices including both semantic and grammatical ones in longer texts to help provide learners with necessary scaf-folds for following complex information. Finally, she provides discussion of text types from upper-level registers such as persuasion and literary text.

In a closing admonition, Silberstein writes:

> In "real life," reading is often part of a series of activities, including locating texts and presenting material orally and in writing. Even in a designated reading class, activities that include speaking and writing are well moti-vated. The pitfall to avoid, however, is using reading as grist for a writing mill, that is, using reading tasks only to provide information about which to write. Reading components of any curriculum should focus on helping student to become better readers. (p. 103)

A Focus on Recent Writings

After these important volumes, an explosion of works erupted on the scene. One of these critical works is *Literacy and Language Teaching* (2000) by Richard Kern. Kern presents an extensive case for the integration of all language skills as well as cultural knowledge in comprehension. He rightly points out in the introduction to his volume that all effective communication requires " 'literate' sensibilities" (p. 5) meaning that in order to use language in the upper registers one has to be able to use reading and writing and cultural knowledge to structure appro-priately sensitive arguments whether that be in oral or written speech. Kern's "broader approach" (p. 6) is directed toward a "coherent curriculum" (p. 5) that meets the needs of learners at all levels from elementary through advanced and eschews the notion that the advanced-level curriculum remain "text-centric literary interpretation" (p. 5). Using the concept of Available Design (p. 30), Kern presses the view of reading—or any of the language functions for that matter—as a process by which a reader organizes (i.e., designs) the world. He refers to "relevant interpretive constraints" (p. 115) that have to be placed on non-native readers by texts generated for native readers; i.e., readers part of the interpretive community. In short, Kern states:

> reading is a dynamic rhetorical process of generating meaning from texts (i.e., realizing them as discourse) that draws on all of one's semiotic resources. Every text a reader encounters is the result of a particular act of design. ... Readers try to understand ... by bringing whatever Available Designs they have (for example, knowledge of language, genres, styles, schemata, and so on) to the tasks of decoding, parsing, and interpreting. (pp. 116–117)

In Kern's framework, acknowledging social factors that influence understanding, he underlines the particularistic nature of understanding. He calls for placing text in a situation and enabling students to take a critical stance toward it and helping readers "to see the basic structures of complex sentences as part of a larger communicative picture" (p. 160). Kern's volume illustrates the differences in perspective that have evolved over time—a growing sense of reader-internal activity that undermines the notion of teaching as a set of procedures.

Another important contribution is *English L2 Reading: Getting to the Bottom*. In this volume, Birch (2002) provides an intriguing, principle-based view of reading in a second language, offering an instructional model focused on the learner becoming an "expert-decision maker" (p. 7). Birch rejects the "psycholinguistic guessing game" metaphor on the basis that the metaphor oversimplifies an extremely complex process and presupposes on the part of the learner more knowledge than they often have from which to make guesses. Birch conceives of second-language reading as entailing cognitive processing strategies in orthography, phonology, and lexicon, and "a knowledge base for language" (p. 6) referred to throughout the book as phonemic images, print conventions, rimes, and so forth. Birch focuses on lower-level processes and painstakingly explores the implications of alphabetics, of differences in writing systems, and of phonology, offering important instructional reminders to teachers about regularities in orthographic systems; in graphemes and phonemes; and about assisting learners in decoding new words. She argues:

> we need to respect the need for ESL and EFL students to have the time and opportunity to acquire automaticity in reading before moving on to

challenging material. To build this time and opportunity into the reading curriculum may mean expanding our notion of the beginning and intermediate student. (p. 147)

Another volume, *Extensive Reading in the Second Language Classroom* (Day & Bamford, 1998), characterizes traditional second-language reading instruction as encompassing grammar/translation; the answering of questions after reading; the teaching of strategies; and extensive reading. In fact, extensive reading provides the foundation for their unitary focus on the teaching of second-language reading. Their volume bases its plan for instruction on the concept of free reading and provides guidance into setting up free or "extensive" reading in the context of traditional language curricula. The volume unabashedly advocates for reading materials written *for* second-language learners, i.e., "language learner literature" (p. 63) and offers examples of rewrites of literary pieces for appropriate levels. This volume illustrates a version of recreational reading programs not uncommon in American schools. In contrast to some of the claims in the Day and Bamford volume, as well as in many studies cataloged in Chapter 3, first-language research indicates that little if any gain in reading has been established through free reading programs (NICHD, 2000). Reading progress must be linked to reading instruction and not just to volume of material. Nevertheless, Day and Bamford's book provides some helpful information about how to engage readers in reading in classrooms—writing reports, giving book talks, reading aloud to other students—and in creating "reading communities" (p. 140). The positive here for future research is examining whether extensive reading with "simplified" books might assist in the building of necessary background knowledge. The whole notion is consistent with the award-winning study from Hiram Maxim (2002) who had students read extended, authentic texts in the context of a basic German curriculum.

Grabe and Stoller (2002) and Koda (2005), mentioned elsewhere throughout this book, also focus in portions of their volumes on the instructional aspects of teaching reading to second-language learners. Grabe and Stoller offer important guidelines for action research, encouraging teachers to interrogate their own teaching, probing the extent to which that teaching and student learning map onto research findings. Helpful guidance is given regarding administering surveys to students to get a sense for their learning of vocabulary, their use of strategies, how they understand rhetorical structures, and how they perceive their growth as readers. Koda specifically discusses comprehension instruction for second-language readers and provides a cautionary note about the wholesale introduction of first-language techniques into second-language reading instruction. She cites concerns about diversity in first-language literacy background; different approaches to strategies based on first-language literacy; distinctions and commonalities between first and second languages; and diversity of interests and purposes for becoming literate in a second language. Hence, she cautions that merely employing a technique that seems to be useful in a native-language classroom is taking a leap of faith that might not be warranted. She does argue, however, based on an extensive review of the second-language reading research literature, for three specific directions for effective second-language reading instruction: highly knowledgeable teachers who are informed about the unique character of the second-language reading process; an understanding of and the inclusion of the first language in second-language literacy instruction; and the inclusion of technology-based solutions into second-language reading instruction.

As I mentioned throughout the earlier pages of this volume, an important concept that developed over the last decade of the 20th century was a focus on literacy. To reiterate, such a focus implies breadth; i.e., in the words of Scarcella (2002) "decoding as well as higher-order thinking—conceptualizing, inferring, inventing, and testing. It entails oral communication skills as well as reading and writing abilities ... Advanced literacy involves knowledge of grammar, vocabulary, pragmatics, metalinguistic knowledge and strategies" (p. 211). *Developing Advanced Literacy in First and Second Languages* edited by Schleppegrell and Colombi (2002) takes a social orientation to its pedagogy. At its heart is a similar ideology to that found in Swaffar, Arens, and Byrnes (1991)—that the task of language instruction is to bring learners to levels of understanding that enable them to internalize information, to critique it, and to recreate it. The Schleppegrell and Colombi volume expands the point well beyond the typical language and literature department into language across the curriculum, including science and social science. With a marked concern for English as a second language literacy in the United States and an unapologetic political agenda regarding the fate of immigrants to the United States, the volume, nevertheless, contains specific instructional procedures regarding the use of advanced discourse features in content areas such as history, social studies, and science as well as specific suggestions about bringing about advanced composition skills. Consistent in spirit with Schleppegrell and Colombi is *Remapping the Foreign Language Curriculum: An Approach through Multiple Literacies* (2006) by Swaffar and Arens. Admittedly, Swaffar and Arens take a slightly different approach, given that the volume is largely directed toward the curriculum within US foreign language contexts and the manner in which literature is taught. They smartly note the importance of a "sequence of learning rather than a sequence of materials" (p. 187). Emphasizing the advanced learner (p. 99) rather than advanced tasks, Swaffar and Arens pursue a specific learning methodology of the précis so that readers come to understand both micro-elements of text as well as discourse structures that reveal literary content and perspectives.

Hudson (2007) refers specifically to *teaching* in his title and yet offers little in the way of explicit instructional strategies. In like manner, Grabe (2009) claims a "theory to practice" organization, yet his volume is similar to Hudson's. Both volumes share a penchant toward reiterating research, speculating about findings, and drawing attention to implications without providing any specific teaching directions. In stark contrast is the Hedgcock and Ferris volume, *Teaching Readers of English* (2009), which reviews the same body of research as Hudson and Grabe, but is deeply specific about teaching direction. Guidelines for teaching are offered throughout the volume such as "Bottom-up Text Selection Considerations" (p. 92); "Guidelines for Timed Reading Programs" (p. 100); "Elements in Understanding Poetry" (p. 269); and "Information Transfer Task Suggestions" (p. 355); among many others. A reader of *Teaching Readers of English* would come away with a set of strategies that enable the conduct of a second-language reading lesson with precision and integrity.

In spite of the volume of work that has been conducted and written regarding instructional approaches to second-language reading in the past decade and a half, several issues that pertain specifically to learning to read upper-register, nuanced text have not been discussed extensively. The first issue is that of *independence*. How can readers read and comprehend with confidence the upper-level, technical material that adult-level, professionally oriented materials demand? Formal instruction, by and large, comes into play in the early stages of the learning process. Research-based teacher guidance is critical, but how readers are actually prepared to gain new useful knowledge sources, enhance their language, particularly their vocabulary level, and gain more nuanced levels of language in the *absence* of a teacher or structured environment is critical. The challenge for learners is to know the knowledge sources they possess that will facilitate accurate comprehension; to know which knowledge sources they possess that might interfere with their comprehension; and to discover ways in which to build new knowledge sources.

A second issue is that of *genre* and *topic*, specifically differences between fictional text and information text for second-language readers. In traditional foreign-language settings stemming from Humanities-based curricula, a substantial diet of literary text was offered. While the use of literary text offers learners the "truly foreign" experience and is, indeed, the most challenging of all types of second-language texts, it also constructs intellectual roadblocks for the reader: the text's topic might not be in the reader's world knowledge store (reading about airplanes in the Middle Ages as an example); the literary text is, by and large, deliberately ambiguous, intentionally open to multiple interpretations; the text will use extremely economical language and tends to have no outside support such as visuals, graphs, and charts; and the text is deliberately cultural. In contrast, information text affords the possibility of a topic that might be in a reader's knowledge store. Such text also claims to be intentionally unambiguous and straightforward. It is often redundant, that is, pictures and graphs may capture information that is already in prose, and the text is often culturally independent—life cycle of snakes; how halogen lamps function, and so forth. Yet how to prepare for an infinite number of topics, often randomly presenting themselves, is extraordinarily problematic. It is to precisely this issue that this chapter now turns.

Illustrating Compensation

In its most concrete, visible, and simple form, language knowledge consists of morphology, syntax, and vocabulary. Surely, the history of language teaching is filled with notions of how to teach these components and the history of language testing is filled with techniques about testing them. In the history of second-language reading, these components have only recently been discussed in terms of their overall contribution to understanding. While forms might convey a past or future tense, the meaning of past or future for how an author constructs a textual message around these notions has only recently been explored in the context of expository prose. Further, how languages realize certain meaningful features, such as mood, to express a wish, a doubt or uncertainty, advice, or to express emotion; or indirect discourse to express distance, is rarely taught in a cross-language fashion or discussed within the context of reading texts as conveying particularly *nuanced* messages. English, for example, is in need of words or intonation to express doubt; Spanish and German, in contrast, need only change a stem vowel. In rapid reading, it is easy for non-native readers to overlook the stem vowel which, for the native reader, may well evoke a particular tone or feeling in the reader that is essentially unwritten. Viewing syntax in its cross-language manifestations, too, is important for second-language readers. While syntax is generally taught in a productive sense of word order, readers must unmask why writers choose to emphasize particular elements of their discourse. The semantic impact of beginning with a direct object rather than a subject needs to be a discussion vis-à-vis meaning, not simply in the pedagogical context of examining and learning and producing the surface manifestation of the sequence of words or in the context of mere efficiency. Determiners in English provide an interesting example of how the most simple morphological features evoke complex conceptual ones. Consider the two contrasting sentences *Tom bought a car* and *Tom bought the car*. Language teachers can explain grammatically that *a* references a generic, non-specific car, while *the* references a specific car. While this is an explanation of sorts, it ignores the semantics of determiners. *Tom bought the car* might evoke a complex set of ideas about that *specific* car. If the sentence is uttered in oral speech one can comprehend multiple things given different intonational patterns. If it is in written form one can fruitfully understand the sentence only in the context of all of the discourse surrounding it. That surrounding discourse might signal that Tom overspent on the car he was captivated by or that Tom is clearly in debt, had been advised not to purchase that particular car, and unwisely ignored the advice. Critical is the evoking of other images, the baggage to use a contemporary expression, that words as simple as *a* and *the* carry with them. Comprehension has to do with *baggage*. The task for advanced language learners is not only to learn words but to create the baggage that they carry with them. It is the baggage, fully packed with images, that distinguishes the upper-level language user from the lower-level going-through-the-motions kind of language user who perhaps only has a carry-on.

In the early pages of this book, I used the term Dust Bowl Empiricism. Every reader of this book knows what dust is, what a bowl is, and what empiricism means. And most North Americans know what Dust Bowl with capital letters refers to. The question becomes what Empiricism in a/the Dust Bowl means. With a negative valence, the expression means in American English "blind, unguided-by-theory observation"; in other words, observing for the sake of observing, a criticism lodged against scientists in American Midwestern universities in the 1930s. With a positive valence, it refers to individuals who conduct careful painstaking detailed data collection. This account might help to explain Dust Bowl Empiricism, but what of the word used in previous sentences, *valence*—a term perhaps familiar only to those who learned it in elementary chemistry? The dictionary explains that valence means *the degree of combining power of an element or chemical group as shown by the number of atomic weights of a univalent element (as hydrogen) with which the atomic weight of the element or the particular molecular weight of the group will combine or for which it can be substituted or with which it can be compared.* This definition does not seem to fit the "Dust Bowl Empiricism" example. The next dictionary definition for valence is *relative capacity to unite, react, or interact with (as with carbon),* while the third is *the degree of attractiveness an individual activity, or object possesses as a behavioral goal.* Definition three provides some insight into the phrase: the valence on a word refers to how much that word attracts other words and of what type to meet the goal of the utterance.

The objective in going through these expressions and words is to walk through examples of what learners actually have to contend with in order to become upper-level users of language. They have to hear or "notice" the word or expression. They have to battle with unreasonable meanings. If they look the word up in a dictionary, they have to interpret and abstract from definitions other concepts that are often being used metaphorically. This is the incredibly arduous reasoning process that often exhausts readers and compels them to capitulate. The result is often an imprecise understanding or, worse, a misunderstanding.

An additional example within a native-language context might be helpful. I was reading a book called *The Conquest of Nature: Water, Landscape, and the Making of Modern Germany* (Blackbourn, 2006) which I had picked up because it claimed to tell the history of Germany based on dams, straightening the Rhine, building canals, and so forth. While reading, I encountered the word *jeremiad* which I pronounced for myself as *je-'rim-i-ad.* I did not know what the word meant and kept on reading. Several chapters later, the word appeared again. Rather than hunting around my house for a dictionary, I did the far more convenient thing—I asked my husband.

"What does *je-'rim-i-ad* mean?"
"What?"
"*je-'rim-i-ad*"
"Let me see that. *jer-ə-'mī-əd.* It's from Jeremiah."
"Oh." [Mental note: "Better look that up in the dictionary."]

Indeed, in the end, the dictionary tells me that Jeremiah was the prophet pessimistic about the future and therefore a jeremiad is a prolonged lamentation or complaint. It took work to learn this word—work that I was unwilling to put in until I was totally embarrassed. I compensated for not knowing the word by asking for an outside knowledge source, but not before I had rationalized that I really did not need the word.

Do you need to know *jeremiad* in order to understand *The Conquest of Nature: Water, Landscape, and the Making of Modern Germany*? After contemplating this question, I conclude that the answer is "no" because I was reading for information, for pleasure, about German waterways. When I saw what the word meant I said to myself, "Oh that's one of those $10 words. Let's see if I ever use it." Yet, on the other hand, if a reader wants to know the genesis of an author's thought and how that author interpreted his own data, the word is important. It evokes the author's understanding of the debates surrounding water use in Germany throughout the centuries and how these debates influenced German perspectives on the environment. Does the reader need to know *Dust Bowl Empiricism* to understand the introduction to this book? Using the same logic as above, the answer is both no and yes. To get at most of the straightforward content in *Understanding Advanced Second-Language Reading* the expression is not even useful, let alone necessary. Yet, to comprehend some of the most fundamental ideology sewn throughout these pages, it is very important to know the expression because it evokes a Midwestern view of *science* that contributes toward understanding everything from the topic to the structure of this volume. Is understanding the word *valence* as critical? Perhaps it is not terribly critical because *valence* was used merely as an illustration. But comparing *valence* and *baggage* might provide some interesting linguistic and sociolinguistic insights into contemporary idiomatic American English. The challenge for the reader is deciding on which words to try to understand and how deeply. Which knowledge sources can the reader draw upon to come to an adequate understanding of a word and how can that reader evolve past adequate understanding into deep understanding? Can research, theory, and technology help us decide which words a second-language reader should try to understand and how to help the reader in that process? These are monumental questions.

A second challenge is posed by first-language literacy. At some level, the term "literacy knowledge" is a catch-all: it refers to what a learner knows about how written language functions and how sophisticated that knowledge is. As the early pages of this book illustrated, the more a reader has in a literate knowledge store, the more that knowledge contributes to explaining performances in second-language comprehension. A mistaken notion on the part of many researchers and teachers is that second-language readers are blank slates—that they must learn literacy again because they are unfamiliar with the language code. In *Reading Development in a Second Language*, notions of print conventions were introduced. The examples in Figure 4.1 elaborate on the point.

Example	Illustration
1	Así como el médico toma una radiografía para analizar internamente el organismo, los antropólogos,mediante el único laboratorio de prospección arqueológica de América Latina, analizarán en marzo un sitio preolmeca del año 3000 A C, ubicado en la costa del Pacifico. El objectivo es identificar con precisión asentimientos humanos utilizando imágenes satelitales y fotografías aéreas a color de alta resolución.
2	• Así como • el médico toma una radiografía para analizar internamente el • organismo, los • antropólogos,mediante el • único laboratorio de • prospección arqueológica de América • Latina, analizarán • en marzo un sitio preolmeca del año • 3000 A C, ubicado en la costa del Pacifico

3	Selbst in Hannover, wo *er Immerhin* 40 Jahre land gelebt
	                        hat, **wissen die**
	           Meisten wenig mit Gottfried
	Wilhelm Leibniz **anzufangen.**

4	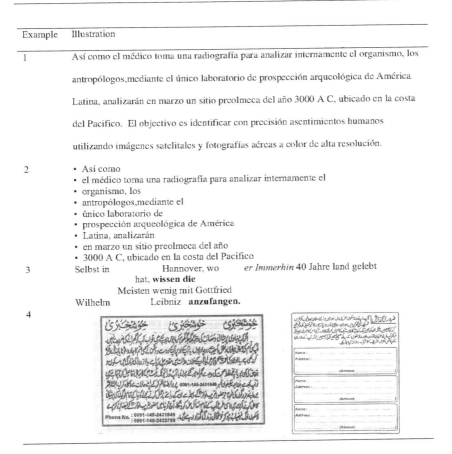

Figure 4.1 Illustrations of conventions and content in Spanish, German, and Urdu

Whether one knows Spanish or not, Example 1 in Figure 4.1 is perceived to be connected text with the concomitant assumption that the text is, indeed, connected and meaningful. Example 2, in contrast, is perceived as a list with varying degrees of connectedness that would need to have lots of information added in order to make a complete text. In reality, Example 1 is identical to the text in Example 2 except that it does not meet standard assumptions of connected text because it is bulleted. The same might be said of Example 3. The text does not meet standard print conventions and, therefore, will be difficult to "comprehend" when, in reality, the text is perfectly reasonable German. A more meaningful example is found in Example 4. Examining the text in Figure 4, one can and does draw a number of inferences without knowing a single word or even a single letter of the language in which the text is written, Urdu. Examining the first line carefully leads one to conclude that the three words are identical. Using background knowledge about the conventions of print, at least in the Western world, some kind of attention-getting device is probably signaled. Next, one notices phone numbers that are indeed from a country outside the United States and one can assume the numbers connect to telephones in the country of origin. Further, because the print is not exaggerated in any way and there are no graphics, one might assume that the message of the text is probably "serious." On the reverse side of the card is more writing—equally serious-looking—a place for names and addresses with "amount" to be filled in.

Whether one can recognize the language or not, in applying general principles of literacy, one recognizes the text as a text, assumes that it contains a coherent message, assumes that it is not a story (witness the telephone numbers listed) and that it is perhaps an ad of some sort because of the three identical words across the top much like "attention attention attention" or "closeout closeout closeout." In reality, the three identical words are "good news good news good news." The reverse of the card has a space for the listing of names, address, and a dollar amount. This configuration seems to be curious and one might respond with "I have no idea of what this card is about. Somebody wants money for sure." Yet, if one then instantiates a religious notion, the card can be interpreted as an indulgence or prayer card, a mechanism used to assist intercessory prayer in many religious contexts. It is cultural or, better said, *subcultural* information that enables comprehension. In fact, the solicitation is for money to support prayer intentions at a particular shrine (Currie, 2006). A person who has that subcultural knowledge (a familiarity with Catholicism or Buddhism, for example) can understand the text at some level *without* linguistic knowledge and a person without that subcultural knowledge who may have *linguistic* knowledge might fail to understand. This act of using literacy and background knowledge in tandem—each supporting the other—illustrates the compensatory nature of language and literacy processes.

Of course, comprehension in upper-level domains cannot be about guessing as the Urdu example implies. Superior-level comprehension is also not about the "gist" or about a broad "sense." It is about precision and exactitude and a self-confidence about content that enable the reader to critically question that content. It is the difference between skimming through a *People, Fokus, Caretas,* or *Cronos* to get a sense of the articles and being able to sustain an understanding of in-depth substantive material such as that found in *The New Yorker, Die Zeit, Le Monde, Revista de Occidente,* and so forth; reading at the superior level is, indeed, the difference between being able to use authentic/unedited information at a professional level such as that found in scholarly journals and merely being able to skim through synopses.

Toward Reader Independence

What I propose is an instructional procedure rooted in the research on second-language comprehension, framed by compensatory theory, and driven by a sense of the interrelationship of all language skills. At some level, what I suggest in the next paragraphs flies in the face of faith-based instructional practices that focus on subskills and hope for the best. As Swaffar, Arens, and Byrnes argued, we have never appropriately acknowledged the positive role of the first language in the comprehension process. In fact, at the higher levels of language learning the role of first-language-based knowledge is perhaps even more powerful than at lower levels because the nature of the upper-level knowledge is much more dense, complex, and complicated. Given that a significant part of learning is understanding how to sift—to look for those things that you are more willing to take seriously—an ability to rely on first-language knowledge is indispensable.

One approach to the knowledge domain problem is to provide learner support on every imaginable topic. In other words, annotations would have to be available on an infinite number of topics in every conceivable language. A more manageable approach is to establish a "set" of topics that might overlap with all other topics. This approach characterizes the curricula of the early levels of most contemporary language instruction. Topics such as the family, celebrations, health and fitness, the workplace, and so forth are routinely covered for their general utility. This approach is also an organizational strategy for "content-based" language courses such as Spanish for the Biological Sciences or French for International Relations or Business Chinese or Business German, which often characterize what might be termed as an intermediate level of language knowledge. Vocabulary is controlled topically and learners interested in the topic are able to garner a deeper vocabulary in an interest area. This curricular pattern is also intended to assist the learner in acquiring the vocabulary level to match a knowledge level that facilitates presentational speech toward a professional orientation well beyond the interpersonal level. But the concern is beyond a mere topic. The upper reaches of proficiency are characterized by an almost hyper-specificity as well as hyper-precision in vocabulary. Specificity and precision are difficult to operationalize in the context of generalizability. Indeed, any instructional setting with the exception of an individual tutorial is a compromise—it tries to accommodate all learners and all learners' needs, which it, of course, can never do. As a result it has to make concessions.

In earlier, perhaps simpler, times the notion of topic was not significant because the upper-level language curriculum was exclusively the literature curriculum. Hence, the vocabulary that was learned was vocabulary related to the learning and using of literary text. Specificity and precision were found in the vocabulary of literary analysis and word learning became codified by century. Readers were often aware of the semantics of a word based on its historic roots and so forth. In this simpler time, the universe of words that readers needed to know was somehow manageable given the parameters of literary study. In the modern era, the manageability of learning a high level of language for literary study has grown into the hyper-complexity of language use for global needs. Indeed, the existence of cost-free materials through the internet contributes to this hyper-complexity. Adding to that complexity is the contemporary acknowledgment that while the world might be a global village it contains many, many languages that effective world leaders need to be able to use. The irony of globalization is that it has not homogenized the world into the *lingua franca* of English but, rather, has emphasized the criticality of being able to communicate with all members of the globe and, essential to the spirit of this volume, of being able to understand them.

The key toward resolving this dilemma—of enabling learners to become sophisticated comprehenders of whichever language they choose—is in creating independence on the part of the learners. Independence comes about by modeling how one learns to comprehend and continues to learn new and more precise words—words in their straightforward as well as their metaphorical meanings. The following proposes a path to independence, one based in the research outlined in previous chapters. The path toward independence must necessarily acknowledge grammatical accuracy, the use of first-language literacy, and a sense on the part of the learner about the state of, and the growth of, their personal knowledge domains.

As an example, suppose that after reading *The Conquest of Nature: Water, Landscape, and the Making of Modern Germany* a reader wants to learn about land reclamation in German history and wisely concludes that reading information *in German* on this topic is the goal. Some access to the topic has already come through his/her native language, suppose English. After all, research indicates that perhaps 20% of what the reader needs is already housed in his/her ability to read in his/her native language. Reading about the topic sets the reader up to think through words that he/she could encounter on the topic in the foreign language. For instance, reading about land reclamation and drainage points toward words such as *swamp, hydrology, canal, locks, drain, pump,* and so forth. The reader should be able to anticipate in all texts that certain words might appear; likewise a reader will *not* be anticipating certain words in the land reclamation domain such as *elephant, birthday party, cathectic, theosophy,* and so forth. The reading of the topic in a first language enhances background knowledge and alerts the reader to particular terms unique to the topic. Before reading in German, the reader might want to look up certain topic-related words or contemplate what these words might be. Chances are that the reader knows the common word for *lock* in German is *das Schloß*. Will the word *das Schloß* appear in a German text on water reclamation? This is a difficult question because the answer is a vague "yes." The word for *lock* in the water reclamation sense is *die Schleusenkammer*, in which *schleus* and *schlos* are etymologically related. A reader would have to be at a very precise level of German knowledge to be able to automatically make these connections.

Instruction should, of course, enable students to become independent and good instruction is good modeling. Hence, teachers should model what students need to learn in order to do what our reader interested in water reclamation is able to do independently. Hence, teachers should enable their students, first, to use their first-language literacy. Imagine assigning the following readings in a Spanish, German, or French setting. "In an Upside-Down World, Sunshine is Shunned" (Rohter, 2002); "Dear Euro, They Sigh (not fondly)" (Erlanger, 2002); and "The 9/11 Inquest: Did Germans Bungle?" (Frantz & Butler, 2002), respectively. All three of these articles come from the *New York Times* from a page 4 regular feature about issues throughout the globe. "In an Upside-Down World, Sunshine is Shunned" relates a story about "what life is like under that hole in the ozone layer" in the city of Punta Arenas, Chile. In journalistic narrative, the article rehearses various kinds of scientific information regarding the danger of ultraviolet rays as well as relating some personal interest anecdotes about whether children can play outside and for how long under the ozone hole. "Dear Euro, They Sigh (not fondly)" is a description of the reaction of Germans to the introduction of the euro which prompted a general belief that prices had increased, using the example that businesses had merely changed the DM sign to the € sign, thereby doubling prices. The subhead in the article makes the point: "Germans are convinced the new currency is costly." "The 9/11 Inquest: Did Germans Bungle?" is a description of German/American tensions brought about by 9/11 bombers having plotted the 9/11 attack in part in Germany. It underlines the tensions with its subheads: "The Germans, says a U.S. official, 'were basically pretty much AWOL'" and "The Americans withheld data 'and now we have proof' a German says."

Students can be asked to read such an article on the web for homework and to prepare for the following class by doing the following task: *If you were reading this topic in [French, German, Spanish], which words would be extremely helpful? Choose 10 and look them up. Be prepared to talk about this article in [French, German, Spanish].* This process is meant to enable students to become wise at their word choice and to efficiently replace what is termed in lower levels of instruction as a "pre-reading activity." Indeed, the task is a complicated level of pre-reading activity in that the material constituting the activity is principally generated by the learner and not by the teacher. The point of reading the text in English is to provide content information, and the vocabulary activity is meant to enable the student to construct a sophisticated vocabulary necessary to talk about the text. Interestingly, in the context of the personal interest portion of the *euro* text, the words *strawberries* and *chives* appear. Certainly students could choose those words to look for if they do not know them, but perhaps wiser choices in the context of an article on currency would be *price gouging, common collective currency,* or *consumer boycott.* In instruction, conducted in the foreign language, students could be asked to share with their peers the words they chose as a means of retelling the article in the foreign language. They could even be asked to write a summary in the foreign language of the article they read in English. Examining the articles written in English about other cultures immediately encourages cross-cultural comparisons and the like, prompting questions such as why a reader of the *New York Times* would be interested in German perspectives on the euro.

A next step is to read authentic texts in the foreign language on the same topic. Cognizant texts for these examples could be "Euro ist kein Teuro" in the *Süddeutsche Zeitung* online, www.sueddeutsche.de, June 4, 2002; "La capa de ozono: Chile en el ojo del huracán" from www.cronica.cl, December 6, 2000, and "Une taupe islamiste dans la police de Hambourg" from www.lefigaro.fr, July 9, 2002. These three texts are not translations, but most assuredly reflect the content of the aforementioned English-language articles from an admittedly different cultural perspective. Students should conduct word searches to see if the words they anticipated to be in the foreign-language text actually appear in the text. They should also be able to reiterate the content of the foreign-language text in the foreign language and make reasonable and reasoned comparisons between the content and form of the two texts. How German or Spanish realize the subjunctive versus how mood is expressed in the English-language article, or why the French would be interested in tensions between Germans and Americans would be examples among many in a high-level discussion centered on text.

Of course, any level of independence would imply that readers would locate their own texts. Imagine a reader wants to read more about *marsh drainage*. One can search *marsh drainage* on the internet to find any number of articles in English on the topic that seem to be important and useful. The reader can then simply use the translation function found in most search engines to translate *marsh drainage* to find its German meaning, *Sumpfentwässerung*. The reader can then scan through the sites offered looking for a relevant German-language text. In summary, the second-language reader should use information housed in the first language about marsh drainage upon which he or she can base the search for important technical vocabulary necessary for comprehension as well as cross-cultural perspectives on the topic. One could imagine that different environmental views take different argumentative stances on the entire issue of marsh drainage. It is the task of the superior-level reader to be able to understand both the technical content and the sociopolitical stance of whatever is contained in the text.

All pedagogical suggestions risk implying that they should be used exclusively. This is obviously never the case. The suggestions made here are consistent with much of the excellent thought that has evolved over the decades about second-language reading in general; about sociocultural implications of an additional literacy; about the relationship of reading and writing; and about discourse and text analysis leading to superior-level performance. In the final analysis, though, the more complicated or technical the material becomes, the more individual-focused and particularlized it must become. Hence, the suggestions are made in the spirit of enabling individual readers to utilize their second-language grammatical strengths, their first-language literacy knowledge, and their expert-level background knowledge to assist them in sophisticated text understanding.

Chapter 5

Second-Language Readers and Literary Text

Understanding Advanced Second-Language Reading now turns to the case of literary reading as an instance of upper-register text understanding. There are two specific reasons for this particular focus. The first is a pragmatic one, rooted in the second-language reading research data base itself. The very few studies that exist with second-language readers interacting with difficult, upper-register tests, indeed, concern the processing of literary text. The second reason is much more critical, yet elusive. Literary text demands of non-native readers that they engage foundational cultural and literary knowledge in order to understand—two knowledge sources that might only exist in an underdeveloped knowledge store. One dimension refers essentially to the *Gestalt* of a particular culture and is, consequently, extremely broad, vague, and uncodified; the other refers to procedural knowledge related to the interpretation of literature and is consequently particularlistic, narrow, and similarly uncodified. Each of these knowledge sources helps to drive the understanding of a literary text. These statements reiterate the arguments made in *Reading Development in a Second Language* for the unique status of literary texts in noting that "it is in literary texts that the implicit knowledge structures, and the unstated cultural heritage, that *all* learners need if they are to develop usable, authentic language skills are found" (p. 185).

The principal question then for this chapter of *Understanding Advanced Second-Language Reading* is how compensatory theory might also help to explain the special case of second-language literary reading by providing a lens into the way in which readers use their available knowledge sources to construct their understandings of literary text. In order to engage with these questions, a previously unpublished longitudinal study that examines readers using their first-language and second-language cultural/literary knowledge is included in the chapter. A final question is a curricular-pedagogical one that parallels that from the previous chapter. *Can compensatory theory help in the development of curricular thought, instructional procedures, and in the acquisition of self-regulatory strategies to enhance second-language literary comprehension?*

As noted throughout this book, significant research in second-language text comprehension has tried to reveal from the reader's point of view the nature and extent of the knowledge structures that the non-native needs in order to either "understand" or to "respond" to texts in an authentic way. To reiterate arguments advanced in previous chapters, three basic patterns have emerged from this research. First, it is clear that the reader's current knowledge base—meaning the first-language cultural and linguistic knowledge base—is a major contributing factor to the reconstruction of a second-language text. This contribution is related principally to first-culture conceptualizations. Carrell (1983, 1984, 1987); Carrell and Wallace (1983); Cohen, Glasman, Rosenbaum-Cohen, Ferrar, and Fine (1979); Connor (1984); Johnson (1981, 1982); Lee (1986); Mohammed and Swales (1984); Steffenson (1988); Steffenson, Joag-Dev, and Anderson (1979); and Zuck and Zuck (1984), among others, all portrayed the second-language reading process as a knowledge-based process. Despite this relatively large number of distinguished studies, the data provided in *Reading Development in a Second Language* suggested that focusing on a reader's knowledge base was overrated and overemphasized, for at times readers had appropriate and relevant knowledge and would fail to use it, and at times they had no apparent relevant or appropriate knowledge and, nevertheless, did not need it for comprehension. Beyond the information regarding prior knowledge, *Reading Development in a Second Language* also provided data clarifying that the first-language knowledge base and second-language grammar base interact with second-language reading proficiency. *Reading Development in a Second Language* pointed out that the interaction takes the form of knowledge being able to compensate for second-language linguistic deficiencies as well as being powerful enough to override actual proficiencies. Questions remained about the psychological state that prompts this type of observed compensatory processing. Finally, a key factor in the compensatory model illustrated in Chapter 2 is a deeper understanding of the role of grammatical knowledge in the second-language reading process. Does grammatical proficiency operate within literary and other upper-register text reading in the way it does with expository text? This question underlines the need to move the spotlight away from the findings of the significant number of studies that investigated the impact a reader's native-language cultural knowledge base has on second-language understanding, and toward other dimensions of the compensatory model. The model in Chapter 2 suggests that a focus needs to be placed on a major portion of reader background, i.e., first-language literacy, in the context of how much raw knowledge of the second language is able to account for second-language literature reading performance and interpretation.

Studies of Second-Language Literary Reading

The "special situation of relatively inexperienced learners attempting to understand and to appreciate literary texts" had my attention in 1991 (p. 23). The interactions of 12 intermediate-level German students with two literary texts, Borchert's (1949) *Nachts schlafen die Ratten doch* and Böll's (1977) *Mein teures Bein*, were examined. At the time the study was conducted these texts were two of the most popular German literary texts read in the United States, based in the belief that the language was relatively "easy" (Ratych, 1985). In my study, learners were asked to read in the original German and recall each story in writing (in the language in which they were most comfortable) and were then interviewed in their dominant language, English, about their understandings. Two findings were reported: first, that readers make decisions early in the text about its "content" based on their own first-language cultural knowledge and assumptions, and that they reconstruct texts on that basis, often swerving well past the mark about actual story content; second, that the knowledge of "known" vocabulary interferes routinely with literary text understanding. In other words, the readers in the study did not exhibit flexible, metaphorical understandings of "known" words. Davis (1992) found a similar phenomenon related to word use. In his study, intermediate-level university students did demonstrate higher comprehension levels when provided with glossed words; ironically, so-called "known" words, however, still remained problematic.

Riley (1993) examined the reading of French folk tales with undergraduate learners of French. The readers were significantly influenced by the organization of the stories: organizational patterns within the folktales more aligned with "expected" English-language story patterns yielded significantly higher recall patterns. Riley also found that the greater the linguistic proficiency of students in French, the less likely they were to be influenced by their first-language organizational patterns. Riley is consistent with Schulz's (1981) findings that linguistic complexity of texts will influence their comprehensibility for second-language learners. In a similar vein, Chi's (1995) investigation encouraged readers to make cultural links between and among two English-language short stories. Consistent with reader-response theory, Chi's approach indicates that helping students link their interpretations between and among texts encourages them to provide more sophisticated interpretations.

Davis also offered important programmatic research about learner attitudes vis-à-vis literature study. In 1992, Davis and colleagues surveyed French and Spanish students about how they perceived literature study in the undergraduate curriculum and why they were studying it. Students reported positive attitudes significantly related to how much leisure reading they did in the foreign language. Importantly, students noted that they believed that the reading of literature would improve their knowledge of the language and their ability to use the language in multiple settings. In a related line of questioning, Davis et al. also reported on French students' beliefs about literature learning. These students reported using literature as a medium for gaining greater cultural knowledge about French-speaking peoples. They showed little awareness/dedication to the "big C" (i.e., Culture) notion of "Great Works."

Fecteau (1999) has conducted the most extensive and sophisticated study of the reading of literary texts found in the research literature. Her study relies admirably on previously published findings: first-language literacy as well as second-language linguistic (i.e., grammatical) level must be included in analyses of second-language reading performances. Indeed, the Fecteau data reconfirm that both sources significantly contribute to second-language literary reading proficiency. More significant, however, is the observation that student performance vis-à-vis literary text in either their first or second language was uneven, indicating that some other variable beyond language or literacy was at play in the student performances. In examining subjects' literacy and literary histories, Fecteau found key differences in their experiences with literature—differences that appeared in subjects' abilities to analyze and interpret the literary texts they were asked to read. Fecteau comments:

> Background knowledge is not limited to cultural or historical facts; it also includes knowledge of literary concepts that may not have been acquired in L1 literature courses. The present findings suggest that certain literary features are not apparent to college students in their L1 or L2, whether because they lack background knowledge or cannot activate it, do not focus on key textual cues or perhaps miscomprehend them, or because these elements are not equally apparent in all texts. (p. 489)

Research suggests that in order to engage learners profitably with literature, they must have a substantial linguistic arsenal—an arsenal that seems to be contextually sensitive. In some contexts, grammar and vocabulary seem to be enough; in other contexts, grammar and vocabulary cannot adequately compensate for other forms of contextual knowledge. Words and forms that appear to be known in some contexts somehow disappear in others. Further, research indicates that the cultural and world-knowledge readers bring can facilitate and debilitate comprehension abilities. In other words, readers with low-level second-language skills have been observed exhibiting high-level comprehension abilities and readers with high-level language skills have been observed doubting their own abilities when the text does not match their knowledge base. Readers overcompensate for language deficiencies with background knowledge or they overcompensate with their linguistic skills for limited knowledge, and other times they do not seem to be able to compensate for any deficiency. A final dimension to the problem space is the apparent independence of second-language learners' literary/interpretive competence from their linguistic and knowledge-based resources.

This state of understanding second-language literary reading—*that* readers use their first-language literacy knowledge, their grammatical knowledge, and their literary-based world knowledge—calls for an investigation of *how* they do this in a compensatory fashion. A possible approach toward developing this understanding is to provide readers with literary-specific background knowledge and to observe how they use this knowledge to buttress their own knowledge sources or to modify them specifically for literary text. The most obvious question then becomes *whether* knowledge of relevant foreign-language literary texts in English translation gets transferred to other texts (not in translation) in an appropriate or authentic fashion and if it does *what* gets transferred. A less obvious question is whether using these texts to enhance students' overall authentic interpretive abilities bears any relationship to their *language-learning* capacities or to their comprehension abilities with other kinds of upper-register texts.

A Study of Second-Language Literature Learning

Compensatory theory and research support for it underlines the absurdity of conceptualizing the reading process in a linear, compartmentalized fashion. The idea of beginning systematic cultural study after beginning to learn a language and concomitantly denying or limiting access to first-language knowledge resources counters the holistic notion of compensation. In arguing for an integrative view of knowledge sources needed for literature learning, Bernhardt and Berman (1999, p. 29) noted the following:

> We often use the concept of the "bridge"; i.e., the bridge course and "bridging the language and literature (re: academic culture) curriculum." This is the wrong model and the wrong image. We will *not* be able to build a better bridge; the farther apart the shores, the weaker the bridge ... We need to adopt a philosophy that either narrows the channel or, better yet, fills it in. This means we need one curriculum that is a language and culture curriculum which becomes increasingly integrated rather than two curricula that get increasingly farther apart from each other.

Bernhardt and Berman highlighted the belief in the symbiotic relationship between language and literature, but urged the probing of a set of pressing questions specifically about language learning. In building up the knowledge base for literature learning and analysis, *can* any inroads into the linguistic/language base be made? *Do* any inroads get made? And do those inroads take learners down the *right* path? By aligning the knowledge base more closely, can positive growth in the linguistic base be stimulated? By allowing readers access to literary/cultural knowledge through their first language, can readers become more proficient at literary reading in their second?

In 1999, Bernhardt and Berman proposed a model of language and culture integration in a beginning German-language program with these questions as a backdrop. The model was based on three convictions: first, that the second-language learning process is developmental and that, therefore, it is misguided to believe that students cannot learn substantive content until they have a full control of the linguistic system; second, that learners should be permitted to use their first-language literacy in the second-language learning process; and third, that it is the ethical responsibility of all German programs to insure that German-language students gain the "rudiments of a cultural-historical knowledge about Germany in more sophisticated ways" (p. 25).

In their model, Bernhardt and Berman developed a syllabus to accompany their department's German-language program, which employed as a basic textbook *Deutsch Na klar!* (DiDonato, Clyde, & Vansant, 1995). The extended syllabus contained Gordon Craig's *The Germans* as a basic sociocultural history; three literary texts in translation: Kafka's *the Metamorphosis*, Goethe's *Faust* and Rilke's *Advice to a Young Poet*; and one opera, Wagner's *The Flying Dutchman*. The model was implemented and a study of student knowledge development follows.

Phase I: Exploring the Impact of L2 Literary Knowledge Provided in L I

Eight first-year university students agreed to participate in the investigation. None of them had had any prior German language learning experience. They participated in the German language curriculum as described above. In other words, in additional to learning the basics of German in a communicative, proficiency-oriented manner, they had read key pieces of canonical German literature in English and discussed them on an electronic discussion board with their professors and classmates.

Within the context of the investigation, learners were asked to read *in English* Thomas Mann's *Mario and the Magician*[1] (1999). Each student participant was asked to read this story at home and not to discuss it with any class members. Each participant was then interviewed individually. The first task was to recall as much of the story as possible in writing in 10 minutes. After the 10-minute period, each was asked to finish with any details that he or she had left out of the original retelling. Three sets of questions were then posed:

1   Talk about ways in which this story reflects the other pieces of German literature that you are familiar with.
2   Given the pieces of German literature that you've read, if you were told that they are the most characteristic pieces of German literature available, speculate on the nature of German literature. What's the style like? What kinds of themes do you expect to encounter?
3   Given the pieces of German literature that you've read, and what you understand as thematic and stylistic content, what is the relationship between this information and your German language learning?

Results

The Recall of the Story

There is a universal character to the patterns of recall. The recalls focus on details of details of the family, the first part of the story. All subjects were also able to go on at length about details of details of all facets of the story in their oral interviews.

Characteristic is the following written recall:

The story started out somewhere in Italy, on the coast, with what I was assuming was a German family of husband and wife, and son and daughter all on vacation at the beach.

They stayed at a nice hotel/resort type place—so nice that it seemed pretty snobby as described when they were asked to be moved after their child showed signs of whooping cough even though the hotel physician affirmed that the child was no longer contagious, etc. Anyway, the management had them moved to please a "more important" guest—a princess or someone with children also.

The vacation kept getting worse. One day on the beach they let their little girl take off her suit and rinse it in the ocean and it offended so many of the natives of the town who were also on the beach that the family was summoned to pay a fine for her "indecent" exposure.

Finally, there was an announcement for a magic show; the kids showed interest, the author expressed worry over the lateness of it in regards to the kids' bedtime, but they attended anyway.

The magician was late on getting on stage *even though it was noted that he was in fact* present, *probably to heighten the anticipation, and to make a better entrance. He was described as being (and said himself) "deformed" some kind of way. He either limped or was semi-hunchbacked—can't recall—and very condescending to his audience, or rather parts of it, where he made spectacles of making certain members of it look especially dumb, etc. A young man in the audience (Giovanotto??) yelled "good evening" to sort of point out that the conjuror hadn't yet done so and he ripped him to shreds from then on. He seemed to be some sort of hypnotist. He made the young man stick out his tongue against his will and later double-up in pain after hearing his "ailment" described to him. Then he moves on to Mario—guesses his profession, then starts talking about the woman Mario loves and how other men love her not as much as Mario. Mario is getting into it, is feeling great pain … The magician ends it by kissing Mario, pretending he's the woman, and then sending him back to his seat, humiliated. Mario, halfway up the aisle, turns all at once shoots the magician, causing an uproar. The family leaves, the kids are thoroughly entertained. They kind of don't know what's going on, but are loving it.*

QUESTION 1: COMPARISONS BETWEEN AND AMONG MARIO AND KAFKA, THE FLYING DUTCHMAN, FAUST, RILKE

Each participant was able to draw clear and astute relationships between and among the texts that he/she had read. Participants commented extensively about the nature of the family in *Mario and the Magician* and of the Samsas in *The Metamorphosis*; compared and contrasted the female characters in *The Metamorphosis* (mother and sister), in *Faust* (Gretchen), and in *The Flying Dutchman* (Senta); reflected on how characters such as Faust and the Dutchman

Table 5.1 Intertextual Themes Articulated by the German-Language Readers

	Metamorphosis	Faust	Flying Dutchman	Letters
Family	x			
Identity struggle	x	x	x	x
Intellectual superiority		x		x
Outside control	x	x	x	
Individuality	x	x	x	x
Women	x	x	x	
Non-rational	x	x	x	
Physical deformity	x		x	

were seeking a personal space; and argued that all of the characters seemed to be at odds with outside forces well beyond their control. Table 5.1 indicates the concepts mentioned by all students (*family*, *identity*, and *outside control*) as well as those mentioned by some.

Advice to a Young Poet was interpreted by all participants as the outlier because of its optimistic flavor.

QUESTION 2: THE NATURE OF GERMAN LITERATURE: ITS STYLE AND CONTENT

There was unanimity among the participants in terms of commenting on the nature of the literary style they read. The term *indirect* was used most frequently meaning that one had to file away a set of details only to use them later in the story. One participant noted that the style was not "'in' the story" but always external to it. As one southern Californian said: "This is really different from *Lonesome Dove*—you know, where there is dialogue and events." *Introspection* and *philosophical* were used also as descriptive terms. In further probing of the participants, these descriptors also referred to tendencies for characters to think through their dilemmas, such as the narrator in *Mario and the Magician*, Faust, Gregor in *The Metamorphosis*, and even Senta in the *Flying Dutchman*, using a method that one anthropology student characterized as "thick description." *Dark* and *pessimistic* were also included in stylistic comments. When asked about characteristic *content*, the common answer was "this is about going bad" and "alienation." Again, each of these pieces of German literature, read in English, was noted as a story of decline, with the exception of Rilke, perceived as the only piece containing optimism. One Nebraskan noted the difference between these pieces of German literature and American literature that "examines the triumph of man over nature."

QUESTION 3: THE RELATIONSHIP BETWEEN HAVING READ THESE TEXTS AND THEIR GERMAN-LANGUAGE LEARNING

For six of the eight participants the answer here was a resounding "no." A relationship between reading German literary texts in English and German-language learning had never occurred to them. The general response in the words of one participant was "that was that culture stuff." Two students responded with an absolute "yes." *Who* these participants were is probably more interesting than that they replied positively.

The first to respond positively and, in fact, with the most detail was the student who had had the most trouble in German-language learning, Joshua. While it is a bit of an absurdity that one refers to a Stanford student having "trouble," Joshua was problematic. He failed a quiz on the separable prefixes (he said he just could not memorize them) and at the end of his course still couldn't differentiate in oral speech between 40 *(vierzig)* and 14 *(vierzehn)*.

Early in Joshua's interview, he said that what was similar in all of the works is that "you could tell they were translated. ... It's not the way an English story would start." This statement could be ascribed to the nature of style and content. But when asked about the relationship between the readings and his German-language learning, he returned to the theme of translation. He said:

> *It has to do with the language. Some things just don't translate. There are ideas that they try to convey in a certain way with word order. Just look at Faust. ...* **Or** *... Just look at that line on page 147: [He reads aloud.]*

> He came forward with a rapid step that expressed his eagerness to appear before his public and gave rise to the illusion that he had already come a long way to put himself at their service—whereas, of course, he had only been standing in the wings.

> *I'm sure that in German that would be much clearer—that the parts and their objects would be related in a different way. ... it's the cases and the word order is what makes the difference. In English you need to use all of those other words; you have to use all the prepositions and stuff in English, but in German you can imply the same thing. ... it really helps me to see how you take your thoughts and put them into German rather than just learning the rules.*

Of course, Joshua is reflecting the agenda of the German course he is in. But interestingly, on a linguistic level, what he says might happen and might help him—did not.

The other student who responded with a clear "yes" to the last question was actually the star student in the class, Karen. She had arrived with an Advanced Placement score of 5 in French and used her French pronunciation to compensate for her lacking pronunciation in German very effectively. With Karen, one could probably introduce a structure a day and she would put it into her linguistic system. Her response was not at the structural level like Joshua's. Karen responded at the semantic level. She noted that the hard part about language learning is the "cultural connotation stuff." She said she saw no practical or cultural relevance to learning to name "the farm animals in French" as in high school. She concluded that students need this type of information from the beginning so "you have a better understanding of what's German even if it's really elementary so you can integrate it into your language."

Phase II: Exploring the Impact of L1 on L2 Literary Reading

During May, 1998, three of the original eight subjects were available to participate in the final phase of the investigation; several had not continued with German and several said that they did not have the time to participate. The three remaining had indeed continued with German-language learning, meaning that each had a total of 30 weeks of instruction, a vocabulary of 1000–1200 words, and an oral proficiency rating of intermediate low. Starting in the 20th week of instruction, these students had begun to work with poetry in German. For this second phase, they were given another story by Franz Kafka, *Vor dem Gesetz*[2] (1970) and a story by Heinrich Böll, *Mein teures Bein*[3] (1977). For this data collection, however, they read in German and still chose to recall in English. Undoubtedly, the original German was well beyond anything these learners could produce or, for that matter, translate on their own. Parallel questions regarding style, content, relationships to other German texts, and most importantly, the relationship to aspects of language learning were probed. These questions were:

1   You have recalled each story in writing. Please recall the story again, filling in parts that you might not have written down and adding interpretive comments along the way.
2   Go back to each text and list five words that you were unsure about—words that you think would have helped you understand each story better.
3   Comment on each text regarding its relationship to other pieces of German literature with which you are familiar; i.e., do these texts have things in common with other pieces of literature you know? Organize yourself according to characters, themes, setting, content, and so forth.
4   You have completed 30 weeks of German language instruction. Talk about your impressions of the German language (vocabulary, syntax, morphological signaling, etc.) making reference to these two stories. To what extent has literary reading helped you to learn German?

Results

QUESTION 1: RECALL PATTERN

Figure 5.1 and Figure 5.2 provide the complete written recalls of the three participants across each text.

Vor dem Gesetz. In the written recalls, the three participants recognize the description of the person and all recognize two characters who ask each other questions. Student 1 gives up. The other two participants provide more

Before something

There's this Tuerhuter, what is that, a door-hat? I don't recognize any of the verbs and most nouns. He says stuff, starts describing his nose and long black beard. I'm completely lost until he asks, "What, then, do you want to know?" and more stuff happens, I have no idea what.
Student 1

A doorman stands before the entrance of his building. He wears a warm fur coat, has a distinctive nose, and has a long black beard. A man from the country (he seems like a country bumpkin) asks the doorman if he can enter the building. The doorman will not let him enter. A conversation ensues between the two and the bumpkin leaves. The man from the country travels a great deal and after some time, he returns to the building. Meanwhile, the doorman had remained day in and day out at his mundane job. Another conversation ensues.
Student 2

A man from far away comes to see a doorman (?) and inquires about the nature of the job. They discuss it a bit, and the doorman allows the man to sit and watch him do his job. The doorman wears a striking coat and has a long black beard. The man watches for a year and a day and the two ask each other lots of questions. They become as close as brothers—the man forgets the "other" doorman, seeing this one as very kind. The man is collecting questions and knowledge in his head for death (?) and the doorman asks what he still wants to know.
Student 3

Figure 5.1 Recall protocols of Kafka's *Vor dem Gesetz*

elaborate and sophisticated recalls. Each gets a sense of the doorman "watching" and the other person staying away and then returning. Each mentions the repetitive nature of the doorman's job. None of the participants offers an interpretation.

Mein teures Bein. In the written recalls, the three subjects mention that the text is about war; i.e., that the man has lost his leg in the war. All three also understand about the veteran's marriage and the part in which the veteran protests that he is not crazy. All three understand that there is something related to shoes, while only one understands the concept of shoe shining, not shoe repair or working in a shoe store. Two mention the comment that "Germans can do anything." In the oral recall, Student 1 explains that she just didn't understand anything. Again, none of the subjects offers an interpretation of any kind.

A man was injured in war and lost an arm or leg (I can't remember which—"Bein"). He married after the war but was unable to work—his wife worked instead and really didn't mind. Then the man was given a chance ... an acquaintance of his gave him a job interview to work in a shoe store. The man claimed that his handicap prevented him from working, but the acquaintance said: "You are a man. You can do everything. You are German. You can do everything." The man nevertheless continually turned down the job ... his acquaintance called him insane, but the man knew who he was.
Student 1

My expensive leg (?)
A man goes to someone who seems to be a doctor complaining about his right leg. The doctor lets him sit down and is suggesting some sort of *Schuhputzen,* something to put in your shoe perhaps to fix whatever the problem is. The guy doesn't like the *Schuhputzens,* he wants his leg—doesn't care if it is expensive. The doctor says he's crazy. The guy says no. The doctor says he's in good health, good heart, etc. except his leg, and he's crazy. The guy says my heart *and* my head are healthy ... I'm not crazy. They continue this exchange, talk about being married and war or something. The guy wants his leg, says he's not crazy, and leaves.
Student 2

Something gives this man a chance—he receives a card and goes to see a man. However, something is wrong with his leg (I think he might have lost it in the war, and has a fake one, or he has damaged it). The man he speaks to asks which one, and he says "right." They discuss whether someone can learn anything—the man says people, especially Germans, can learn something. Then the man tries to clean his shoes, but the guy with the hurt leg won't let him. He wants a higher price. The shoe shiner kindly says that he is crazy. He says he can tell the guy is 29 and in good health (of heart and head) but his leg is 70 and very sad. The guy agrees, but says he is not crazy. He tries to explain though the shoe shiner keeps repeating "any time is short." The guy talks of a man—a friend—who got married, but was OK on money because his wife was healthy and could work. This guy was a brave soldier.

Then, he talks of losing the leg in battle—if he hadn't, all the officers (and he gives their ages) would have died. Now they will live and serve until they're 80 (like Hindenberg).

Finally, the shoe shiner asks if he wants to take a seat. He says "no" and leaves.
Student 3

Figure 5.2 Recall protocols of Böll's *Mein teures Bein*

Table 5.2 Self-Reported Vocabulary Needs across Two German-Language Texts

	Student 1	Student 2	Student 3
Mein teures Bein			
	Beamte	Bein	Miete
	Sache	Amt	Rente
	Schuhputzen	Zettel	Stiftengehen
	Rente	Schuhputzen	Totschießen
	Schwierigkeit	Lag	Gewischt
		Sache	
Vor dem Gesetz			
	Gesetz	Gesetz	Gesetz
	Türhüter	Bückt	Türhüter
	Schwierigkeit	Merke	Eintritt
		Heimat	Einlass
		Beobachten	

QUESTION TWO: VOCABULARY

Table 5.2 outlines the self-reported vocabulary deficiencies. There is little commonality between and among the subjects beyond those words found in the title of each text. Ironically, most of the words listed (with the exception of *stiftengehen*, *gewischt*, *bücken*, and *Einlass*) are found in the first-year textbook that all of the students were just completing.

Notable is that even when students ostensibly knew parts of words such as *Schuh* and *putzen*, they did not seem to be able to put the two concepts together. Further, they did not seem to be able to engage in both the literal and metaphorical sense of *teuer* (expensive, costly). Student 3 gets closest in her recall by remarking "It's the story of a leg, but not the entire story." She is never able to make the metaphorical leap even when pushed in the interview.

QUESTION THREE: INTERTEXTUAL RELATIONSHIPS

In parallel to Phase 1, students drew astute connections between and among characters in the texts. They were always able to justify the conclusions they drew with detailed textual evidence.

Table 5.3 outlines the links that each subject made between the texts they read in German and the German texts in English translation with which they were

Table 5.3 Intertextual Relationships Articulated by the German-Language Readers

Student 1	Mephistopheles and Faust	the Beamte and the cripple
Student 2	Gregor	the cripple
Student 3	Gregor	the cripple
Student 1	*Vor dem Gesetz*	the Dutchman
Student 2	*Vor dem Gesetz*	the Metamorphosis
Student 3	*Vor dem Gesetz*	Kant

familiar. Student 1, even though he/she was the least able of the students to recall much of what he/she read in German, drew interesting parallels between the relationship between Mephistopheles and Faust and the official and the crippled veteran, as well as between the man in the Kafka piece and the flying Dutchman. She reported in the interview a dominance scenario in the former case as well as the playful and sarcastic tone of the interchanges and the stupefying helplessness of the characters in the latter. Students 2 and 3 reported the link between Gregor and the crippled veteran. All three subjects diverged in the interviews by linking the character in *Vor dem Gesetz* to the Dutchman (mentioned above), to the absurdity in *The Metamorphosis*, and to the writings of Kant, information acquired in a philosophy course, not a German course.

QUESTION FOUR: LANGUAGE

With the question regarding the extent to which literary reading helped in the learning of German, results were mixed. One participant responded principally at the affective level: "After 30 weeks I'm sure that with a dictionary I could have read this with full understanding. I recognized all the structures and tenses. Literature helps you get used to the sentence construction." A second student responded with a 15-minute discourse on Latin and Spanish compared with English and then launched into the question of identity. Because identity is such an issue in German literature, he argued, the introductory language-learning materials in *Deutsch Na klar!* that were used stressing "identity" (meaning descriptions of students, their families, their daily routines, what they study, and so forth) were culturally compatible with the pieces of literature the students had read. A third student focused exclusively on grammar in literary form: "Literary reading helped me learn structure within sentences and word order because it makes it more natural. I'm much more comfortable with verb placement and modals because it's in paragraphs not sentences. The other thing that's cool about German is how the words get stuck together."

Implications for Compensatory Theory

The Participants as Readers of Literature

The participant German learners were good and astute readers who were able to draw clear and convincing comparisons between and among the texts that they read. All comparisons were documented with a good sense of the textual elements. Providing additional evidence for questions raised by Fecteau (1999), the participants in this investigation seemed to have a "literary interpretation" dimension within their personal literacy. In the all-English phase of this investigation, the participants started to create a "German space" for themselves. Consistent with previous research, they started with their L1 base of *Lonesome Dove*, the farm animals in French, and the American theme of man's triumph over nature. But after only 10 weeks of exposure to the integrated curriculum, they nevertheless were able to articulate intra-German perspectives. At the stylistic level, too, the students demonstrated a usable and useful knowledge base from which to embark for comprehension and interpretation. Expecting an American-type story line is a false expectation that will often lead one in the wrong direction when reading and interpreting German literature. Expecting to collect information that will be of use later in the story is an important concept to hold onto in many German-language literary contexts. The participants in this investigation seemed to have acquired these culturally consistent concepts throughout their German literary readings in English as well as in German.

The Participants as Readers of German

When reading in German, the participants seemed to be able to use their German fairly effectively. Given that they had had only 30 weeks of instruction and no grammar or dictionary tools to use while reading the Kafka and Böll texts, they were able to capture a core of the authentic, unedited German texts they read. Even the participant who claimed she understood nothing re-constructed the raw outlines of the story in front of her.

This investigation provides additional insight into the exceptionally problematic nature of vocabulary use in a second language. I noted in *Reading Development in a Second Language* that:

> second-language learners have a store of words to which they attach meanings. In a real sense, the meanings are frequently unidimensional in nature—the one word, one meaning mentality pervading much second-language teaching. When materials are presented to students, "contextually relevant" meanings are generally provided. This implies that a word such as *Stock* in German may be glossed as "floor (of a building; ex first floor)." The gloss does not include an alternative meaning such as *stick*, a perfectly plausible "meaning" yet irrelevant in the context. ... a risk on the part of the nonnative is not knowing alternative meanings and getting "stuck" with encoding an appropriate meaning in an inappropriate context. (p. 78)

Consistent with the Davis research, this investigation highlights the urgency of flexible word knowledge for readers of literature. It also underlines for instructors that assuming word knowledge even of so-called simpler "first-year" words can be presumptuous. This finding helps to explain some of the lower-division/upper-division conflicts. Lower-division faculty "know" that students have been taught and have learned certain words; upper-division faculty disparage lower-division for "not having taught anything." Perhaps the issue is actually the developmental difficulty that students face in expanding their vocabulary beyond the one-word/one-meaning model into a flexible, metaphorical one.

The Participants as Learners of German through Literature

The participants articulated both their interest in, and the need for, culture learning. Again, consistent with Davis's work, the participants seemed to be seeking cultural knowledge and believed they would understand German-speaking people more fully if they had contact with literature. None of the participants referred to an interest in literary criticism qua literary criticism. Of the original eight participants in this study, seven of them studied in Berlin for a quarter. One of the final three participants, Student 1, in fact, became a German major. In other words, all participants indicated a more than superficial interest in German culture and German-language learning.

Yet, the question of language learning remains. None of the participants articulated that if they read more literature, their language would be enhanced. One wonders where the disconnect occurs. Perhaps literature is provided too early, introducing a high frustration level into the curriculum; perhaps literature is introduced too late and in a fragmented fashion sending the message that it is indeed something different and disparate. Perhaps the root of the problem lies in a beginning curriculum that does not focus on dimensions of sophisticated and complex text adequately or in an upper-division curriculum that makes no provision for substantive language learning.

Toward a Pedagogy for Second-Language Literature Learning

The field generally refers to the symbiosis of literature and language. This investigation fits under the first definition of symbiosis: the close union of two dissimilar organisms. In both phases of this investigation, literature learning helped feed literature learning and language learning was there too. The literature learning did not seem to harm the language learning in any way. What is still up for question, though, is whether the field will be able to produce a curriculum compatible with the second definition of symbiosis: the intimate living together of two dissimilar organisms in a mutually beneficial relationship. In Phase 1, for only two of the subjects did there seem to be an acknowledgment of a beneficial relationship. One conclusion, then, is that literature learning only assists literature learning and interpretation. But only time and continued investigation of these questions will provide satisfactory answers. Perhaps sustained and extensive literary learning does enhance language knowledge. At this time, no credible evidence of this is available. Given the enormous amount of curricular time devoted to literature study, the wisdom of this time allocation should be brought under scrutiny in future research. But even more critical is exploring whether this time contributes to the learning and understanding of other upper-register texts.

At one level, the study is simplistic in that it investigates priming effects. A curriculum was aligned with a curriculum and there was positive transfer. In other words, the farm animals to a Kafka interpretation? No. Kafka in English to Kafka in German? Yes. But what of the educational character of using literature as a primary language and literacy learning tool? Literary texts are inherently ambiguous. The kind of interpretive arsenal that one must acquire in order to cope with these ambiguous texts is enormous. A large amount of time was expended reading in English in order to hone interpretive skills. Certainly, understanding or having exposure to some prototypic German characters such as Gregor, or Faust, or the Flying Dutchman, should enable learners to have a culturally genuine reference group for further and future interpretations. Providing this authenticity should certainly enhance learners' comprehension and interpretive skill. A set of *shoulds* does not necessarily translate, however, into interpretive action. As emphasized in *Reading Development in a Second Language*, "An understanding of how learners approach these texts, whether their teachers are aware of these approaches, and whether these approaches merely facilitate the façade of understanding … or the development of real understanding must be developed" (p. 185). The question yet to be answered is whether there is a way of viewing literature learning and teaching through a compensatory lens and whether such a perspective would bring about learners more able to cope with highly nuanced, upper-register text.

The curricular struggle over the place and role of literature in the American foreign-language curriculum is arguably a key flash point that plagues the field. Any number of treatises describes the history and evolution of literary study with respect to language study; its link to sociopolitical events such as wars and immigration; its ties to linguistics, sociolinguistics, and applied linguistics; its connection to high culture endeavors juxtaposed against practical proficiency; and its association with education rather than training. Barnett (1991), Benseler (1991), Bernhardt (1994b), Henning (1992), Hoffman and James (1986), James (1989), Kramsch (1985), Lide (1990), Muyskens (1983), Peck (1992), Rice (1991), Shanahan (1997), and Swaffar (1988), among others, have all outlined, discussed, and debated the tensions that conflate to form the educational landscape of the American foreign-language curriculum with a particular emphasis on literature study. With the rise of the cultural studies model and its seemingly more encompassing perspective contrasted with the narrowly defined agenda of literary analysis, the struggle has become more public and more toxic. For more than a decade now, this academic stand-off has seen literature-oriented academics argue that communicative approaches encroaching on the curriculum have led to ignorance of the *belle lettres* while language-oriented academics question the privileged status afforded literary texts as appropriate vehicles for learning. Kramsch and Kramsch (2000) have thoroughly and definitively synthesized the perspectives of academics on all of these issues for the past century.

Each of these sets of discussions is fundamentally academic. Each perspective acknowledges the critical importance of the other yet somehow remains conflictive. This conflict is bitterly ironic. It is essentially a faith-based conflict—one that relies on belief and folk wisdom rather than actual evidence. Beliefs range anywhere from the "enhancement of life through the beauty of literature" argument through literature constituting the most difficult and, therefore, most important second-language learning task to the "importance of being an educated person conversant with great works" contention. Surely, each of these principles, as well as others, holds a particular truth value. Yet, despite these beliefs the field has very little research-based evidence about the symbiosis that supposedly exists between language and literature. Only a virtual language/ culture sociopath would argue that literature should be eliminated from the curriculum. No matter how attached members of the profession are to practicalities, they will ultimately passionately argue that all learners should be given and must be given the opportunity to read and enjoy literary texts. Shanahan (1997), for example, articulates that the field knows very little about the educational character of starting with language learning and gradually moving toward upper-register, literary texts. How knowledge of language and literary interpretation should be aligned; whether alignment is a worthy goal; how a learner comes to learn to interpret literary texts—texts that are deliberately ambiguous; how one can acquire the requisite knowledge structures for the non-native interpretation of a literature—all of these areas are murky at best. The intention of this chapter has been to try to provide some modest insight into these complex and exasperating arenas.

In teaching contexts, scholars have focused on language programs and on the literature curriculum essentially as univariate problems, each with its own set of independent issues. There is, of course, discussion and debate about whether the proficiency-based, interpersonal level of discourse taught in the first- and second-year language curriculum actually can lead to the development of a discourse that permits the development of a language of and for literary discussion. Further, there is subtle and not-so-subtle discussion of the nature and structure of the cultural knowledge base necessary for literary analysis. On the subtle front, avoidance is employed: the "they will pick it [i.e., necessary cultural knowledge] up as they go" method. The not-so-subtle approach has been characterized as an accumulation of culture capsules often delivered in the concept of the bridge or "introductory" culture class (Shumway, 1995). The field recognizes that these crash course solutions are problematic. One need only look at the number of presentations and sessions at professional conferences that examine the issue of the bridge—how to get students out of language courses and rapidly into the advanced coursework that focuses on upper-register texts. Accompanying these discussions of curriculum design are pedagogical contributions designed to problematize and then resolve instructional issues surrounding the use of literary texts for language learners. Birckbichler and Muyskens (1980), Bretz (1990), Davis (1989, 1992), Esplugas and Landwehr (1996), Haggstrom (1992), Harper (1988), Hedgcock and Ferris (2009), Knutson (1993, 1997), Purcell (1988), and Shook (1996), among others, provide the field with sets of practical suggestions for introducing literature to language students; for working with students struggling with literature study; and for applying theoretically consistent pedagogical approaches to the study of literature. Recommendations include using reader-response as well as critical theory approaches to engage learners with literature early in their language- and literature-learning careers. Critical is that these refer to using literary texts as *vehicles* for language learning. None of these writings refer to non-natives trying to understand literary texts as representative instances of texts in the upper reaches of discourse.

The question still remains of learning in order to comprehend and interpret complicated literary text. The suggestions brought forward in Chapter 4 are focused on readers needing to learn an independence; i.e., readers who need to be able to self-regulate so that they can access with confidence all of the appropriate knowledge sources they need in order to explore the full expanse of second-language literary and other upper-register texts. This chapter has argued that a systematic approach that enables readers to apply relevant first-language knowledge to their second-language literary reading is critical toward bringing readers into self-regulating control of literary reading and interpretation. A corollary to the arguments set forth in Chapter 4 is to use a similar set of principles for literature instruction. I mentioned in an earlier chapter that during the writing of early stages of this book, a rash of mining accidents occurred—in China, Mexico, and Canada, as well as in the US State of Utah. One could imagine asking learners to read an article in English such as "With 65 still entombed at Mexican Mine, Ache Deepens," from the *New York Times*, March 3, 2006. That article described not the mining accident itself but its aftermath and the affective reactions to that aftermath. The story begins with "There is no hope at the mine here now, only the anguished wrung-out ache to recover the bodies of their loved ones, to put an end to the waiting, the praying and the tortuous talk of miracles" (McKinley, p. 4). Students could again be asked to prepare a set of vocabulary that they believe best reflects the key points in the article, especially focusing on how affect is expressed within a journalistic content and how they believe affect is expressed best in the language and culture they are learning. They could then move as described in Chapter 4 to a similar piece of journalism from the target language and then move into literary pieces such as *El Chiflón del Diablo* from Victor Montoya or *Das Bergwerk von Falun* by E. T. A. Hoffman or *Germinal* from Emile Zola. The point is to help students become astute enough to cope with different registers in different genres; to enable them to work independently within these upper-register genres, and to demonstrate to them how they can fruitfully use their strongest and most immediate resource, i.e., their native language, to buttress them through the arduous process of understanding and interpreting foreign-language literary texts. Readers will ultimately need to be able to grapple with questions such as what is identifiably literary in a particular text versus another, or where interpretation is *literary* per se versus a part of relatively straightforward narrative analysis. The structure put forth here provides a deliberate sequence to enable students and their teachers to discover and construct a satisfactory justification for their understandings.

My argument here and its corollaries are admittedly rooted in reasoned, best personal judgment based on a compensatory view of second-language reading. How second-language readers learn to assert and withhold judgments about upper-level, complicated text; how they intellectualize across the boundaries of linguistic knowledge, knowledge of literary conventions, and appropriate cultural knowledge that is uncodified, subtle, and invisible; and how they build a legitimate, defensible interpretation remain unexplored. That is a critical territory that must be conquered if we are to make progress in second-language reading research in the years to come.

Notes

1   *Mario and the Magician* is a story of a family on vacation in Southern Italy; the family is in conflict with the local culture from the moment of their arrival. They decide to attend a magic show. The magician is a hypnotist who mesmerizes the apparently "normal" intelligent audience. The magician hypnotizes an array of audience members and ultimately decides to humiliate one of the audience members, Mario, who is a waiter that the family knows, and Mario leaves the stage and shoots the magician.

2   *Vor dem Gesetz* can be best described as a timeless document on the inaccessibility of law for the common person. The story takes place at the entrance of a legal office, where a guard denies entry to a man from the countryside. When he senses the villager's astonishment and dismay, he explains to him the intricacies of the legal system, which has a guard at each level. The villager sustains his curiosity somehow and wants to make his symbolic entry to the law; yet, overwhelmed by the guard's description, he decides to wait till he is granted permission. The guard allows him to squat at the entrance. Years pass by, and the guard becomes the villager's only perception of the law. When the villager is about to die, he makes the observation that no one has ever applied to enter the door since he did. The guard yells at him and declares that the entrance was meant only for him. Each individual has his/her own private legal or bureaucratic threshold, where one must wait to be granted entrance.

3   *Mein teures Bein* is a short story about a German soldier's interaction with a (German) bureaucrat. Set in the post–World War II milieu, the story lays bare the inefficacy of bureaucratic attitude towards the compensation of loss or, in the specific case of the protagonist, physical injury. The soldier's right leg was shot and had to be amputated. On receiving a notification from the government office, he shows up. The officer in charge offers him a position as a shoe shiner at the Platz der Republik. The soldier declines on the grounds that he lacks the skills for it, moreover, he would like to have a job that pays more. The officer responds to this rather vehemently. He gives him a long lecture telling him exactly how much money he would be able to make. Despite the officer's interruptions, the soldier presents an equally precise mathematical response, trying to convince the officer that the cost of his leg is being underestimated. The conversation comes to an end with the officer re-offering the position to the soldier. The soldier declines it a second time and leaves.

Chapter 6

Assessing the Learning and Teaching of Comprehension in a Second Language

Assessment has become a word that evokes panic on the part of students afraid they will not meet a set of external standards, disgust on the part of teachers claiming to lose valuable instructional time due to administering excessive numbers of assessments, and frustration on the part of the public hoping that schooling meets its intentions. While all three sets of parties have legitimate arguments against the notion of assessment, arguments that have become increasingly politicized, the views fail to acknowledge a key fundamental of teaching: teachers and students must know whether students are able to do what they are being taught to do. Often overlooked in this arena is teacher performance; that is, whether teachers are employing instructional strategies that bring about student learning. Anyone who has ever taught a language knows that just because students are able to perform linguistic tasks at a sentence level in the controlled environment of a classroom, does not necessarily mean that those same students can perform in more complex environments. The corollary is also true: just because teachers bring in reading materials and then ask students questions about the materials, does not mean that students are developing sophisticated comprehension abilities.

This chapter in *Understanding Advanced Second-Language Reading* takes up the concept of assessment where *Reading Development in a Second Language* left off. *Reading Development in a Second Language* focused on the concept of using recall in a first language to gain insight into how learners were comprehending written materials, and demonstrated a scoring scheme based in propositional analysis in order to generate a convenient score. *Understanding Advanced Second-Language Reading* returns to this particular issue to demonstrate more clearly how to generate a scoring matrix, which to many readers of *Reading Development in a Second Language*, appeared to be extraordinarily unwieldy. But it goes beyond the original recall scoring approach in *Reading Development in a Second Language*. It demonstrates a holistic scoring procedure to explore greater efficiency in gauging readers' abilities. This chapter is, however, not only about gauging readers. Unlike *Reading Development in a Second Language*, this volume opens a discussion of *teaching* reading. The field seems to know a lot about procedures. As noted earlier, Hedgcock and Ferris (2009) provide a remarkable array of procedures and activities that teachers at all levels should explore. The field knows far less, however, about effective presentation that brings about a high level of proficiency. This chapter acknowledges that research provides few if any insights into effective teaching in the reading arena, most assuredly none when considering the learning and teaching of upper-level, highly sophisticated text. The chapter tries to begin to remedy this deficit by providing some self-report data about what students say is effective in the performance of their instructors and what instructors report as effective. It ends with a suggested protocol for evaluating the effective teaching of second-language reading in the upper registers.

Reiterating Approaches to L2 Reading Assessment

Reading Development in a Second Language pointed out that large-scale reading comprehension assessment in academic contexts generally entails the administering and scoring of machine-readable responses, most often, multiple-choice or forced-choice fill-in-the-blank in nature, to a set of random reading passages. It discussed at length the use of the cloze procedure as well as the research on the impact of content questions on learners' comprehension. Almost a decade after the publication of *Reading Development in a Second Language*, *Assessing Reading* (Alderson, 2000) appeared. *Assessing Reading* put forward the advantages and disadvantages of the catalog of conventional measures of reading comprehension in a second language in even greater detail than *Reading Development in a Second Language* did. *Reading Development in a Second Language* had also brought testing theory to bear on the issue of reading tests, indicating that the more passages and the greater the number of questions, the better the test (Brown, 1976); the Alderson volume conducts a much more thorough and thoughtful review of some of the psychometric issues concerned with second-language comprehension assessment. Further, Hedgcock and Ferris (2009) as well as Grabe (2009) refer to assessment, rehearsing many of the ideas and arguments set forth by previous volumes.

Assessment is an arena in which a significant intellectual rift exists between this volume and other writings. *Understanding Advanced Second-Language Reading* takes as a research-based premise that first-language use is absolutely critical in all dimensions of the second-language comprehension process. By implication, assessment must consider the role of the first language and probe the impact of using a first-language literacy in understanding comprehension products. Further, given that most language teachers across the globe are *foreign*-language teachers, familiar with the language of their students, it is critical that language researchers permit and discuss the use of the L1 in L2 assessment, rather than ignoring it. Ironically, even Hedgcock and Ferris (2009), the most enlightened of recent volumes on the subject of second-language reading, acknowledge the L1/L2 relationship, yet fail to even mention how the L1 can function in assessment. In a reference to the use of recall, they never mention the use of a first, or dominant, language, only to the use of a second. Ironically, they do admit that using a non-dominant or second language is "a fairer test of writing (or oral production) than of L2 comprehension" (p. 356).

Practitioners have generally lamented that the scores generated in conventional tests have little immediate and practical value because no matter how lengthy and complex a test, the score says little more than "the score." But perhaps more important is the issue that practitioners and researchers alike admit in hushed voices—that being able to complete the conventional comprehension tasks does not always mean that the students "understood" a passage. I often return to the classroom experience that pushed me into second-language comprehension research: students had read a passage in German about Martin Luther that mentioned Luther's advocacy for individual freedom, his effort to liberate himself and others from powerful and political church leaders, his translation of the Bible into the "people's" language, and so forth. A student remarked (after having answered in German all of my content questions about the passage accurately) how interesting the passage was—she didn't know Martin Luther King knew German. Indeed, large-scale studies such as Anderson, Bachman, Perkins, and Cohen (1991) and Gordon and Hanauer (1995) provide non-anecdotal evidence of the same phenomenon: when subjects were asked to think aloud in a reading test situation, there was an incongruence between their performance on questions and their actual construction of the text. Gordon and Hanauer remark: "Responses were at times correct for reasons that did not reflect reading ability" (p. 320).

An assessment strategy that permits a full range of responses; i.e., a score and some insight about the reader, are what current theory and practice continue to demand. *Reading Development in a Second Language* advanced an alternative in second-language reading contexts—the use of recall as a measure of reading comprehension that is both quantitative and qualitative. The immediate recall protocol procedure outlined in *Reading Development in a Second Language* argued that with little, if any, test-development, practitioners are able to ask students to read an array of passages in the foreign language and to provide extensive responses to those passages through immediate or even delayed recall in their dominant language. Practitioners are able to examine the recall patterns within the context of individual language structures as well as within the context of passage topic. *Reading Development in a Second Language* argued that being able to examine student performance carefully enables teachers as well as students to diagnose grammatical and vocabulary abilities that contribute to comprehension, or perhaps more importantly, impede comprehension at an extremely sophisticated level.

The first part of the first paragraph of this chapter can serve as a model for performance and for the assessment of that performance via the development of a text matrix. After reading the first two sentences of the chapter, Amy K. recalled in the following manner:

> *Assessment evokes panic, disgust, and frustration. Students panic because they are afraid of tests. Teachers are disgusted because they think they spend too much time testing, and taxpayers are frustrated because they're not sure school is worth it. But no matter what, teachers and students need tests.*

Examining the recall indicates that Amy K. understood key points and also reconstructed key elements such as *public* becoming *taxpayers*; *a set of external standards* becomes *tests*; and so forth. The recall also indicates that the reader failed to mention the position that all stakeholders "*have legitimate arguments against the notion of assessment.*" The question here, as in all comprehension assessment, becomes a value judgment regarding how accurate the recall is— whether it captures a legitimate sense of the passage. Depending upon proficiency level, of course, the section on *arguments against* might or might not be important. For a lower-level reader, perhaps the main points about each group mentioned are most important; for the upper-level reader, perhaps the finer points of the politicization of assessment is a more significant notion to glean. To reiterate, what is "important" in the text is a value judgment on the part of the assessor. Any good assessment should be driven by the quantity and quality of the information the particular assessor actually wants to gather based on his/her purpose, objectives, curriculum, and so forth.

As *Reading Development in a Second Language* indicated, the recall procedure lends itself to the generation of a quantitative score, which, for example, eases comparison between and among readers. *Reading Development in a Second Language* illustrated three different matrix types. The first, based in the notion of hierarchical text structures, is extremely precise and elaborate and can take many hours to construct. The second and third are similar in appearance: one is weighted, the other not. To construct such a scoring matrix, the text should be read aloud with pauses noted. If the text is electronic, it is easy for the matrix developer to hit the Enter key at every pause. In this instance, the procedure results in a list of 29 pausal units. The resulting analysis is the following:

> *Assessment/* has become a word/ that evokes panic/ on the part of students/ afraid they will/ not meet/ a set of external standards/ disgust/ on the part of teachers/ claiming to lose/ valuable instructional time/ due to administering/ excessive numbers of assessments/ and frustration/ on the part of the public/ hoping that schooling/ meets its intentions./ While all three sets of parties/ have legitimate arguments/ against the notion of assessment,/ arguments/ that have become increasingly politicized,/ the arguments/ fail to acknowledge/ a key fundamental of teaching:/ teachers and students/ must know whether students/ are able to do/ what they are being taught/ to do.

In order to complete the matrix, the list of pausal units should be pasted into an Excel spreadsheet as in Table 6.1. Automatic formatting then enables the development of a spreadsheet that includes the names of all persons reading the passage. Obviously, once a template is made for each class or course, it can be used over and over with a mere "cutting and pasting" from text to new text. If scoring is to be weighted, each pausal unit should be ranked on a 1–4 scale from least important to most important to the text's meaning. The 4's should provide essentially a telegraphic version of the text. Again, a full account of weighted scoring is provided in *Reading Development in a Second Language* with an accompanying explanation that, statistically speaking, there was little difference between weighted and unweighted scoring.

The next step in the process is to match the reader's recall to the propositions listed. In the case of the recall above, the student, Amy K., receives a score of 15. This score is well within the bounds of expectation in recall. *Reading Development in a Second Language* cited the evidence that in free recall, recalling around 50% of the propositions in any given text is a high-level achievement.

The development of the matrix illustrated in Table 6.1 took less than one minute, with an additional minute to cut the list of propositions, to paste them into

Table 6.1 A Sample Scoring Matrix Based in Text Propositions

	Amy	Joan
Assessment	x	
has become a word		
that evokes panic	x	
on the part of students		
afraid they will not meet	x	x
a set of external standards,		x
disgust	x	
on the part of teachers	x	
claiming to lose	x	x
valuable instructional time	x	x
due to administering	x	
excessive numbers of assessments,		
and frustration	x	
on the part of the public	x	x
hoping that schooling	x	x
meets its intentions.		
While all three sets of parties		
have legitimate arguments		
against the notion of assessment,		
arguments		x
that have become increasingly politicized,		x
the arguments		
fail to acknowledge		
a key fundamental of teaching:	x	
teachers and students	x	
must know whether students	x	
are able to do		x
what they are being taught	x	x
to do.		

Excel, and to use the automatic format routine. Comparing this with the necessary hours and hours in development time necessary for generating multiple-choice or even short-answer assessments indicates that propositional analysis is far speedier. The evaluation of the readers listed took in total four minutes. Of course, the matrix illustrates a snippet of a paragraph. The longer the text, the longer the time for assessment that should be allocated.

Time is in fact the oft-cited issue with using immediate recall as an alternative assessment mechanism. While recall does provide lots of "items" across many passages, it can be relatively time-consuming to score (Deville & Chalhoub-Deville, 1993). In *Assessing Reading*, Alderson returns to this point a number of times, noting "the rather obvious limitation from the point of view of much large-scale or even classroom assessment is that such techniques are time-consuming to apply" (2000, p. 339). Some significant work has been conducted on automated computer scoring mechanisms. While a system is still not completely user-friendly, it is not too many generations away from completion (Heinz, 1992; 2004). Of course, not all practitioners are in a position to be able to use computer assistance at all times. Hence, practitioners with many student performances to assess are often left with a bad choice. They are often stymied because of the constraints of resources with a superficial score that is not terribly useful.

The challenge then becomes one of maintaining the idea of using a reader's recall to gather important data regarding his/her comprehension and being able to even more quickly assess the comprehension level than by counting all propositions. To put the challenge into a question form, *can an intuitive approach that places learner reading performances into blunt, unsophisticated categories such as "not good"; "OK"; "on target" place readers in the same category that more careful, time-consuming scoring strategies do?* The key issue, of course, is whether or not instructional programs can abide by particular research principles in second-language comprehension and reach the decisions they need to reach quickly and efficiently. My colleague, Karin Crawford, and I took up this challenge by asking whether it is possible to "rate" comprehension rather than to "score" it and to determine a ranking that is consistent with careful scoring. Specifically, *is it possible to rate reading samples holistically—much like the holistic assessment of writing—and obtain the same distribution of ranks generated by the sum of scores on individual propositions? Further, are raters sensitive to the same types of linguistic and vocabulary features that a scoring matrix can make visible?* Does any of this matter anyway? Our investigation also gave us the opportunity to probe in a slightly different fashion the relationship between grammatical knowledge and reading comprehension ability.

Rating Rather Than Scoring

In order to begin to answer the question of rating as a more efficient assessment measure of using recall protocols, a reading comprehension task in German was administered to 69 college freshmen all with experience in learning German at the secondary school level. The passage was a 250-word authentic text entitled "Die Verwandlung" (The Metamorphosis), from Günther Wallraff's book *Ganz unten* (1990). It contains an obvious intertextual reference to Kafka and relates the author's concern about the treatment of guest workers in (at the time) West Germany. In order to understand the treatment these workers receive, the author ran an advertisement in a newspaper seeking a menial-level job. The author described himself as a foreigner and went so far as to disguise himself to look darker, including getting dark-colored contact lenses made for himself. Students were asked to read the passage and, when they believed they understood as much of the passage as possible, to recall it in writing in the language in which they felt most comfortable. In all cases, the language chosen was English. The total number of propositions in the passage was 78. The ratio of words to sentences was 14. All performances were scored and re-scored against a scoring grid based on the propositions in the passage. Interrater reliability was .96. As in previous studies, the scoring grid also indicated clear bands of performance across the passage—two particular sentences were generally not acknowledged in recall. These sentences contained three nouns that seemed to be obscure and low-frequency verbs in an infinitive construction (Table 6.2 and Table 6.3). Further, these two sentences illustrated in the tables of the scoring grid were predictive of high performance. That is, if a reader recalled either sentence "*Sie können die zahllosen Zumutungen nicht mehr verdauen*" [They can't tolerate the unreasonable demands] or "*Viel war nicht nötig, um mich ins Abseits zu begeben, um zu einer ausgestossenen Minderheit zu gehören, um ganz unten zu sein*" [It didn't take much to push me to the side, to belong to a shunned minority, to be totally downtrodden], then the probability of obtaining a high score for the reading of the entire passage was indeed substantial.

The 69 recall performances were then randomly distributed across five raters. The five raters were asked to rank the performances and place them into categories, preferably low (1), middle (2), and high (3), indicating the relative rankings. Raters were told that they did not have to use three categories—that it

Table 6.2 Scores Generated from Propositions 26–36 of the Text, "Die Verwandlung"

	Student 6	Student 7	Student 8	Student 9	Student 10
Sie können					
die zahllosen Zumutungen					
nicht mehr					
verdauen					
Sie haben kaum eine Chance	x		x		
auf dem Arbeitsmarkt	x	x	x		x
Es gibt für sie	x	x			
hier aufgewachsen	x			x	x
kein wirkliches Zurück	x	x			
in ihr Herkunftsland	x	x		x	x
Sie sind heimatlos.		x			x

Table 6.3 Scores Generated from Propositions 56–73 of the Text, "Die Verwandlung"

	Student 6	Student 7	Student 8	Student 9	Student 10
Viel war nicht noetig					
um mich ins Abseits					
zu begeben					
um zu					
einer ausgestossenen					
Minderheit					
zu gehoeren					
um ganz unten					
zu sein					
Von einem Spezialisten					
liess ich mir					
zwei duenne	x				x
sehr dunkel	x				
gefaerbte Kontaktlinsen					
anfertigen	x				x
die ich Tag und Nacht	x				x
tragen konnte					

might be possible that in their random group all performances would be rated as equivalent. The correlation between scoring and rating was calculated, resulting in a value of $r = .71$.

The correlation was not particularly inspiring; also not uninspiring. Further, when the raters were interviewed in order to get a sense of the relationship between their intuition about the "quality" of the reading performance versus what was indicated by the scoring grid, none of the raters noted the two sentences that seemed to be key to "high" performance on the passage. In addition, the raters noted that they felt too constrained by the three-category system, some noting that they had to place too many persons in the middle group. As a result, two additional participants were asked to rate all of the passages—this time on a four-point scale. This action improved the correlation of the scores and the ratings to a more acceptable $r = .78$ ($p < .01$). The relationship between these ratings and the grammar score was also of considerable interest. The correlation between grammar and the recall score was .46; between the grammar and the rating, .44 ($p < .01$ in both cases).

Of course, a one-passage study is always dubious—one does not know whether the performances (either the original reading performances *or* the raters' performances) were idiosyncratic or not. The next part of the probe, then, was a replication using a different passage. It appeared, on the basis of the first probe, that "rating" is a genuine possibility. If this finding were to hold, then practitioners would have at hand a convenient measure that was also rich in data on individual students. On the other hand, however, if sophisticated raters are unable to locate the true difficulties in passages, rating passage performance is not substantially better than using conventional assessment tools.

A second authentic German passage of 250 words and 105 propositions was selected from Volker Borbein author of *Menschen in Deutschland* (1995). The word to sentence density was 12. This passage concerned isolation in modern society and pointed toward answering machines as significant evidence of this isolation. Fifty-six first-year college students read and recalled the passage, each choosing English as the language of recall. All 56 recalls were scored; the inter-rater reliability of this scoring was .97. Next, five raters were engaged and asked to place each recall into one of four categories described as: 1—not on target; 4—absolutely on target; with ratings of 2 and 3 somewhere in the "almost" and "not quite but almost" ranges. The average relationship between and among raters was .87.

The same analytic procedure was followed with this text. The relationship between the recall score and the rating was $r = .66$ ($p < .01$). In contrast to rater performance within the first part of the probe, raters did seem to be sensitive to that portion of the passage that would predict high performance: *Die Werbung bemüht sich um ihn, der Staat holt viel Geld aus ihm heraus. Reiseunternehmungen tragen der Tatsache Rechnung, daß die Zahl der Alleinlebenden die Zahl der Haushalte mit zwei oder mehr Personen bald überholt wird. Seine Beziehungen haben nie länger als ein paar Monate gedauert, die längste hielt immerhin fast zwei Jahre.* This group of sentences had high predictive power that enabled readers to understand the text at a sophisticated level. In addition, the relationship between the ratings and the grammar score remained of considerable interest. The correlation between grammar and the recall score was .35; between the grammar and the rating, .37 ($p < .01$ in both cases).

Each set of findings is consistent: there is a substantial correlation between the measures of careful scoring and rating performances. This indicates that, by and large, the two methods tap the same set of reading behaviors. In each case, too, the relationship between the reading performances (either careful scoring or rating) and the grammar scores is much less substantial. This correlational evidence indicates that a discrete point grammar test and a holistic reading assessment do not tap overlapping behaviors. This finding reaffirms the data cited repeatedly in previous chapters—grammatical knowledge accounts for an important and large part of the variance in second-language reading performance; it does *not*, however, account for the majority of the performance. Relying on grammatical knowledge as an indicator of reading ability falls short time and time again.

The evidence presented here suggests that rating reading performances through the written recall of passages is a productive and efficient means of assessing reading in a second language. There is further evidence that the rating could be more satisfying than scoring, for a simple score sheet does not indicate whether or not the student understood the context of the text. For example, in the text used in the second phase, a subject recalled primarily cognates and lists from the text about social isolation, able to recall *stillness, bare feet, beer, food, microwave,* etc. This strategy of listing without coherent sentences was used by students recalling the passages in both the first and second phases of our investigation. The listing strategy demonstrates a potential weakness of the scoring method: readers might recognize the words and receive a medium range score, but not understand the import of the text. With each text used, there were subjects who did not recall a great number of words, but who understood the basic idea of the text and who were able to provide an accurate interpretation. Yet, there were also subjects, for example, who understood that the passage was about a bachelor who enjoyed his freedom and time alone, and various other details, but did not recall a congruent number of items. This text, in particular, is a good example of the benefits of rating over scoring, because the difficulty, except for a few passage segments, does not lie in the vocabulary. Rating in this case gives a better sense of the reader's ability to connect meaning to grammar. This is a possible explanation of the discrepancies in a few cases between the score and the rating; the rating provided a more accurate assessment.

The rating methodology depends on scorers who are sensitive to grammatical, idiomatic, and other elements that present a challenge to learners of German. In order to understand how raters perceive the rating task, the Borbein passage was presented to experienced teachers of German. All but one identified some element within sentences 12 through 14 that would determine whether or not the students had a sophisticated reading ability of German as well as any additional difficulties. One rater in particular was able to pinpoint precisely the elements in the text that were key in determining the distinctions between ratings of 2, 3, and 4: the subjunctive ("*Muetter hätten ihn gern als Schwiegersohn*"), the unusual use of the genitive and difficult vocabulary ("*Reiseunternehmen tragen der Tatsache Rechnung*"), and the use of the future perfect ("*überholt haben wird*"). Only one of the subjects was able to understand all of these elements in the reading passage, and then not even fully correctly. If a rater was not sensitive to these grammatical and vocabulary complexities, rating would present a difficulty. In fact, the least experienced teacher could not identify elements in the passage that distinguished between high-performing and lower-performing readers. This teacher was only able to approach the text as a whole, saying that if a student were able "to piece it *all* together," she would be high performing. When pressed to identify a passage in particular that might be distinguishing, the teacher eventually chose "*Er hat sich nie binden wollen oder koennen.*" This passage was not recalled by those given a rating of 2 and by some given a 3 rating; however, their ability to understand was not related to the relatively simple modal construction but, rather, whether they understood the passage previously mentioned above. It seems as though the inability to recall this relatively simple passage is determined by the external context of the status of social isolation.

After the completion of the interviews with teachers to get a sense of whether they could identify the elements in the text that careful scoring indicated were predictive of difficulty, a careful review of all the recall protocols was conducted in order to gain a general idea of the range of linguistic performances within each rating (1 through 4). In other words, if there is some match between what careful scoring and teacher sensitivity reveal, is there also a relationship between actual linguistic performances and ratings?

The qualitative analysis was conducted within the four rating categories. Within the level 1 ratings, there was always a perfect correlation between the score and rating for the low recalls. In this low category, subjects only had the basic knowledge of a man around 50 who is buying an answering machine. The sentences recalled were those of simple structure with SVO and some basic vocabulary items were also recalled, such as "*Freiheit*" [freedom]. In the level 2 category, a low- to mid-performance rating, subjects understood more of the passage without necessarily being able to recall segments written in tenses other than the present indicative. A greater array of vocabulary items was included with some edging toward the present perfect and simple past. Knowledge of relative pronouns and prenoun inserts was not in evidence.

Within level 3 ratings, subjects' recalls included elements from sentences 12 and 13 but were not exactly correct. Subjects were able to recall the past tense of sentence 14, and there is evidence of knowledge of the subjunctive. Generally the full context was correctly understood as a story about a man who has never had to care for children, and so forth. A greater command of German vocabulary is in evidence. Within the highest level of ranking, subjects were still generally unable to recall sentences 12–14 correctly; however, the rest of the text was recalled almost literally, including relative clauses and prenoun inserts. These recalls "read" as high performances.

This type of analysis indicates that it is important to have four categories in which to rate the recall. This better reflects the range in learner performances and allows one to distinguish between those students who just cannot read in the second language and those who understand the basics but not much more. Such analysis also potentially yields some insight into the linguistic dimension of second-language reading proficiency.

These data inspire confidence that one can, indeed, continue with a holistic assessment, getting it rated (rather than "scored") in a timely fashion without sacrificing the most important data set—the actual performance of real readers. Further, it is important to understand in second-language contexts the parameters of those relationships and to continue to make these distinctions in performance assessments. But is this a call to reject careful scoring and to move toward the intuitive approach? No. The raters were not consistent across the two passages in their abilities to isolate what actually caused readers difficulty. Whether this is a reading question or a teacher development question remains; until we have teachers who can reliably isolate features—even in the modern era teachers will report word length and sentence length as primary factors—we will need to encourage and insist on a careful analysis of student reading performances. This investigation also underlines that the concept of "grammar" continues to be ambiguous and daunting. A reader cannot read without it; at the same time, decontextualized grammatical knowledge seems to hold only a tenuous relationship with comprehension abilities. A critical conclusion is, indeed, that in assessment one cannot rely on a grammar score to provide useful information about literacy. Yet, ironically, a look at which parts of German readers used in their recalls reveals some dimensions of language development as well as the impact of the grammatical syllabus on reading proficiency.

Rating seems to be a useful technique for trained practitioners sensitive to grammatical structure and discourse features. It is quicker and perhaps taps instructor intuition, making it a potentially more satisfying source of knowledge for instructors. It is, however, not terribly useful as a diagnostic tool. It does not help to locate sources of error. An instructor must "guess" at those sources. And psychometrically, of course, rating brings with it restricted scales—scales that make quantitative analysis problematic. *Scoring*, in contrast, would seem to be a better technique for inexperienced practitioners who need to acquire sensitivity to microlevel features of grammar and discourse. Careful propositional scoring requires the scorer to make relatively few decisions and provides direct evidence of grammatical and vocabulary difficulties. It is useful as a pedagogical and diagnostic tool. Psychometrically, scoring generates elaborate scores that can reveal variance across readers. Scoring is, on the other hand, extremely time-consuming and potentially misleading for it cannot reveal holistic understanding. Of course, which factors, or combination thereof, are driving the generation of both scores and ratings continue to be sources of challenge and exploration. As in all research and instruction, wisdom should prevail. Until we fully understand the second-language comprehension process, we will be forced to generate and interpret scores and ratings about which we are not fully knowledgeable. Naturally, decisions made are always associated with opportunity costs. The issue is to understand which opportunity to choose at which cost and to interpret results accordingly.

Assessing the Teaching of Comprehension

The topic of scoring versus rating provides a perfect platform for launching a discussion of effective second-language reading teaching. The data discussed above point to very real differences between the assessment abilities of experienced and inexperienced instructors: the more experienced the instructor, the more sensitivity to micro-level features of text that play important roles in distinguishing between high-level and lower-level comprehension performances. The question remains, however, of whether this kind of sensitivity on the part of a teacher leads directly to being able to impart this sensitivity to students. In fact, acquiring this level of sensitivity is precisely what students need to acquire in order to become effective comprehenders. And yet, *what do we actually know about teachers and how they teach comprehension? And what do we know about teaching effectively in the upper registers? What is the relationship between effective comprehension teaching and the effective teaching of productive dimensions of interpersonal and presentational language? Do they "look" the same in a classroom performance?* These are important questions for the remainder of this chapter on assessment.

Ironically, there is a good deal of common folk wisdom, unfortunately not widely or sufficiently documented, about what one would expect to see in an effective basic language class. Above all, in an effective basic language class the students are talking. They are, in fact, talking more than the teacher. In addition, one would expect to encounter in an effective language class a lot of group work—a structure that enables students to talk with each other over an extended period. Finally, effective classrooms tend to have a clear structure to lessons that all students can anticipate—an introductory portion that reviews known or previously learned materials and an intermediate portion built on the opening section that introduces new or difficult material. After the practice of a new concept, a wind-down period ensues that enables learners to exit the class on a positive, confident note. Learners often praise this kind of explicit structuring as it enables them to negotiate the often difficult terrain of language learning. They also often praise the explicitly articulated nature of the objectives of language learning. In other words, effective instruction is more often than not tied to making learners aware of precisely what it is that they are to learn and to use and they are given tasks that clearly enable the learning (Light, 2001).

This description of basic language teaching highlights the key impetus behind all teaching—student learning. Further, if as I argued in the introductory pages of this volume, second-language reading is critical for an educated citizenry, then that learning also has to be about engagement—in other words about getting learners involved in the subject matter so that they have it with them the rest of their lives. One might question whether a life without a knowledge of calculus or golf or physiology is fulfilled, yet unquestioned is a life without literacy—that is a fundamentally different matter in the modern world for the analytic skills it brings with it that should and, more critically, need, to last a lifetime.

In returning to the compensatory model of second-language reading, one should be able to probe whether an instructor accounts for the first-language literacy knowledge base. Does the instructor, as suggested in Chapter 4, enable readers to rely on what they can read in their first language as a linguistic and conceptual anchor? Does the instructor fully understand the nature of the strategies individual readers employ, such as whether they use a dictionary, what type of dictionary it is, whether the person turns to hypertext environments, using translation software, and so on and so forth. In the case of upper-level reading instruction, does the instructor probe readers' knowledge of literary forms and devices such as understanding metaphoric language or how to analyze a poem for rhyme and meter, or how they understand the ironic subtleties in journalistic commentaries? The compensatory model also suggests that excellent instruction should be sensitive to the linguistic dimensions of the text at hand. Is the instructor able and willing to focus on microfeatures of the text, asking the students to understand why an author chose a particular grammatical form (why is the subjunctive form found in this particular sentence?) or a particular word or turn of phrase? Most assuredly in literary instruction this type of pedagogic strategy is key. Finally, the compensatory model argues that there is an array of background knowledge that surely comes into play in comprehension. For the advanced second-language reader, the key question for their teachers is whether the background knowledge the reader possesses is sufficient and whether it is appropriate. Teachers need to be sensitive within the context of individual readers toward the interaction of the first-language base with the second as it operates at the conceptual level. How do teachers remain aware that second-language readers are at times able to retrieve the information from second-language texts that is compatible with first-language cultural patterns, but often not able to retrieve incompatible information? In other words, readers read from their first-language conceptual base and understand what "makes sense to them." Further, we know that second-language readers use the sociohistorical factual knowledge that they have with second-language texts. At times, as noted throughout this volume, compensatory behavior is extremely helpful, but it can also be destructive to constructing an accurate and complete construction of any given text. Again, teachers must have these concepts in mind when working with individual readers.

Another critical point that teachers must take from the research and from the compensatory model is the manner in which the individual's knowledge base interacts with second-language linguistic abilities. As noted in previous chapters, the interaction can take the form of knowledge compensating for but also overriding linguistic deficiencies. That is, readers with low-level second-language skills can in some contexts exhibit high-level comprehension abilities because they can use their knowledge to compensate for their linguistic deficits. At the same time, however, their knowledge might lead them to *over*compensate and, thus, denigrate or negate actual language skills. That is, readers with high-level language skills can doubt their own abilities when the text does not match their knowledge. If readers are good at high-level textual analysis, to be most specific on the point, their skills will assist them or, better said, help them to compensate, even within a very restricted linguistic frame. It is clear that learners will develop their interpretations within the context of the sociocultural knowledge that they carry with them. This knowledge is not necessarily appropriate or relevant, but it is, however, all that readers often have as an interpretive base. When second-language readers misinterpret, teachers not well-informed in theory and research often judge them as not being sophisticated or not well-educated, when those teachers should recognize that a reader's misinterpretation may be rooted in inappropriate background knowledge for the interpretive text at hand. These points have been reiterated continually throughout this volume in order to underline the multivariate and recursive nature of second-language text processing.

If instructors proceed in their teaching according to what we know about the process of reading in a second language, we will see lessons in which instructors uncover the conceptual representations of text that readers construct. Then, after uncovering the representations, we should see instructors who realign the representations of readers when these are inappropriate. We should see instructors who look for and diagnose misunderstandings arising from cultural misconstructions, linguistic deficiencies, and from the conflation of the two. We should see instructors who know how to proceed in terms of sociocultural knowledge, in terms of linguistic knowledge, and in terms of literary or interpretive analytic skill. This type of perspective on the L2 reading classroom has rarely if ever been discussed in the literature. Planning within a compensatory framework is, however, critical in bringing about instruction that is consistent with the research base and that brings students to higher levels of linguistic proficiency, cultural appreciation, and comprehension.

Exploring Effective Second-Language Literature Teaching

Much of the above is unsatisfactory speculation given that there is little empirical evidence that the suggestions evolved from compensatory theory translate easily into effective pedagogical practice. The irony is, however, that in spite of this lack of research and the dearth of attention to upper-level reading comprehension teaching within the field, many high stakes decisions are, in fact, made on the basis of the teaching of second-language reading. These high-stakes decisions are made within the context of promotion and tenure files in language and literature departments. Indeed, all of these files contain statements from both peers and students about teaching effectiveness—teaching that is largely based in the instruction of upper-level texts; principally literary and cultural texts. Hence, in the spirit of trying to gain greater understanding in the context of effective teaching, I asked a set of questions of peers who, as part of their second nature as tenured professors of literature, "assess" literature teaching, peers who are senior and eminent literary scholars who have sat on untold tenure and review committees and have made a career's worth of difficult decisions.

My interview protocol was to probe what they look for in teaching evaluations. Theoretically, this would provide an inductively derived outline of characteristics of effective literature teaching. After three of these interviews, I saw little point in continuing. When interviewed about what each person looks for in effective literature teaching I got themes and variations of the following type:

> Hey, I look to see whether the instructor was attentive; i.e., did he show up for class on time? Did he hold regular office hours? Did he seem to talk to the students when they wanted to talk? Did he have a syllabus? I want to make sure that the class happened and that the kids were reasonably satisfied.

I asked some questions about the assessment of the content and the structure of the course offered. The general answer was "I assume that if the person got hired, the content is OK; I couldn't do anything about that anyway even if it weren't." Then I asked my interviewees how they can tell from the evaluations whether the students learned anything. The answers I received fell into the following category: "You can't. If they [students] tell you they'd take another course from the person, I assume they learned something."

This response is highly consistent with the research on student evaluation of teaching. That research literature reports that student evaluations of teaching are measures of student affect. In other words, teaching evaluations measure how the students feel about themselves at the end of the course. If the instructor has paid a lot of attention to them and considered their needs, and the students believe they will get a high grade, then the evaluations are positive. It is not unreasonable, then, that the interviewees noted concerns about office hours "availability." The research literature provides further documentation of this in studies that indicate that the more frequently evaluation is done within a course, the higher the end-of-term evaluations. The emphasis is on "more frequently"—the interim evaluations can be thrown in the waste basket, never seen by the instructor, and the students will believe that this is a demonstration of "caring" on the part of the instructor and, therefore, rate the teaching higher. Obviously, what I had hoped to find from my interviewing of literary scholars were ideas about excellence in literature teaching and, by extension, other upper-register text teaching. I heard nothing more than what we know already—generically—about teaching.

I then moved to another data source for trying to create generalizations about effective teaching from individual cases. I reviewed sets of letters written by students regarding the tenure candidacy, promotion to tenure, and promotion to Full Professor papers of five colleagues in commonly and uncommonly taught languages. I looked at letters from a total of 85 students; 47 undergraduates and 38 graduate students. Eighty-four of the letters were supportive of the literature professor under consideration. Again, I was looking for descriptions of "effective teaching" which is, in many ways, a subtext for "learning." As might be predicted, the letters from the students cross-validated what the research on teaching evaluations says. The overwhelming majority of student comments were about how they felt in instruction with the person or how they were "treated" by the instructor in question. Almost 100% of the letters praised an "open atmosphere" in which students felt free to express their own ideas without inhibition. Many of the letters praised instructors' abilities at including the comments of "all" students and of leading discussion without dominating it. There were comments such as sincerity in listening to student opinion and, of course, accessibility after and outside of class.

But what of my question, *How do you know if you learned anything?* The word "learn" or "learning" or a reference to "I didn't know that before and now I do" was found in seven of the 84 letters. Six of the seven letters used the word "help" such as, "The instructor helped me…" The help offered, which I argue can be taken as a version of learning, was always in the context of making connections. "The instructor helped me make a link between this piece of literature and that; between this historic event and that; between this theory and that interpretation." There was another consistent set of comments. Fourteen of the letters praised the ability of the instructor to meet "different intellectual needs." Some of the letters referenced the difficulties of having graduates and undergraduates in classes; others the difficulty of students at various linguistic levels.

I concluded my informal investigation by thinking about 85 student letters, 84 of which were extremely positive. Does this mean that we should conclude that "all is well; let's not fix it if it's not broken?" The dilemma we face is that all student evaluations are not extremely positive; many of our assistant professors are trapped in generic teaching evaluations that perhaps tap "effective teaching" in lecture courses, but perhaps not. Further, upper-level foreign-language literature courses are small—that creates certain advantages (small courses always get better ratings than large courses; non-required always get better ratings than required), but also puts our instruction and instructors into teaching evaluation limbo. Do we really want to base tenure and promotion decisions on how students feel about themselves? Yet at all levels of the promotion process, teaching evaluations are taken extremely seriously—frighteningly seriously given that we have so little research-based information on the assessment of teaching upper-level, complicated texts. A further consideration is the assessment of students' performance in these upper-level, reading-based classes. They deserve to know what it is, specifically, that they will learn, what it is they have not yet mastered, and, more importantly, *how* to master it. Students report that they are in the upper-level literature classes because they believe their language skills will improve. They are owed an articulate statement on what the instructor is trying to accomplish and how that attempt will be assessed.

This chapter ends with a viable, though untested and unresearched, framework for the assessment of upper-level reading instruction. A first step is to consult the clients, that is, the students, who have a store of knowledge about instructors. Table 6.4 includes questions and commentaries that should be elicited from students. These probes are targeted at the key areas of compensatory processing: language knowledge, literacy knowledge, and, specifically for upper-level students, engagement. Any assessment of teaching needs to probe with students whether their language use improved and became more sophisticated and whether their confidence was enhanced with regard to literary/critical material. Table 6.5 is a corollary protocol for peer assessment of teaching. It presupposes expertise in areas such as student proficiency level and its relationship to the difficulty level of the material. Any instructor of upper-register material should grapple with the heterogeneity of topic knowledge and background experience that learners have and should be held responsible for accommodating these different knowledge bases. A second key area involves the assessment of how well readers are able to understand highly nuanced language forms and how to enable learners to acquire an understanding of such forms. In upper-level instruction, learners tend to "know" all of the grammatical forms. Understanding their subtleties is a different dimension to their learning. A final critical area is how the teacher approaches and assesses student analytic ability. The protocols in Table 6.4 and 6.5 are intended to commence a theory- and research-based direction in the assessment of high-level comprehension instruction in second languages.

Table 6.4 Student Assessment Protocol of the Teaching of Advanced Second-Language Reading

Evaluating topic knowledge

Was this course your first experience with the topic of X?
If no, please comment on your prior experience with the topic.
If yes, please comment on how your instructor prepared you for this new topic.

Evaluating language knowledge

Was the linguistic level of the material that you read targeted at your comfort level or your frustration level?
If at your comfort level, how did the instructor challenge you to become more sophisticated in your use of language?
If the material was at your frustration level, how did the instructor help you to become more comfortable with the language?
Did you learn to use [insert language] more effectively?

Evaluating literary knowledge

Was this course your first experience with literary analysis?
If no, please comment on your prior experience with learning to analyze literature.
If yes, please comment on how your instructor prepared you to analyze literature.
Do you feel prepared and confident to read independently in this area?

Evaluating engagement

Will you use what you learned in this course in the future?
If no, why not?
If yes, how will you use the material?

Table 6.5 Peer Assessment Protocol of the Teaching of Advanced Second-Language Reading

Evaluating topic knowledge

Was the topic aligned with the experience of the students in question?
If no, how did the instructor compensate for student inexperience?
If yes, how did the instructor provide a more sophisticated experience for the students?

Evaluating language knowledge

Was the linguistic level of the material in the course matched to student linguistic level?
If the material was at the student comfort level, how did the instructor challenge students' linguistic abilities?
If the material was linguistically frustrating for the students, how did the instructor compensate for this and assist students?
Did the students become more astute in their use of [insert language]?

Evaluating literary knowledge

What is the students' experience level with literary analysis?
How did the instructor prepare students for literary analysis?
Did the instructor enhance students' knowledge of literary analysis?

Evaluating engagement

Are students continuing with additional courses in literature?

Assessment and evaluation will probably always remain flashpoints in any teaching area. Teachers want students to succeed and are loath to criticize; students want teachers to like them and they too, therefore, are reluctant to be severe in their assessments. Yet, assessment is the key to driving excellence in teaching and learning. Students need to understand what it is that they are to learn; how to go about that learning; and how precise they are in the reading of upper-register texts. Teachers' roles are to establish environments in which each reader as an individual can progress in the learning of language and culture arena to achieve the analytic skill necessary to read, comprehend, and use upper-register texts for future learning.

Chapter 7

Continuing to Research Second-Language Reading

I began this book by invoking Huey's (1908) ethic and I will end with this spirit. Huey expected all of us to participate as a community in improving reading instruction. He fundamentally believed that research was the path to bring about improvement. *Reading Development in a Second Language* set forth research directions in the area of research design and in curriculum and instruction. The first task of this chapter is to discuss whether the challenges for research and teaching set forth in *Reading Development in a Second Language* were ever met. But Huey was not one to look backward. Hence, to remain with his ethic, *Understanding Advanced Second-Language Reading* ends with an outline of a research program that follows many of the research directions cited in the volume and that principally emphasizes the work to be done within a compensatory framework.

Toward Criteria for Quality Research

Reading Development in a Second Language set forth recommendations for the conduct of second-language reading research. A feature of excellent research in second-language reading that has been implemented in the data base is the consistent use of authentic text. The days of observing readers under conditions that do not represent what they will do outside of instruction seem to be over. Yet other issues mentioned, principally seated in a lack of responsiveness to previous theory and research, remain of concern. In other words, many studies even today seem to be conducted within a vacuum rather than being in dialog with past and potential work. This contention held true with a number of the studies listed in Chapter 3 that re-explored what seemed to be the same issue over and over without revealing new perspectives. *Reading Development in a Second Language* also lamented the use of single measures of comprehension, noting that "there is no perfect measure of reading comprehension. Every measure is flawed; each measure provides one perspective. Therefore, multiple measures are necessary to provide a more than unidimensional picture" (Bernhardt, 1991, p. 224). And yet multiple measures were rarely employed within individual studies over the past years. Beyond a lack of multiple measures is the lack of multiple texts. A reading study employing one text from the universe of texts runs the risk of disadvantaging subjects due to a particular topic or style. Subjects must be given multiple opportunities to display their proficiency in reading. A third key issue noted in *Reading Development in a Second Language* was a failure of studies to position their subjects toward the text(s) they were asked to read. That volume noted that we needed to analyze reader performances under different "cognitive and affective stances, and while accomplishing different reading goals ... Each of these conditions and circumstances implies a potentially different set of processing strategies and concomitant different set of performance data" (p. 225). No study outlined in Chapter 3 observed the same readers under different conditions or with different dispositions. This state remains of major concern because it is clear that literacy is linked to different kinds of social conditions.

As I noted in Chapter 3, I tried to re-articulate these concerns in a contribution to a special issue of *Reading in a Foreign Language* (Bernhardt, 2004). Yet, progress regarding appropriate research design has been slow. There are several reasons for this. Often, young researchers interested in the topic of second-language reading are either schooled in second-language acquisition *or* in reading, but rarely in both. This leads to studies that might meet certain criteria but not appropriate ones for the particular area. Second-language acquisition researchers might focus on language variables and ignore the reasoning behind using multiple texts in a study. Reading researchers might focus on the texts and ignore the level of the reader's first-language proficiency or the nature of the first languages involved. A second reason for second-language reading researchers having failed to establish a common research tradition is that, as I mentioned earlier, both related fields, second-language acquisition and reading, have been slow to acknowledge the importance of the field itself. These fields have not demanded rigor because they generally ignore any findings from the data base. Again, while this might appear to be tautological it is, perhaps, more the nature of a vicious cycle of dismissal. In fact, in my early career it was next to impossible to get a study of second-language reading published in a number of journals; hence, the only research outlet available was often edited books and conference proceedings. This situation meant that a substantial number of studies that were quite good tended to be ignored because they were buried in what might be called non-elite, non-refereed volumes A third reason is related and that is the demands of publishing. In the *Handbook of Reading Research, Volume II*, Mosenthal and Kamil (1991) remarked on this phenomenon:

> University constraints often play an important role in determining what approach to progress reading researchers adopt ... . In order to produce the necessary volume of research, assistant professors can be tempted by the expediency of choosing validating research over interpretive research. Because it provides for a ready-made set of variables and operational conditions, validating research often yields highly predictable (and

publishable) results at much less the effort than might be the case for interpretative research. (pp. 1039–1040)

Mosenthal and Kamil go on to contend that while these kinds of publications might help the individual researcher progress, they often do not contribute to progress in the field of reading. Their view might explain why there are many studies in certain areas—studies that often seem to be indistinguishable one from the other. While careful work across multiple languages and populations is important, that work should be progressive in nature rather than constantly a replication of what has come before; it should bring in new views and new perspectives rather than repeating established ones. In *Reading Development in a Second Language*, I commented that naivety in research designs is forgivable, but carelessness is not. Under the rubric of naivety, I listed not using newer research methodologies or technologies for data collection. The more serious issue is the careless one or a "lack of responsiveness to new data" (Bernhardt, 1991, p. 224). I often review for journals and repeatedly see studies that fail to allow subjects to use their stronger language in assessment; or that fail to delineate the language backgrounds of subjects; or that continue to use cloze as an assessment technique even though it has been discredited. The area of second-language reading is too important to accept reading studies that are not fully informed by the data base. In addition, I often see bibliographies filled with decades-old studies or I see studies that do not grapple with any theory whatsoever. It is as if the studies are conducted in a vacuum and that vacuum excludes the context where a particular study contributes to the whole of progress in the field.

We clearly need as a profession to establish research criteria that meet the needs of the unique situation of second-language reading. These quality criteria must meet the demands of both reading research and second-language acquisition research. Some criteria are listed in Table 7.1. The criteria try to capture our need to garner information across different text types as well as across language and literacy backgrounds. They also try to reinforce the notion that all research studies must be respectful of the intricacies of an array of languages and, therefore, should always include native informants as part of a research team.

Table 7.1 Research Criteria for Studies of Second-Language Reading

Specification of first-language literacy level
Measurement of second-language grammatical level
Delineation of first-language backgrounds of subject population
Explanation of the linguistic relationship of the cognizant first and second languages
At least one member of the research team able to use the cognizant first and second languages
Subjects' comprehension assessed in their dominant language
Multiple texts employed
Multiple measures employed

Finally, there is the critical issue of how we pose questions. Brantmeier (2004b) noted that:

> analysis of variance (ANOVA) is the most widely used statistical procedure in quantitatively-oriented second-language reading research. This is because, as depicted by the research questions, L2 reading researchers often investigate the relationship of many different independent variables with dependent variables and are concerned about the variation between and within groups of variables … ANOVA has been employed in analyzing data for inferential purposes. (p. 57)

She adds an example: "prior research that examines a comprehension assessment test for L2 reading may have shown that success on the test is related to factors such as topic familiarity levels, gender, type of assessment task, etc." *Understanding Advanced Second-Language Reading* argues, however, for a different way of conceptualizing the second-language process—not as a compilation of factors independent of one another, but rather as a set of factors that influence each other. Brantmeier takes on the point: "Perhaps more inquiries about L2 reading comprehension should be concerned with the amounts and types of variables that are superior, or more influential, in producing higher levels of reading comprehension." She notes that a multiple regression perspective, while not different from analysis of variance mathematically speaking, can offer a perspective that enables us to see how much of the reading process we are able to explain within investigations and how much is outside the investigation; i.e., "residual." The compensatory model is about how much influence we can account for and how much is still unexplained.

New Questions on Old Topics

All academic books raise more questions than they answer; *Understanding Advanced Second-Language Reading* is no exception to this rule. This chapter returns to the narrative in Chapter 3 for conceptual organization. For while this volume advocates compensatory processing and a view of reading that tries to understand variables in relation to each other rather than independent of each other, it acknowledges that the majority of the data base remains focused on individuals' variables. These remain important variables that we must come to understand in greater detail.

Questions Related to Background Knowledge

There is no question that the knowledge a reader possesses has an influence in the reading process. How this knowledge operates and whether it determines or obfuscates comprehension are the issues. Research questions suggested might be: *When does a reader revert to relying on background knowledge? What role does background knowledge play in upper-register text processing? Is this role perhaps more or less significant than in lower-level text processing; i.e., is the compensatory share larger or smaller? How do the readers of an upper-register text know when to distance themselves from background knowledge in order to assess knowledge implied by the author?* I have been extremely careful throughout this volume not to invoke military dimensions of second-language reading or of its importance within the intelligence community and yet, the variable of background knowledge is absolutely crucial in this arena. *Does believing in a bit of knowledge remain so powerful that one cannot read beyond it? How does one learn to use background knowledge but to remain suspicious of it?*

Another category of questions relates to what background knowledge actually is. I struggled with this issue while trying to categorize studies. Indeed, knowing how to use an analogy is a bit of background knowledge; but that knowledge could perhaps be more conveniently categorized as literacy knowledge. Topic interest also entails background knowledge; if a reader has no interest in a topic one might assume little background knowledge. An alternative way of posing such a question would be: *Is topic interest, in fact, an affective factor and more related to motivation that to actual concrete topic?*

Questions Related to Technology

The studies outlined in Chapter 3 that examined uses of technology are important. They have begun the complex process of trying to understand the interaction of a second-language reader with technology-based tools. Throughout this volume I have referenced texts found on the internet and have used the argument of technology on which to base my view that it is technology itself that has caused the explosion of second-language readers. While I have asserted this we still do not know *how many readers across the globe regularly access information in a language other than their mother tongue?* One could investigate this question by probing the number of hits on particular websites.

The studies listed provide overwhelming evidence that readers believe in the power of technology. They accept and expect technology-based tools. Yet the exact nature of these tools and their configuration remains unclear. Studies seem to point toward particular kinds of configurations, for example, electronic dictionaries. *Are word-based rather than picture-based configurations truly superior? Or is the efficacy of electronic configurations dependent upon variables such as register, topic, and/or reader proficiency level?* Re-asking many of the questions already posed, but within better-designed studies that include measures of literacy and multiple passages and tasks would provide the confidence we need for future materials development. Additional questions regarding word look-ups, the density of textual look-ups and so forth could all be probed within the context of technology-intense second-language reading studies.

Technology exhibits dilemmas corollary to those facing definitions of background knowledge. Substantial overlap will occur between variable focus. For example, *when a reader navigates through hyper-text, are the navigation strategies unique to the second-language context or are they strategies simply deposited from first-language strategies?* In order to answer this important question, one would need to track second-language readers reading hypertext not only in their second language but also in their first.

Questions Related to Strategies

Separating specific second-language reading strategies from general first-language literacy strategies is absolutely key in making progress in the arena of strategies. Merely finding strategies at use in reading is tantamount to discovering that a text is involved; such a finding reveals little about strategy use. Some of the studies highlighted in Chapter 3 indicated findings that would not, indeed could not, be found in first-language reading, such as translation. *Is translation the key second-language reading strategy? Do readers of upper-register texts continue to use translation as a strategy or do they suspend it in upper reaches, having enough cognitive capacity and confidence not to resort to it or to find it superfluous? Should we perceive the use of prior knowledge as a "strategy"? Are there second-language versions of prediction or interpretation strategies? Should we understand compensation in terms of strategies?*

Expert–novice think-aloud studies could provide some insight into this critical topic.

Questions Related to Testing

Large-scale test development in languages other than English such as Spanish and Arabic as a foreign language would be helpful in gauging the progress of readers from lower levels into much higher registers. Moreover, approaching the question of rating versus scoring in a more substantive way beyond the data offered in Chapter 6 would also be important in establishing the efficacy and efficiency of that particular technique. Questions of the relationship of second-language reading and writing might also be fruitfully pursued within the rating framework.

Questions Related to Intrapersonal Variables

Affective and personality variables remain as variables that tend to fascinate yet rarely contribute to a resolution. Well-designed studies that enable research to factor out features such as language and literacy knowledge and, most probably, also topic, would then allow researchers to perceive affective/internal variables such as interest, motivation, and gender.

Questions Related to Transfer

The area of *transfer* illustrates the difficulty of proposing a question related to one apparent variable when the question might be primarily about a different area such as *strategies. Can L1/L2 transfer and strategy use be separated?* In Chapter 3, I already highlighted some key questions regarding transfer, arguing that the question should not be whether there is transfer but, rather, how this transfer takes place. *Is the L1/L2 link always used as a strategy? Is transfer perceptible through the reaches of upper-register reading?* Again, well-designed think-alouds would be helpful in pursuing these questions.

Questions Related to Phonological Processing and Word Recognition

I have mentioned repeatedly throughout this volume that we understand very little about the precise nature of phonology in second-language reading. Indeed, it is eminently clear that phonology plays a role *but how close is that phonology to the L2 phonology? Does phonological processing continue to play a role in upper-register text comprehension? Does phonology become more native-like as a second-language reader progresses into the upper reaches of text understanding?*

Questions Related to Instruction

Large-scale instructional programs such as extensive reading need to be conducted under experimental conditions in order to glean which features of the program bring about the reported vocabulary and comprehension increases. Merely continuing to describe extensive reading programs, for example, without comparing them with other programs offers little. The claim that extensive reading leads to vocabulary gains requires a measurement of vocabulary level before implementing extensive reading and a comparison with other ways of acquiring vocabulary before we can claim the efficacy of extensive reading with confidence. Further, the recall protocol procedure has never been examined experimentally. I have asserted its efficacy and can testify to its usefulness, but it needs to be examined within the context of other instructional approaches as well as within the context of teacher development. *Does the recall protocol procedure help teachers to "see" what is going on in second-language comprehension? How do teachers learn to glean how their students are conceptualizing second-language texts? Does this ability to perceive student comprehension processes actually assist learners in their comprehension?* The précis idea offered by Swaffar and Arens for approaching the learning of upper-register texts should also be investigated. *Does a specific focus on text structures, as is highlighted by a précis technique, enable readers to independently create a précis and, more importantly, does being able to do so enhance their comprehension abilities?* The studies listed in Chapter 3 also indicated that certain teaching strategies such as instruction in word retention were helpful and should be examined within the context of true experiments. Grabe (2009) and Hudson (2007) each list effective first-language instructional strategies that should be investigated in L2 contexts.

Questions Related to Vocabulary

No area within second-language reading is more critical than an understanding of vocabulary learning *within the context of reading.* As I have noted earlier, studies conducted in isolation of how words are retained are necessary but not sufficient. We need far better understandings of how learners go about word acquisition; how they understand cognates versus non-cognates; how they learn high-frequency versus low-frequency words; and how they seek the assistance of technology, specifically through electronic or hand-held dictionaries, while reading. But most importantly, we need to begin to understand how and when learners can acquire a metaphorical use of words. To understand upper-register text processing will be to understand how ambiguous, multiple-meaning "easy words" can be understood in their metaphorical contexts. The learners discussed in Chapter 5 reading literary text had not yet met with this flexibility. How and when that ability develops is critical toward understanding upper-register text processing. Even studies as rudimentary as probing how many concepts learners across an array of proficiency levels have for a given word such as "lock" or "chair" or "*sabandija*" or "*hoyo*" would perhaps provide some clues about how metaphor and vocabulary depth develop.

Questions on Upper-Register Text Processing

Expert–novice think-aloud studies have been mentioned repeatedly in the previous paragraphs as ways of approaching new questions of background-knowledge utilization, strategies, L1/L2 transfer, and vocabulary use. Clearly, such an approach is equally, if not more, appropriate within the context of examining how second-language readers cope with extensive, opaque, and nuanced texts—texts that only the highly educated native speaker is expected to engage with. We need to look toward users of such texts in order to understand how they approach them, which knowledge sources they use, how they suspend judgment and then formulate it in order to construct an interpretation.

A further question then becomes: *What of interpretation? How does one evaluate an interpretation?* Because advanced-level readers rarely have to reveal an interpretation, except perhaps in literary or journalistic circles, we have very little understanding of how well an advanced-level second-language reader might be reading. Similar to the assessment of reading in other settings, the measures we have are inevitably indirect. But if we as a profession have no sense or concern about how we would judge the quality of upper-register reading, i.e., interpretation, we have little imperative to continue our research. Beyond conducting expert–novice studies, we will also need to probe expert readers about their understandings of metaphorical language; their use and understanding of particular grammatical structures; and explore whether they revert to native language processes. Using both a free and probed think-aloud methodology might enable us to finally confront some of the complexities of upper-register texts.

But what of upper-register texts themselves? Can they be cataloged, characterized, or organized in some manner? In the same manner that we have come to conceptualize instructional text, teachers need to have a refined sense of what constitutes an upper-register text. *Is it the structure, the vagaries of low frequency vocabulary use, quantity of metaphorical and/or intertextual reference that make an upper-register text upper register? How do we help to develop in teachers such sensitivities?* And then, of course, there is the eternal question of the literary text. *What separates it from other upper-register texts and how can a second-language reader learn to identify its subtleties?* These questions are meant to be research questions, not rhetorical ones. We need to confront and explore such questions if we are to gain a thorough understanding of the second-language reading process. Examining expert thought processes across an array of upper-register texts within the topic field of the expert as well as outside that expert's topic field might bring us to a better understanding of what a novice reader must do in order to become expert at second-language text processing.

Questions on the Model of Second-Language Compensatory Processing

This book has been fundamentally structured around the concept of compensatory processing and its conceptualization in Chapter 2, stated explicitly in Figure 2.7. The conceptualization calls for exploring second-language reading within the context of first-language literacy knowledge as well as second-language grammatical knowledge as critical variables about which we seem to have some reliable knowledge. Future research that takes these variables into account while examining "other" variables will help to clarify the nature of those "other" variables. Further, there is much to understand about the mechanism of compensation. Only future research will indicate whether that theory most fruitfully characterizes the second-language reading process from novice to very advanced stages, whether it needs to be extensively modified or, for that matter, dispensed with to make room for a newer model with greater explanatory power.

Pursuing all of these questions as Huey reminded us takes many hands in many lands. I will end this volume with my thinking about the compensatory model within the contexts of observations I have continued to make, specifically about the "language knowledge" variable.

Questions Related to Morphosyntax

One of the earliest-researched variables in the reading and psychological literature about reading is morphosyntax (Huey, 1908). Early researchers examined the manner in which readers perceived words, word formations, and how the context in which words were found influenced the recognition of further words. This tradition of examining text-based dimensions of reading and comprehension continued throughout the 1960s into the early 1980s, with a number of researchers investigating the relationship between certain kinds of morphosyntactic combinations; their "psychological complexity" (Huggins & Adams, 1980, p. 87); and their impact on text comprehension. Important work using garden path sentences (*The old man the boats*) probed how readers disambiguated various syntactic patterns (Huggins & Adams, 1980, p. 98). As reading research has become complexified with the integration of more socially oriented variables in the past 20 years, research into morphosyntactic features of text (how words in strings relate to each other) has faded. While this phenomenon may be, in part, the result of social variables that I discussed in Chapter 1 taking the main stage, as well as the realization that research should be based on naturalistic rather than constructed text as reviewed in Chapter 3, it might also be due to the fact that the English language is, syntactically speaking, relatively inflexible without many inflections. Word order is by and large SVO and there is relatively little variance between spoken and written syntax (VanPatten, 1996). Consequently, in a monolingual, English-speaking context, morphosyntax may be a relatively inconsequential variable because readers and listeners are attuned to a predictable, strict word order and to relatively few inflections. Readers of English are confronted with issues far more daunting than word placement such as spelling patterns, homophones, and allophones when they construct meaning from text. It could well be that the issues of inflection and word order reveal little if anything startling and that urgent questions in this regard have already been asked and answered.

The area of morphosyntax has taken on new dimensions and urgencies, however, with a growing awareness in both research and practice that reading instruction and theory must be able to accommodate a multilingual view of reading. Recent scholarship has underlined the recognition that the English-speaking view is limited to generalizations only about English-language reading within its cultural and linguistic space which varies radically from other sociocultural spaces. Accepting this recognition is crucial toward developing understandings of readers who must learn to comprehend in multiple linguistic contexts because "languages vary as to whether they mark case or not and whether or not they have 'free' word order" (VanPatten, 1996, p. 38).

I wanted to continue my explorations of how English-speaking readers learn to apply their knowledge of the morphology and syntax of Spanish and German in their Spanish and German reading comprehension. Spanish and German provide key linguistic points of commonality and difference with English. Spanish (although a Romance language) appears on the surface to be more closely related to English than German (although the latter two are Germanic languages). Using Spanish affords the opportunity to examine the interaction and influence of relatively uninflected languages with fairly strict word order (Spanish and English) against a backdrop of a highly inflected language with relatively free word order (German) compared with an uninflected, strictly ordered language (English). I wanted to gain some understanding of how and when readers engage their formal knowledge of these linguistic dimensions, in order to continue to try to understand the relationship between formal language knowledge and comprehension in a second-language context.

Of course, the field of second-language acquisition possesses a significant and critical literature on the acquisition of morphology and syntax. Most studies, however, are conducted either in speaking, writing, or with grammaticality judgments. That is, studies focus on the productive skills to note when particular forms are internalized by learners (see Hawkins, 2001; Odlin, 2003). Intuitively, it would seem that morphosyntax, or the way in which words relate to each other, would be a key variable in predicting second-language reading comprehension. Support for this belief is derived from the work of Odlin (1989) and Kern (2000). Evidence within second-language contexts predicts that the impact on the comprehension process of readers moving between predictable and unpredictable word order, for example, is significant. Languages such as German, Russian, or French exhibit degrees of flexibility in word order and, consequently, readers cannot merely rely on word meaning to comprehend, but must understand the signaling relationships between and among words (Kern, 2000). Odlin (1989) notes that second-language learners from flexible word order languages have higher numbers of production error rates when learning rigid word order languages. Odlin further hypothesizes that learners from rigid word order languages have higher error rates in the receptive language skills, namely reading and listening. The qualitative analyses on which I built the 1991 model (Figure 2.4) yielded a complementary perspective. As I noted in Chapter 2, readers would reveal a fairly discombobulated English syntax in their recalls, often failing to recognize which word an adverb was actually modifying or who was doing what to whom. In fact, in Figure 2.4 syntax is the language component that appeared to be operating in a counterintuitive fashion—the more proficient the learner, the higher the probability of committing morphosyntactically based errors.

In Chapter 2, I also referenced a set of specific studies that examined particular grammatical features. My own work in eye movement that examined native; non-native, highly fluent; and non-native, nonfluent readers reading the same texts in German is one example. I found that native German readers read in a relatively linear fashion; non-native, non-fluent readers put German into their own syntactic rules for word placement; and non-native yet fluent readers were somewhere in the middle—not mentally rearranging German words, but certainly spending more time in areas of the text that both natives and the non-fluents were simply skimming (Bernhardt, 1987). Native readers of German also directly fixated on endings of words, in contrast to readers of English who move from content word to content word, indeed, seeing function words but rarely spending more than 100 milliseconds on them (Carpenter & Just, 1977). While that work examined the L1 and L2 processing of German, Berkemeyer (1994) examined the extent to which the unambiguous knowledge of a particular morphosyntactic feature, anaphora and cataphora, could predict comprehension. Indeed, among both native and non-native readers, explicit knowledge of the particular form correlated with comprehension. Work by Fraser (2000) within this same tradition examined pronoun usage. In German, pronouns are marked for case and gender. In most cases, these pronouns are referential, performing anaphoric and cataphoric functions. In other cases, "they are without meaning and are just performing a grammatical function" (p. 287). Her findings are consistent with Berkemeyer's with the added dimension that learners sought *meaning* even within pronouns that filled only grammatical functions. This finding brings the positive perspective that second-language readers do, indeed, search for meaning and are not mere translators from form; it also brings the caveat that readers must develop a strategy of differentiating between form and meaning.

Work in Spanish by VanPatten and Cadierno (1993) and Cadierno (1995) has been conducted from a different yet complementary theoretical view: the relationship of meaning to form. It takes the perspective of using comprehension processing to support the acquisition of particular forms. VanPatten and Cadierno examined object pronouns and word order in Spanish. In their experiment, they found that subjects in a treatment group that had explicit instruction on the manner in which the particular grammatical forms in focus realize themselves had significantly higher comprehension scores. In a parallel study, Cadierno looked at the processing of the past tense forms in Spanish, conducting an experiment that removed lexical references to tense (such as "yesterday" or "tomorrow") and that relied exclusively on grammatical form to understand the utterance. In the case of each of these studies, subjects who learned the formal dimensions of either adverbials or past tense forms in Spanish were more able to complete comprehension tasks than those relying on lexical means alone. Significant work within this paradigm has been summarized and analyzed in VanPatten (1996).

Yet these studies, all of which use statistical means to make claims about the relationship of grammatical form to successful reading comprehension in a second language, are insufficient in clarifying the extent to which a knowledge of form aids comprehension or, indeed, which forms in a given language are most predictive of comprehension ability. Even in the most recent and comprehensive review of second-language reading research (Koda, 2005), no study is mentioned that focuses on the relationship between the nature of linguistic forms and the comprehension of paragraph-level discourse and beyond. It is not enough to know that morphosyntactic knowledge is important or a contributor to second-language reading comprehension. An important step is understanding the nature of morphosyntactic patterns that predict second-language reading comprehension and whether generalizations about morphosyntax hold consistently across languages with different morphosyntactic realizations.

I set out, as a result, to once again explore morphosyntax. I asked 133 students who opted to use German as the language in which they would complete the Stanford Language Requirement to release their grammar and reading test (a recall in English) scores. The grammar test consisted of two parts. Part 1 of the test consists of 30 multiple-choice items. Twenty-three of the 30 items focus on single grammatical operations. Seven additional items test specific word order placement. Part 2 of the test consists of 39 items. Four of the items focus specifically on rules for ordering words; the remainder contains items in which one must perform two form class operations simultaneously. The reliability of Part

1 measured by coefficient alpha is .87 and of Part 2 is .90. I asked the students to read three authentic texts. Text 1 is about the dilemmas of single parenting (268 words), text 2 about the difficulties of foreigners in Germany (194 words), and text 3 (200 words), the beginning of a chapter in *Der Vorleser* (*The Reader*)—the Bernhard Schlink (1995) novel. These texts were chosen according to three criteria. They had to be authentic (i.e., no editing for the benefit of the non-native reader); around 250 words in length; and representative of texts that students would encounter in their second year of German-language study. The texts were chosen by a professor who teaches regularly in the second-year program.

As a measure of syntactic complexity, the ratio of words to sentences was calculated. The *foreigner* text is syntactically simplest with an average of 13 words per sentence; *single parents* has an average of 16 words per sentence; and the section of *The Reader* an average sentence length of 24 words. Another view on text difficulty is provided by the number of propositions per passage. *Single parents*, the longer text, has the greater number of propositions ($N = 137$); *foreigner*, $N = 78$, and *The Reader*, $N = 53$. Counting propositions is a way of measuring total content. It is unsurprising that expository, information texts have a relatively high content load. I used multiple regression in order to employ several variables to predict another variable. In this case, Part 1 and Part 2 of the grammar exam were used to predict the comprehension scores. Part 1, the 30-item test (essentially of morphology), stepped in in all cases with the highest correlation: .52 in the case of *single parents*; and .5 in the *foreigner* text; and .82 in *The Reader*. In each case, Part 2 of the test (the items with more complicated morphology) added virtually no predictive power. In the final analysis, the prediction from Part 1 of the comprehension scores on *single parents* and the *foreigner* text is practically identical: around 26%. Yet, Part 1 is an even more profound predictor of comprehension of *The Reader* text: 63%. In all cases the predictive power came from the first part of the grammar examination that tested "simpler" grammatical forms.

I then set out to examine the same question within the context of Spanish. This time, I examined the performances of 83 students who opted to use Spanish as the language in which they would complete a university language requirement. The students took a multiple-choice test of three parts and then read two authentic texts in Spanish. The assessment of their ability to understand the text was recall in English. Part 1 of the test consists of 36 multiple-choice items. Part 2 of the test consists of 41 items; Part 3, 25 items. The reliability of Part 1 measured by coefficient alpha is .83; of Part 2, .86; and of Part 3, .90. The Spanish test has a structure similar to that of the German test in that it fundamentally tests knowledge of form. A difference is, however, that the items on the Spanish grammar test used are in context. For example, in order to test formal and informal command structures, a cue is given such as "Imagine that you are babysitting for a Spanish-speaking family." Then there are items such as: "*Sr. Alonso, 'write' your telephone number*," "*Carlo, don't 'play' football in the house*," in order to assess learners' knowledge of the difference in grammaticality for formal and informal commands. Two authentic texts were used. Text 1, "*archeology*" contains 304 words and describes the way in which modern technology has enabled more sophisticated investigations of pre-olmec culture in Latin America. Text 2, "*oral legends*", 392 words, focuses on the importance of the oral tradition in Latin American culture and retells two legends; the former text is straightforward exposition and the latter "soft" expository. As a measure of syntactic complexity, the ratio of words to sentences was calculated. The ratio of words to sentences in Text 1 is 27.6 and in Test 2 is 15.7 meaning that Text 1 is considerably more syntactically dense. Another measure of text complexity is total number of propositions. Text 1 contains 96 propositions and Text 2, 108. These texts, like the German texts, were chosen according to three criteria: authenticity (i.e., no editing for the benefit of the non-native reader); 250–300 words in length; and representative of texts that students would encounter in their second year of Spanish language study (i.e., an introduction to all basic grammatical forms in Spanish with an active vocabulary of approximately 2000 words).

Multiple regression was used again to develop a prediction. It indicated that Part 1, the 36-item test (essentially of present tense) steps in in both cases with the highest correlation: .224 in the case of Text 1; .408 in the case of Text 2. Within the context of each case, Part 2 and Part 3 of the grammar test contribute some minimal amount of prediction of the reading comprehension scores.

Do these two data collections merely indicate once again that formal language knowledge matters in the second-language comprehension process? This conclusion on its surface may be interpreted as an uninteresting and obvious fact. Yet, the phobia that infects both first- and second-language teaching and research, that focusing on grammar or micro-elements of language redirects critical energy from meaning, has led the field to overlook that grammar or microelements of reading carry actual meaning. As I noted repeatedly in Chapter 3, in the second-language reading data base there are lots of studies about the construction of meaning; about the synthesis of knowledge throughout passages; about authentic and non-authentic text; about background knowledge; and the like. But very few present data about the actual formal language knowledge that learners bring to the task of second-language reading. Yet, in the context of findings from these two data collections, if the variance attributed to language knowledge were removed from the significant effects of most of the studies outlined and reviewed in Chapter 3, the very same studies might not reveal the significant findings they claim. Future studies clearly need to probe basic grammatical proficiency in a language before making claims about other factors that contribute to comprehension or its breakdown.

Beyond the fact that language knowledge was a critical factor in each data collection in this study lies the consistency in both the German reading and the Spanish reading of the nature of the grammatical forms that were significant predictors. The simpler grammatical forms assessed on each test contributed to the greatest prediction on all of the authentic texts used in the study. At first glance, this finding would appear to be a bit illogical. A logical assumption would be that the more difficult or more complex part of the grammar tests would be the better predictors of the performances on the authentic reading passages used. Yet, a possible explanation is the consistency of this finding with what is known about beginning readers in their first language—they must have control over the basic code. In other words, one cannot control the latter parts of the grammar tests (such as past perfect tenses or pronoun placement in dependent clauses) without having automaticity on the forms from the earlier parts on which the more complex forms are built. The complexity in the latter parts is not about new forms but about using multiple sources of the same forms simultaneously.

The data also indicate the criticality of verifying findings across multiple languages. The English-readers reading German did not perform in the same manner as the English-readers reading Spanish. It is important to consider and account for the very real differences between performances on the German texts and the Spanish texts. The German data provide additional evidence for the remarkably consistent finding about "language knowledge" predicting around 30% of any given second-language comprehension performance. In a field which has relatively few concrete, replicable findings this finding stands out. Yet, the Spanish grammar data, while statistically significant, appear to explain far less of the variance than the German grammar data. It is possible, of course, that the German grammatical exam provided a more relevant and concrete measure of individual grammatical forms needed to predict performance on the integrative measure of comprehension of these particular texts than the Spanish grammar test, which might not have isolated forms directly important to the reading passages at hand. It may also be that the nature of the forms tested in the Spanish exam were too simple, providing little variance between and among the subjects studied. But a contrastive analysis of German and Spanish that segregates salient forms in the two languages for native readers of English provides more interesting explanatory clues.

Examining the present data set against the backdrop of previous data generated on the cognitive processing of German reveals remarkable consistency, even though the texts, the students, the data collection methodology, and 20 years separate the two. I argued 20 years ago that what separated fluent from non-fluent in German was not vocabulary use, but the ability to "see" the really important morphological elements—not the "*das*" in "*das Mädchen*" (signaling both nominative and accusative cases), but the "*dem*" in "*dem Mädchen*" (signaling dative). Reader performance looks different in the context of German due to the surface structure and the complex morphological nature of German. The morphological elements are critical; without them, there is no way to indicate the difference between actor and agent; a "first noun is agent strategy" (VanPatten, 1996) employed by many learners is not helpful. Hence, "knowing" different grammatical elements in German predicts comprehension performance. But what of Spanish? As noted earlier, Spanish (for the native English reader) is much more transparent syntactically and morphologically. This perhaps helps to explain why vocabulary seems to be so critical in the understanding of Spanish for English-speaking readers. Grammatical form is simply not as critical as it is in other languages; readers can much more effectively proceed to a lexical compensatory strategy, rendering, within the context of my investigation here, a much lower, yet significant, prediction. This interpretation would be consistent with Brisbois' (1995) French language study that found grammar accounting for only 3% of the variance in comprehension and vocabulary accounting for nine times that amount of variance. In any case, the data underline the problematic nature of making pronouncements generically about the reading process, unless verified across different languages of different structures and configurations.

Caveats and areas for future research are always important to consider. It might be fruitful, for example, to be more precise in isolating items on grammar tests that appear unambiguously in reading passages. Yet, given that within the context of connected text there are rarely forms that are unambiguously anything, this direction might not be a productive way of thinking about the research problem. Acknowledging the impact of form for form's sake in the context of comprehension research might be a better use of research time. Further, while the studies used reliable tests, item analyses need to be conducted on both the Spanish and the German tests. It is possible that there is a lurking validity problem in the grammar tests such as failing to isolate forms that test morphosyntax versus vocabulary items. If so, the predictive values of each might be called into question. Further, the number and variety of cross-linguistic contrasts must be significantly increased within the reading research data base. Being able to examine second-language readers across a number of languages within a tightly controlled context will provide the field with the insights that it needs to understand more fundamentally the differences between reading first- and second languages.

Questions Related to Genre

But, finally, the significance of the literary text in German and the soft expository text in Spanish is remarkable. Anyone in literary criticism will indeed argue that literary texts are unique. We have significant empirical evidence for this in the performance of these readers. But what is so significant is that it is not a random conceptual dimension that makes the performance of these readers unique in comparison with their performance on the expository texts vis-à-vis the grammar test. In fact, had I hypothesized about this earlier, I would have assumed that the relatively simple grammar test would have had little relationship to the literary text; I would have chosen a much more obtuse explanation as a matter of fact. The evidence offered here is that simpler predicts more complex. Apparently because literary text consists of significantly more conceptual and generally highly economical language, the grammatical form load is perhaps more significant than in expository texts in which a reader can compensate with content as well as background knowledge. In other words, in expository texts there are elements related to the text both reader-external and reader-internal that can potentially compensate for deficits in grammatical knowledge. Not so in literary text, or certainly not to the extent that these elements exist for exposition. Because literary texts often suspend the physical world and because they are structured in ways that rarely include compensatory assistance in the form of pictures, graphs, or visual structuring aids, readers have little left from which they can compensate. What they are left with for compensation is linguistic form and whatever literary knowledge they might already possess. This particular case of two opposing genres read by the same subjects who were also measured in their grammatical knowledge lends credibility to thinking about second-language reading as a compensatory process. But it also places in dispute the distribution of how much variance should be attributed to grammatical knowledge. Had literary texts been used upon which to build the model posited in Chapter 2, then perhaps the factors would have been distributed dramatically differently, but that is precisely why we, many hands in many lands, must continue to pursue an understanding of second-language reading with rigor and vigor.

Conclusion

This volume tried to focus the field's attention toward upper-register text processing, which perforce directs it toward a genre focus. Yet a genre focus would be a misstep if that focus were so narrow that it excluded conceptualizing grammatical knowledge, prior literacy experience, and perhaps another array of personal/affective variables. To return to the model of second-language reading as posited, we need to understand how this array of variables, both known at the moment and yet to be discovered, interacts and assists each other throughout the development of second-language reading proficiency; how readers can best be sustained in that development; and how teachers can develop their own sensitivities and understandings of the process they try to teach.

Appendix to Chapter 3

Survey of studies investigating second-language reading in adolescents and adults

Reference	Theme	Subjects & Texts	Language	Findings
Abu-Rabia, S. (1996)	Attitude and culture	150 total: 80 Jewish and 70 Arab 14–15-year-old students from central Israel; 3 stories	L1/L2: Arabic, Hebrew	• Texts with familiar cultural content elicit higher reading comprehension scores than texts with unfamiliar cultural content. • Attitudes of readers were found to be primarily instrumental rather than integrative.
Abu-Rabia, S. (1998a)	Attitude/cultural background	210 Israeli Arab students; 10th grade; 6 stories counterbalanced	L1/L2: Arabic, Hebrew	• Familiar cultural content leads linked to higher comprehension scores.
Abu-Rabia, S. (1998b)	How culture influences reading comprehension	74 8th-grade Arab students (14–15 years old) from Israel, learning Hebrew as L2	L1: Arabic L2: Hebrew	• Familiar cultural content leads linked to higher comprehension scores.
Abu-Rabia, S. (2003)	Memory function; 2 passages	47 10th-grade & 11 high school students; 39 L1 Hebrew speakers, 8 L1 Russian speakers; English was L3 for all passages	L1: Hebrew, Russian L2: English	• Correlation between a large working memory store and reading and writing proficiency in English.

Author	Topic	Sample	Language	Findings
Akamatsu, N. (2003)	Orthographic influences	49 fluent ESL readers; 12 passages	L1: 18 Chinese, 16 Japanese, 15 Persian L2: English	• Non-alphabetic groups slower than alphabetic. Compatibility of orthography leads to higher processing speeds.
Alessi, S., & Dwyer, D. (2008)	Comprehension & vocabulary development; 1 text	76 undergraduates at the intermediate level	L1: English L2: Spanish	• Vocabulary before reading leads to greater speed, but not comprehension. • Vocabulary during reading leads to greater comprehension, but not speed.
Allan, A. (1992)	Measuring test-wiseness in L2 reading test takers	51 first year Hong Kong polytechnic students	L1: Cantonese L2: English	• Readers used diverse test-taking skills. • Some validity to the instrument studied.
Al-Othman, N. M. A. (2003)	Online L2 reading rates and comprehension	25 post-graduate ESL students, aged 27–39; proficiency levels ranged from intermediate to upper intermediate	L1: Arabic L2: English	• Speed of reading online texts linked to reading comprehension. • Limited computer experience affects comprehension scores.
Al-Seghayer, K. (2005)	Technology and reading comprehension	40 university-age ESL learners: 2 passages	L1: no information L2: English	• Highly structured and visible hyper-text mapping preferable to unstructured.
Anderson, N. J. (2003)	Online L2 reading strategies in ESL/EFL	247 L2 English students (131 EFL students in Costa	L1: Spanish L2: English	• Survey of Reading Strategies (SORS) modified for online reading techniques of readers of L2.

Reference	Theme	Subjects & Texts	Language	Findings
		Rica; 116 ESL students in USA) with proficiency levels from beginning high to high intermediate		• Problem-solving strategies appear to dominate. • No significant differences between the strategies of the EFL group as compared with the ESL group.
Anderson, N., Bachman, L., Perkins, K., & Cohen, A. (1991)	Construct validity of reading comprehension test	28 US college students enrolled in ESL program (out of 65 total). 9 beginning level, 10 intermediate level, 9 advanced level; 15 reading passages	L1: Spanish L2: English	• Construct validation must be determined through multiple measures. • Synthesis of measures provides important insight in comprehension.
Auerbach, E. R., & Paxton, D. (1997)	L2 acquisition tools, classroom instruction	Undergraduate students	L1: English L2: Various	• L2 learners who investigate L2 processes improve their learning. • Investigating processes helps critical thinking.
Barry, S., & Lazarte, A. A. (1998)	Prior knowledge, text type, and reading comprehension	48 high school students of Spanish as FL, divided into two groups: high knowledge (HK)	L1: English L2: Spanish	• Readers with prior knowledge of a content area develop complex and correct mental models. • Syntactic difficulty and topic influence model building.

Study	Focus	Sample	Language	Findings
		and low knowledge (LK): 3 reading selections		
Bell, F. L., & LeBlanc, L. B. (2000)	L1 or L2 glosses; technology	40 university students of 3rd-semester L2 Spanish; 1 passage	L1: English L2: Spanish	• Readers prefer glosses in the L1. • Readers have a high comfort level with computer-based reading. • Language of the gloss not related to L2 comprehension.
Bell, T. (2001)	Extensive reading, speed, comprehension	26 Yemeni adult elementary-level ESL learners; 2 texts for speed; 3 texts for comprehension	L1: Arabic L2: English	• Extensive reading develops speed and comprehension.
Bengeleil, N. F., & Paribakht, T. S. (2004)	Reading and lexical inferencing	17 (7 advanced, 10 intermediate level) university medical students in Libya	L1: Arabic L2: English	• Subjects of different proficiency levels use similar clues for inferring word meaning. • Higher proficiency learners are more successful at inferencing.
Berkemeyer, V. (1994)	Anaphoric coreferents and text comprehension	4 native and 50 American readers of German; 1 text	L1: English L2: German	• Correlation between referencing system and comprehension. • Knowledge of referencing system and comprehension linked to language proficiency.
Bernhardt, E. B., & Kamil, M. L. (1995)	L1/L2 transfer	187 US Airforce Academy students total: 130 beginning	L1: English L2: Spanish	• Literacy and language knowledge significant contributors to L2 reading. • Language knowledge is a stronger predictor

Reference	Theme	Subjects & Texts	Language	Findings
		(1st semester), 24 intermediate (>5 semesters Spanish), 33 advanced (>7 semesters Spanish); 35 short texts		than literacy. • Threshold and interdependence hypotheses need to be consolidated.
Block, E. (1992)	Comprehension monitoring	25 college students (16 proficient, 9 non-proficient readers); 1 text	L1: Chinese, Spanish L2: English	• Monitoring in L1 and L2 similar. • Differences in monitoring linked to reading ability not to language proficiency.
Brantmeier, C. (2003a)	Prior knowledge, topic interest, enjoyment, gender	86 5th-semester L1 English intermediate learners of Spanish in a university Hispanic culture class; 2 texts	L1: English L2: Spanish	• Affective factors not linked to L2 reading comprehension. • Some evidence for gender differences in L2 reading comprehension.
Brantmeier, C. (2003b)	Gender variables	78 intermediate-level university students (29 male, 49 female) in a "bridge" course on Hispanic culture; 2 texts	L1: English L2: Spanish	• Topic familiarity linked to gender positively affects reading comprehension.

Study	Topic	Description	Languages	Findings
Brantmeier, C. (2003c)	Gender and strategy use	78 L1 English university students of L2 Spanish, 5th-semester class, intermediate level; 2 passages	L1: English L2: Spanish	• Gender not related to processing strategies. • Gender-based prior knowledge affects certain text understanding.
Brantmeier, C. (2004a)	Gender and passage content	68 university students enrolled in advanced Spanish grammar & composition course; 2 passages	L1: English L2: Spanish	• Females demonstrated higher comprehension of gender-related texts.
Brantmeier, C. (2005a)	Anxiety	92 university students of advanced level Spanish grammar and composition	L1: English L2: Spanish	• Of 4 language areas, reading produces the lowest reported level of anxiety. • Anxiety increases with tests. • Anxiety lessens with an increase in proficiency level.
Brantmeier, C. (2005b)	Prior knowledge, text and test type	(1) 53 native Costa Ricans in advanced EFL classes in Costa Rica; (2) 102 university students of intermediate Spanish in US; (3) 138 university students of advanced Spanish in US; 2 passages	(1) L1: Spanish, L2: English; (2) & (3) L2: Spanish	• Prior knowledge is a more important variable than analogical reasoning.

Reference	Theme	Subjects & Texts	Language	Findings
Brantmeier, C. (2006)	Components in the reading process	104 native speakers of English; 1 lengthy literary text	L1: English L2: Spanish	• Recall ability linked to passage interest.
Brisbois, J. E. (1995)	L1/L2 transfer	131 native English-speaking US Air Force Academy students enrolled in French (88 beginners and 43 upper level)	L1: English L2: French	• Provides evidence of a threshold. • L1 literacy buttresses L2 reading. • Vocabulary a significant component of grammatical knowledge.
Camiciottoli, B. C. (2003)	Metadiscourse and ESP reading comprehension	55 Italian intermediate to upper intermediate university students of economics	L1: Italian L2: English	• Readers demonstrated little awareness of metadiscourse in a professional-level text. • Teaching metadiscourse might influence text understanding in content areas.
Carrell, P. (1991)	L1/L2 transfer	120 total: 45 native Spanish speakers (US college students); 75 native English speakers studying Spanish at US college; 4 passages counterbalanced	L1: Spanish L2: English	• L1 reading and L2 proficiency impact comprehension. • Size of impact varies according to particular groups.

Study	Variables	Participants	Languages	Findings
Carrell, P. L., & Wise, T. E. (1998)	Prior knowledge, topic interest, gender	104 ESL students at an American university; 10 passages	L1: Various L2: English	• Some gender differences in topic. • Prior knowledge and interest related to comprehension although neither is dominant.
Carrell, P. L., & Connor, U. (1991)	L2 reading text type	33 US college students (23 undergraduate, 10 graduate) enrolled in ESL instruction program; 2 reading passages	L1:Chinese, Spanish, Hindu/Urdu, Indonesian, Korean, German, Serbo-Croatian, Greek, Italian, Hebrew, Vietnamese, Japanese L2: English	• Descriptive texts easier to read than persuasive. • Descriptive essays written at higher levels than persuasive. • Some gender differences noted.
Chan, C. Y. H. (2003)	Background knowledge, language proficiency, and L2 reading comprehension	214 students from universities in Hong Kong and mainland China; intermediate & post-intermediate levels of L2 English; 2 cloze passages	L1: Cantonese L2: English	• The study's results show that the effect of cultural content on L2 reading comprehension depends on the reader's level of L2 proficiency. • Prior knowledge positively affected the reading comprehension of intermediate L2 readers, but had little or no effect on more proficient readers.

Reference	Theme	Subjects & Texts	Language	Findings
				• L2 language proficiency is more important than prior knowledge of cultural content to L2 reading comprehension. • More advanced L2 proficiency has a compensatory effect on lack of background knowledge, and less proficient learners depend more heavily on prior knowledge.
Chi, F.-M. (1995)	Intertextuality as a strategy	10 Taiwanese EFL college readers; 2 short stories	L1: Taiwanese L2: English	• Invoking intertextuality provides complexity in responses to literary texts.
Chikamatsu, N. (1996)	L1 orthography and L2 word recognition	62 total: 45 American college students, 17 Chinese college students (native speakers of Chinese). All participants enrolled in 2nd semester Japanese language course in US	L1: Chinese L2: Japanese	• Language-based strategy differences for word recognition. • Chinese readers relied on a visual strategy. • English readers used phonological strategies.
Choi, I.-C., & Bachman, L. F. (1992)	Adequacy of IRT models	1400 students taking the TOEFL test, and 1000 students taking the FCE from eight	L1: Portuguese, French, Arabic, Chinese, Japanese,	• Less restrictive IRT models reject fewer items than Rasch modeling does.

Study	Topic	Participants	Languages	Findings
		countries	Spanish, German, Thai L2: English	
Chu, H.-C. J., Swaffar, J., & Charney, D. H. (2002)	Culture-based text structures	120 Taiwanese college freshmen; 120 Taiwanese college seniors; 4 passages	L1: Chinese L2: English	• Subjects unaware of culture-based rhetorical differences. • Some rhetorical conventions influence comprehension.
Chun, D. M. (2001)	Technology	23 university students taking a second-year German course; 2 passages	L2: German	• Readers preferred hypertext with glosses immediately available over online dictionaries. • Higher comprehension noted for the combination of attached glosses and online dictionaries.
Chun, D. M., & Payne, J. S. (2004)	Technology	13 L1 English college undergraduates taking 2nd-year German; 1 short story	L1: English L2: German	• Readers with low phonological memory look up words more frequently than readers with high phonological memory. • Readers learn to rely on glosses in an electronic environment.
Chun, D. M., & Plass, J. (1996)	Technology	160 US college students total who were 2nd-year university German students (in 3 studies); 1 short story	L1: English L2: German	• Visual and verbal glosses more helpful than verbal alone. • Vocabulary and comprehension are related.

Reference	Theme	Subjects & Texts	Language	Findings
Davis, J. N. (1992)	L2 literature	25 US college students in an intermediate level French class; 1 chapter	L1: English L2: French	• Drawing on personal experience is helpful in L2 literacy comprehension.
Davis, J., Gorell, L., Kline, R., & Hsieh, G. (1992)	Attitudes towards literature	175 US college students enrolled in French and Spanish	L1: English L2: French, Spanish	• Positive attitudes toward literature reading correlated with recreational reading. • Negative correlation between cultural knowledge and literary interpretation.
DeBot, K., Paribakht, T., & Wesche, M. (1997)	Vocabulary	10 Canadian college students in an ESL class (various L1 backgrounds who use French as their official language of study); 1 text	L1: Various e.g., French, Chinese, Persian, Spanish, Vietnamese, Arabic L2: English	• Readers used similar strategies for inferring the meaning of unknown words.
Degand, L., & Sanders, T. (2002)	Linguistic markers, L1/L2 reading comprehension	54 undergraduate participants (31 L1 French, L2 Dutch; 23 L1 Dutch, L2 French); 18 expository texts counterbalanced	L1: Dutch, French L2: Dutch, French	• Some causal relational markers positively affect reading comprehension in the L1 and in the L2. • No advantage in L2 comprehension over L1 comprehension noted in using relational markers.

Study	Focus	Participants	L1/L2	Findings
Donin, J., Graves, B., & Goyette, E. (2004)	Text type, L1/L2 relationship	16 L1 English male officers participating in L2 French military language program (9 at beginning of intermediate series; 7 at end of intermediate series); 4 texts	L1: English L2: French	• No relationship between text type and reading speed. • L2 proficiency affected reading time. • L1 narrative texts more memorable than expository text in either L1 or L2.
DuBravac, S., & Dalle, M. (2002)	Text types	47 undergraduates in 4th-semester course on French reading and oral communication; 2 expository, 2 narrative texts	L1: English L2: French	• Expository texts led to more miscomprehension for students. • Narrative texts led to generation of more inferential questions.
Dussias, P. E. (2003)	Parsing strategies	University students: 31 native Spanish speakers with English L2, 32 native English speakers with Spanish L2; L2 for both groups superior level; monolingual Spanish & English comparison groups	L1: English, Spanish L2: Spanish, English	• L1 and L2 readers use local references for resolving ambiguities.

Reference	Theme	Subjects & Texts	Language	Findings
Dykstra-Pruim, P. (1998)	Independent reading; children's	40 first-year university students of German; multiple books	L1: English L2: German	• Beginning readers report positive attitudes toward reading L2 children's literature. • Reading L2 children's literature enhanced knowledge of culture.
Ercetin, G. (2003)	Technology	84 intermediate & advanced-level students of English for academic purposes at university; 1 text	L1: Various, e.g., Arabic, Spanish, Japanese, Korean, Chinese L2: English	• Hypermedia assists comprehension. • Intermediate learners use more hypermedia than advanced. • Verbal glosses preferred over pronunciation and visual assistance. • Topic annotations accessed more often than word-level.
Everson, M. E. (1998)	Word recognition	20 university first-year CFL students with no prior (heritage or the like) exposure to L2	L1: English L2: Chinese	• Link between pronunciation and meaning for Chinese learners.
Everson, M., & Ke, C. (1997)	Strategies of intermediate and advanced L2 learners	7 total: 5 "intermediate" 3rd-year college students studying the Chinese language; 2 "advanced" graduate students enrolled in	L1: English L2: Chinese	• Decoding differences based in L1 orthography. • High-level comprehension linked to oral skills.

Study	Focus	Participants/Materials	Languages	Findings
Fecteau, M. L. (1999)	L1/L2 transfer; literature	42 US college students enrolled in introductory French literature course; 2 texts	L1: English L2: French	• L1 recall predicts L2 recall. • No relationship between proficiency and recall. • L1 recall more significant than L2 proficiency when reading literary text.
Felser, C., Roberts, L., Marinis, T., & Gross, R. (2003)	Processing strategies	University students, advanced speakers of English as L2	L1: Greek, German L2: English	• Ambiguities resolved by meaning-based information, not by structural characteristics.
Fender, M. (2008)	Fluency and word recognition	16 Arab learners of English; 21 additional ESL (non-Arabic speaking) learners	L1: Various L2: English	• Knowledge of English word structure may be beneficial for Arab learners of English.
Flaherty, M. (1998)	Visualization and verbalization; design memory	30 native English-speaking university students of Japanese	L1: English L2: Japanese	• Long-term retention of *kanji* linked to memory for abstract designs.
Fraser, C. (2007)	Comparison of L1 and L2 reading rates and task performance	2 university student groups of native Mandarin Chinese speakers with L2 English, total of 95 participants; 10 short expository texts	L1: Mandarin Chinese L2: English	• Reading rate differs in L1 and L2. • Contextual difference in various reading tasks.

4th-year Chinese; 1 text

Reference	Theme	Subjects & Texts	Language	Findings
Fraser, C. A. (1999)	Lexical strategies and word retention	8 Francophone university students with intermediate ESL proficiency	L1: French L2: English	• Some lexical strategies demonstrate better results in retention rates than others.
Fukkink, R. G., Hulstijn, J., & Simis, A. (2005)	Technology and word learning	41 Dutch 8th-graders (13–14 years old) with intermediate L2 English	L1: Dutch L2: English	• Computer assistance leads to quick lexical access. • Word access can become faster but not necessarily automatic. • No relationship between rapid lexical access and comprehension.
Gascoigne, C. (2002)	Strategies	16 L1 English novice learners of L2 French; university students	L1: English L2: French	• Readers use L1 strategies in L2. • Readers report comfort level with longer L2 texts. • Study rejects threshold notion.
Gascoigne, C. (2005)	Comprehension and grammar	56 university students enrolled in beginning French classes	L1: English L2: French	• Relationship between grammatical knowledge and meaning-based tasks.
Ghahraki, S., & Sharifian, F. (2005)	Proficiency and text type	92 Iranian university-level students majoring in English; Michigan Test of	L1: Farsi L2: English	• Higher levels of reading ability include distinguishing between fact and interpretation.

Source	Topic	Participants	Languages	Findings
Ghaith, G. (2003)	Cooperative learning and affect	56 Lebanese high school students (15–16 years old); 1 text	L1: Arabic L2: English	• Cooperative learning did not have an impact on affective variables. • Cooperative learning was positively related to reading achievement.
Godev, C. B., Martinez-Gibson, E. A., & Toris, C. C. M. (2002)	L1 vs. L2 in testing	80 3rd-semester, undergraduate students of Spanish; 1 text	L1: English L2: Spanish	• Test questions and responses should be permitted in the L1.
Gordon, C., & Hanauer, D. (1995)	Comprehension task and mental modeling	28 10th-grade high school students studying EFL in two Israeli public high schools; 4 parallel versions of 1 text	L1: Hebrew L2: English	• Test questions and methods affect readers' construction of texts.
Graden, E. (1996)	Teachers' beliefs	6 secondary French and Spanish teachers (3 Spanish teachers, 2 French teachers, 1 teaches both)	L1: English L2: French, Spanish	• Teachers consider L2 use important for effective reading. • Classroom context does not necessarily facilitate reading.

Note column note fragment: English Language Proficiency (MTELP) determined proficiency group; 5 texts, 9 paragraphs

Reference	Theme	Subjects & Texts	Language	Findings
Hacquebord, H. (1999)	Diagnostic testing for reading comprehension assessment in L1 and L2	569 students in first year of secondary education in the Netherlands (Dutch as L1 = ~65%; Dutch as L2 = ~35%)	L1: Various L2: Dutch, various	• Test was reliable for both L1 and L2 students.
Hammadou, J. (2000)	Analogies and prior knowledge	~163 university students of French or EFL; 2 texts	L1: French/ English L2: French/ English	• Analogy negatively influenced comprehension regardless of learner group. • Comprehension was linked to proficiency level and prior knowledge.
Hanauer, D. I. (2001)	Importance of focus-on-form for language learning	20 female Israeli college students (20–24 years old); all were participating in, or had completed, advanced EFL reading course; none with degrees in English or Hebrew lit.; 1 poem	L1: Hebrew L2: English	• Response to, and perception of, poetry linked. • Poetry reading can assist cultural awareness.
Harrington, M., & Sawyer, M. (1992)	L2 working memory	advanced L2 learners	L1: English L2: Japanese	• Larger working memory linked to higher comprehension measures.

Source	Topic	Sample	Languages	Findings
Hayashi, K. (1999)	Extensive reading	100 Japanese students of EFL at the college level	L1: Japanese L2: English	• Extensive reading leads to higher comprehension than instruction alone. • Proficiency increases linked to more top-down strategies.
Hayati, A. M., & Pour-Mohammadi, M. (2005)	Dictionary use	45 Iranian university EFL students at intermediate level; 4 passages	L1: Farsi L2: English	• Monolingual dictionaries are useful. • Bilingual dictionary use leads to increases in L2 reading comprehension.
Hirai, A. (1999)	Listening rate and reading rate for L2 learners	56 Japanese college students of English with varying proficiency levels; 7 prose passages	L1: Japanese L2: English	• Listening and reading rates comparable when subjects equalized for proficiency level.
Hirvela, A. (2005)	Technology	2 Korean students of ESL at an American university	L1: Korean L2: English	• Learners need formal instruction in completing computer-based reading and writing tasks.
Hitosugi, C. I., & Day, R. (2004)	Extensive reading	14 English-speaking post-secondary students	L1: English L2: Japanese	• Extensive reading related to significantly higher comprehension scores on a test of Japanese reading. • Affect positively enhanced in extensive reading program.
Hoover, M. L., & Dwivedi, V. D. (1998)	Grammatical processing, L2 & L1 reading	48 L1 French and 48 L2 French (highly fluent) university students	L1: English, French L2: French	• Faster L2 readers more efficient in syntactic processing than slower readers. • Slower readers react to syntactic patterns not in their L1.

Reference	Theme	Subjects & Texts	Language	Findings
Horiba, Y. (1996)	L1/L2 transfer	66 US college students from 2 universities (Intermediate L2, Advanced L2, L1 Japanese and L1 English)	L1/LS: Japanese, English	• L2 readers more text-based than L1 readers. • L2 readers have difficulty distinguishing between different levels of coherence.
Horst, M. (2005)	Extensive L2 reading and vocabulary acquisition	21 adult immigrant learners of ESL; proficiency levels from elementary to intermediate high	L1: Arabic, Chinese, Farsi, Korean, Polish, Spanish, Russian L2: English, French L3: English	• Extensive reading in linked to gains in vocabulary. • A methodology to measure vocabulary growth offered.
Hudson, T. (1991)	Content-based instruction	364 total REST Project college students; 152 who received reading for content comprehension	L1: Spanish L2: English	• Reading in a content area enhances comprehension.

		instruction; 212 students with no content comprehension instruction		
Hui-Tzu, M. (2008)	Vocabulary acquisition and retention	25 3rd-year male students with intermediate-level English proficiency; 4 articles on 2 themes	L1: Chinese L2: English	• Focused vocabulary exercises needed alongside learning vocabulary thematically.
Hulstijn, J. (1993)	Vocabulary	82 grade 10 and 11 students total in 2 studies; chapter in a book	L1/L2: Dutch, English	• Words determined to be relevant were looked up more frequently than words regarded as unimportant. • Words with contextual support were looked up less than words without. • Word look-up partially correlated with vocabulary knowledge. • No relationship between the ability to infer words from context and looking up words.
Iwahori, Y. (2008)	Extensive reading	33 high school learners of English	L1: Japanese L2 English	• Extensive reading benefits reading rate and overall proficiency.
Jiménez, R. T. (1997)	Strategies	5 middle school students	L1: Spanish L2: English	• Students can be taught cognitive strategies. • Culturally compatible materials preferable.
Jiménez, R. T., García, G. E., &	Metacognition		L1: Spanish L2: English	• Three effective strategies identified: transfer of information between L1/L2; translating

Reference	Theme	Subjects & Texts	Language	Findings
Pearson, P. D. (1996)				from L1 to L2; and making use of cognate vocabulary.
Johnson, K. E. (1992)	Teacher beliefs	30 ESL teachers (secondary, elementary, and adult level programs)	Not specified	• Teachers often take a functional orientation to L2 reading instruction.
Juffs, A. (1998)	L1/L2 transfer	17 Chinese; 17 Korean or Japanese; 17 Romance adult ESL students on advanced level; compared with 17 monolingual English native speakers	L1: Chinese, Korean, Japanese, Romance, English L2: English	• L1 and L2 speakers approached sentence parsing in similar ways. • L1 parsing strategies affect how learners process sentences in L2.
Kamhi-Stein, L. D. (2003)	Affective factors	4 female bilingual, L1-Spanish speakers; college freshmen; all "underprepared" for language demands of college courses (as measured by verbal SAT, English part of	L1: Spanish L2: English	• Reading behavior is influenced by subjects' attitudes and opinions of their home language. • Subjects' beliefs about reading determine active reading behavior.

Study	Topic	Sample	Language	Findings
Kasper, L. F. (2003)	Technology	ACT exam; Cal. State Univ. Engl. Placement Test); 2 texts No information	L1: not specified L2: English	• There is a positive correlation between online hypertext reading in the L2 and higher L2 reading scores. • Online L2 reading results in more time on task leading to improved performance on reading tests.
Kern, R. G. (1994)	Translation as a strategy	51 US college students enrolled in 3rd-semester French class	L1: English L2: French	• Low-ability groups use translation more than high-ability groups. • Translation decreases with time in learning. • Translation is a helpful strategy.
Keshavarz, M. H., Atai, M. R., & Ahmadi, H. (2007)	Content and linguistic simplification	240 Persian speakers; 4 versions of 2 texts	L1: Persian L2: English	• Prior knowledge and proficiency level were primary predictors in comprehension and recall performance. • Text simplification not helpful in increasing comprehension scores.
Khaldieh, S. A. (2001)	Icraab and vocabulary in AFL reading comprehension	46 university students of AFL; one 330-word text	L1: English L2: Arabic	• Knowledge of vocabulary had significant effect on performance. • Reading comprehension rests mainly on knowledge of vocabulary, not in knowledge of icraab.

Reference	Theme	Subjects & Texts	Language	Findings
Kim, M. (2004)	Literature	9 students aged 18–30 enrolled in a university intensive English program course focusing on L2 reading & speaking skills; 1 short story	L1: not specified L2: English	• Literary texts can make the L2 reading experience more enjoyable for learners while increasing their communicative ability in the L2. • Literature provided a context to engage in extended meaningful discourse in the target language.
Kim, S.-A. (1995)	Vocabulary and prior knowledge	108 Korean high school students; 1 text	L1: Korean L2: English	• Texts with more difficult vocabulary tended to have lower recall. • Pre-reading instruction had an effect on recall performance.
Kitajima, R. (1997)	Strategy training	43 students total (28 US college students enrolled in a 4th-semester Japanese course, 15 control students)	L1: English L2: Japanese	• Strategy training in coreferential ties can have positive effects on Japanese text comprehension.
Knight, S. (1994)	Dictionary use	105 US college students enrolled in 2nd-year Spanish; 4 texts	L1: English L2: Spanish	• Students who had access to electronic dictionaries learned more than those who did not. • High verbal ability students learned more words than low ability students.

Study	Focus	Participants	Language	Findings
Ko, M. H. (2005)	Glossing	106 undergraduate Korean speakers; 1 text	L1: Korean L2: English	• Dictionaries particularly helpful for low verbal ability students. • Students with dictionary access spent more time reading passages than those without dictionary access. • No difference between L1 glosses and no glosses at all. • L2 glosses lead to better reading-comprehension test performance. • Subjects reported a desire for L2 glossing.
Koda, K. (1993)	L1/L2 transfer	46 US college students enrolled in 1st-year Japanese language program (all had at least 3 years of previous L2 experience and no prior exposure to Japanese	L1: English L2: Japanese	• L1 reading skills interact with L2 specific linguistic features.
Koda, K. (1998)	L1/L2 transfer and orthography	Beginning-level ESL students at American university: 20 L1 Korean speakers, 20 L1 Chinese (Taiwan) speakers	L1: Chinese, Korean L2: English	• Korean readers demonstrate a strong relationship between reading comprehension, decoding, and phonemic awareness. • Direct relationships not found among Chinese ESL students.

Reference	Theme	Subjects & Texts	Language	Findings
Koda, K. (1999)	Orthography	40 university students (20 L1 Chinese; 20 L1 Korean) enrolled in intensive, beginning-level ESL classes	L1: Korean, Chinese L2: English	• L1 background affects orthographic sensitivity.
Kol, S., & Schcolnik, M. (2000)	Technology	47 university students of EAP in Israel; enrolled in course intended to prepare them to read academic English extensively; one 4-page text	L1: Hebrew L2: English	• Readers with technology-based training could read as well from a screen in the L2 as they could from traditional paper media.
Kondo-Brown, K. (2006a)	Affective factors	43 speakers of English, university level; 2 texts	L1: English L2: Japanese	• Self-perception and motivation relate directly to reading comprehension and *kanji* abilities. • Motivation to learn and to read Japanese were positively related to the learning of *kanji*. • Word-level deficiencies negatively impact motivation to read.

Study	Focus	Participants	Languages	Findings
Kondo-Brown, K. (2006b)	Inference of unknown words	42 English L1 students; 1 narrative/ 1 expository text	L1: English L2: Japanese, *kanji*	• Proficient students are more successful at inferencing, often as good as heritage learners, although they frequently guess incorrectly. • Phonological knowledge aided in inferring unknown *kanji*.
Kramsch, C., & Nolden, T. (1994)	Text reconstruction	30 low-intermediate US college students of German; 1 text	L1: English L2: German	• Text reconstructions indicate that readers re-evaluate test events; restructure information; and relocate a story's meaning.
Kroll, J. F., Michael, E., Tokowicz, N., & Dufour, R. (2002)	L2 lexical development and fluency; relationship between L1 and L2 naming and translation tasks	Experiment 1: 59 L1 English students of college-level French Experiment 2: 31 students in intensive summer university language courses in Spanish and French	L1: English, French, Spanish L2: French, Spanish	• Less-proficient L2 group was slower and made more mistakes in naming words in and translating words into the L2 than a group with higher L2 proficiency. • L1–L2 translation was slower than L2–L1 translation. • Bilinguals achieved higher scores on L1 reading span tests. • Bilinguals scored lower on L1 naming tasks than beginning L2 learners.
Kweon, S.-O., & Kim, H.-R. (2008)	Extensive L2 reading; vocabulary acquisition	12 Korean intermediate-level university students of English	L1: Korean L2: English	• Extensive reading significantly increases vocabulary acquisition. • Vocabulary items acquired in extensive reading are also retained.
Lai, F.-K. (1993)	Summer reading programs	226 Hong Kong secondary school	L1: Chinese L2: English	• Summer reading program yielded improvements in reading comprehension,

Reference	Theme	Subjects & Texts	Language	Findings
		students (Grades 7–9); participants had variable amounts of English learning; 40 readers		reading speed and writing development for many participants. • No improvement in reading speed and writing accuracy in the lower-ability groups noted.
Laufer, B., & Hadar, L. (1997)	Dictionary use	123 total: 76 EFL high school students and 46 university EFL learners.	L1: Hebrew L2: English	• Learners with higher skills in dictionary use are able to extract more information from a monolingual dictionary, while less skilled dictionary users are not as likely to use the monolingual part of a bilingualized entry. • Average learners may use the monolingual part of an entry for comprehension purposes, but might find it difficult to use it for production tasks.
Lazarte, A., & Barry, S. (2008)	Effect of L2 academic emersion on reader recall and reading strategies	Study 1: NES group: 79 USA undergraduates; NSS group: 35 Peruvian students Study 2: 26 female NES Spanish teachers; 2 extracts	L1/L2: English, Spanish	• Native Spanish speakers have better kernel recall and pauses than native English speakers. • Native English-speaking teachers with high exposure to academic immersion have better recall than those with low exposure.
Lee, J. F. (2002)	L2 grammatical forms and	181 college students of 2nd-semester	L1: English L2: Spanish	• Comprehension and input processing are determined by frequency of future tense;

Author	Focus	Participants/Materials	Languages	Findings
	comprehension	Spanish; 3 texts		subjects' attitude toward task; and reading context.
Lee, S.-K. (2007)	Form-focused textual enhancement	259 Korean high school juniors; various texts	L1: Korean L2: English	• Meaning-focused reading classes can enhance comprehension and the learning of form.
Leeser, M. (2007)	Topic and working memory	94 adult university student learners of accelerated, introductory Spanish; 4 narrative texts	L1: English L2: Spanish	• Relevant background knowledge enhances L2 reading comprehension. • Readers' ability to make form-meaning connections also influenced.
Leffa, V. (1992)	Technology and glosses	20 beginning level college students enrolled in two English courses, and representing various departments (selected from pool of 43 students); five 100-word passages	L1: Portuguese L2: English	• Electronic glossary was more efficient than the traditional dictionary. • The electronic glossary was not difficult to learn to use.
Leow, R. P. (2001)	Input enhancement and success of L2 reading	38 first-year students of college-level Spanish; 1 text	L1: English L2: Spanish	• No difference noted between written input enhancement and unenhanced written input. • Subjects' level or depth of attention and kinds of processing used on L2 reading tasks attributed to the readers' level of grammatical awareness.

Reference	Theme	Subjects & Texts	Language	Findings
Leow, R. P., Ego, T., Nuevo, A. M., & Tsai, Y.-C. (2003)	Textual enhancement	72 university students of first-year Spanish (broken down into two groups: 41 experimental (enhanced) and 31 control (unenhanced)); 2 texts	L1: English L2: Spanish	• Enhanced L2 texts did not result in higher levels of recognition of targeted verb forms over unenhanced texts. • No correlation between enhanced texts and either reading comprehension or intake. • Readers successful in recognizing present perfect over present subjunctive verb forms.
Leung, C. Y. (2002)	Extensive reading	1 Japanese speaker	L1: Japanese L2: English	• Subject improved vocabulary knowledge and reading comprehension, while also developing a positive affect toward reading.
Liu, J. (2004)	Visuals and reading comprehension of high-level texts	107 adult ESL learners enrolled in American university	L1: majority Spanish, Arabic, Japanese, Chinese, Korean L2: English	• Scores of low-level subjects who read high-level text with comic strip enhancement were much higher than low-level students who received high-level text without comic strip. • High-level subjects' reading comprehension of high-level text not improved by inclusion of comic strip.
Lumley, T. (1993)	Sub-skills in L2 reading	Total of 158 non-English speaking	L1: Various, e.g., Chinese,	• Agreement among a group of five experienced EAP teachers for matching

Study	Focus	Participants	Languages	Findings
	comprehension tests	background (NESB) students; 90 overseas students, 50 Asian students from a local English language center, and 50 post-grad students from Eastern Europe. 5 experienced ESL/EFL teachers rated items on an EAP test	Indonesian, Japanese, Korean, Thai, eastern European languages L2: English	subskills to individual test items and assessing difficulty. • Significant correlation between teachers' perceptions and Rasch IRT analyses of test items.
Lund, R. (1991)	Listening/reading comparison	180 US college students in 3rd-semester German courses; 1 text	L1: English L2: German	• Beginning and intermediate readers of German outperformed listeners in comprehension. • Repetition helped readers more than listeners. • Readers recalled more propositions at each level, but listeners recalled a greater proportion of main ideas.
Luppescu, S., & Day, R. (1993)	Dictionary use	293 Japanese university students; 1 short story	L1: Japanese L2: English	• Students using dictionaries did better on vocabulary tests than students who did not. • Use of dictionaries did not always relate to correct answers on comprehension questions.

Reference	Theme	Subjects & Texts	Language	Findings
Maeng, U. (2005)	Reading strategies in L1 and L2	5 advanced-level L2 English Korean graduate students at an American university	L1: Korean L2: English	• Participants transfer many L1 reading strategies when confronted with reading tasks in the L2. • Strategies used by subjects in L2 English reading mirror successful strategies of L1 English readers. • Kinds of strategies used differed depending on whether the text was in L1 or L2.
Marinis, T., Roberts, L., Felser, C., & Clahsen, H. (2005)	Syntax	University students, aged 17–46. 34 L1 Chinese speakers, 26 L1 Japanese speakers, 24 L1 German speakers, 30 L1 Greek speakers. Control group of 24 L1 English speakers	L1: Chinese, Japanese, German, Greek L2: English	• Non-native speakers of English often neglect syntactic information when processing L2 texts. • Syntactic processing influenced by L1.
Mason, B., & Krashen, S. (1997)	Extensive reading	Study 1: 60 college students in Japan Study 2: 4 EFL college classes (128 students) in English literature	L1: Japanese L2: English	• Extensive reading students in Japan made significant gains on a cloze test. • Readers in an extensive reading program did better than traditionally taught students. • Extensive readers who wrote English summaries improved more on cloze tests

Author/Year	Focus	Participants/Materials	Languages	Findings
		Study 3: English response group, Japanese response group, comparison group; 30 books		than the comparison students. • Extensive readers responding in Japanese made higher gains in reading speed and writing over their counterparts.
Maxim II, H. H. (2002)	Extensive reading	59 American university students, beginning German learners; novel	L1: English L2: German	• Students demonstrated an ability to read full-length authentic L2 text in 1st semester. • Students in a conventional curriculum and those in the extensive reading program performed equally well on tests.
Mills, N. (2006)	Self-efficacy and reading ability	95 college students enrolled in 3rd- or 4th-semester French; 15 passages	L1: English L2: French	• Self-efficacy in reading is positively associated with reading proficiency.
Mokhtari, K., & Reichard, C. (2004)	Academic reading strategies, metacognition, L1/L2 relationship	350 undergraduate university students (209 Moroccan, 141 American) at US & Moroccan universities, enrolled in courses of study where the language of instruction is English	L1: Arabic, English L2: English	• Groups from different social contexts displayed similar patterns of strategy awareness and reported usage. • Differences in repeated reading, monitoring, and predicting noted.

Reference	Theme	Subjects & Texts	Language	Findings
Mori, S. (2002)	Affective factors	447 Japanese speakers, university students	L1: Japanese L2: English	• Interest and motivation to read are linked. • A unique L2 motivation was undetected.
Mori, Y., & Nagy, W. (1999)	Context vs. morphological analysis as reading comprehension strategies	59 undergraduate & graduate students in intermediate/pre-advanced Japanese	L1: English L2: Japanese	• Successful reading comprehension achieved when students had access to both contextual clues and words in isolation/*kanji* clues. • Words in isolation and context use not correlated. • Proficiency related to context, but not to *kanji* use.
Morrison, L. (2004)	Comprehension monitoring and L1/L2 reading proficiency	52 undergraduate FSL students (two different L2 tracks: French immersion (FI) and core French (CF)); 3 passages	L1: English L2: French	• Comprehension monitoring transfers across languages. • L1 and L2 reading proficiency are closely linked to monitoring performance.
Nakada, T., Fujii, Y., & Kwee, I. L. (2001)	L1/L2 literacy; neuroscientific research	20 subjects (20–29 years old): 10 L1 Japanese speakers (5 highly literate in L1 and L2 English); 10 L1 English speakers (5 highly literate in	L1: English, Japanese L2: English, Japanese	• Same cortical structures used when reading in both L1 and L2. • L2 is a "cognitive extension" of the L1.

Study	Focus	Subjects	Language	Findings
Nassaji, H. (2003)	Text processing strategies	60 adult ESL learners (graduate students in Canada), native Farsi speakers	L1: Farsi L2: English	• Word recognition and phonological processes plus syntactic and semantic processes played a role in differentiating between skilled and less-skilled ESL readers. • Lower-level word recognition skills are crucial to successful L2 reading comprehension.
Nassaji, H. (2004)	Vocabulary knowledge, lexical inferencing strategies	21 adult intermediate ESL learners of varying L1 backgrounds	L1: Chinese, Spanish, Persian, Portuguese, Arabic et al. L2: English	• Level of vocabulary knowledge mapped onto the frequency and kinds of strategies learners used and their success. • Depth of vocabulary knowledge is key in lexical inferencing.
Nishino, T. (2007)	Extensive reading	Two 14-year-old Japanese	L1: Japanese L2: English	• Subjects enhanced their motivation to read as a result of their increased confidence, fluency, independence, enjoyment, and other factors. • As subjects grew older, their motivation to read actually declined.
Oded, B., & Walters, J. (2001)	Depth of processing & reading comprehension	65 Israeli undergraduates in an EFL reading comprehension class (43 at advanced low	L1: Hebrew L2: English	• Subjects asked to perform more difficult assessments (such as summarizing text) had higher scores than subjects asked to do less challenging tasks. • Finding was particularly salient for

(Note: top of table) L1 and L2 Japanese)

Reference	Theme	Subjects & Texts	Language	Findings
Oh, S.-Y. (2001)	Text type	level; 22 at advanced high level) 430 (105 excluded from main study) Korean 2nd-year high school students, intermediate EFL level; 6 texts	L1: Korean L2: English	lower-level learners. • Elaboration facilitated reading comprehension for students of high and low proficiency.
Ozono, S., & Harumi, I. (2003)	Logical connectives and L2 reading	60 Japanese university students of EFL (high, medium, low proficiency); 6 texts	L1: Japanese L2: English	• High-proficiency group performed consistently even when confronted with text with missing logical connectives. • Low-proficiency group showed varied success depending on the type of logical connective.
Parel, R. (2004)	Inferencing strategies	302 "low language proficiency" (measured by Swansea Vocabulary Test) Canadian 10th-grade high school ESL learners	L1: Various L2: English	• L2 text comprehension is enabled by a minimal L2 vocabulary foundation that triggers morphological analysis. • Inferencing strategies and contextual guessing are more important to L2 reading proficiency than a broad knowledge of L2 vocabulary knowledge.
Paribakht, T. S. (2005)	Lexicalization	20 university ESL	L1: Farsi	• L1 lexicalization of L2 texts might be

Study	Focus	Participants/Materials	Language	Findings
		students; 6 paragraphs	L2: English	a strong component in L2 reading comprehension and vocabulary building.
Paribakht, T. S., & Wesche, M. (1999)	Vocabulary	10 intermediate-level university students of ESL; 1 text	L1: French, Chinese, Farsi, Spanish, Vietnamese, Arabic L2: English	• Subjects ignored most of the unfamiliar L2 words while reading. • Inferencing was the most readily used strategy when words were not ignored.
Park, G.-P. (2004)	Listening/ reading comprehension	168 students in university English conversation class, all with at least 6 years of ESL study in secondary school	L1: Korean L2: English	• Reading and listening comprehension are different from each other. • Linguistic and prior knowledge significantly influenced listening comprehension. • Only linguistic knowledge influenced reading comprehension, while prior knowledge showed a moderate effect. • Question types were shown to have little or no effect in listening, while linguistic knowledge and prior knowledge did influence it. • Question types and linguistic knowledge were important in reading comprehension, while prior knowledge had little or no influence. • Reading tests were easier than listening tests.

Reference	Theme	Subjects & Texts	Language	Findings
Parry, K. (1991)	Vocabulary	4 ESL college students (1 Japanese, 2 Greek, 1 Korean) who were enrolled in an introductory anthropology class	L1: Japanese, Greek, Korean L2: English	• A wide range of strategies can be used to learn vocabulary. • Amount of reading related to vocabulary size.
Parry, K. (1996)	Culture	20 secondary school students in Nigerian group; 25 college students in Chinese group; 7 passages.	L1: Nigerian, Chinese L2: English	• Reading strategies are influenced in part by cultural factors. • An interaction between high-level schemata and low level textual cues and cultural differences in strategies was found.
Perkins, K., Gupta, L., & Tammana, R. (1995)	Tests	70 students enrolled in English classes; 29 items	L1: Various e.g., Japanese, Chinese, Arabic, Korean, Spanish, Thai, Turkish, Urdu, Hebrew, Indonesian, Wolof L2: English	• Neural networks useful in predicting item difficulty with consistency and accuracy on standardized reading comprehension tests.

Study	Focus	Sample	Languages	Findings
Phakiti, A. (2003)	Gender	384 Thai university students of EFL	L1: Thai L2: English	• Men and women showed no difference in reading comprehension performance or implementation of cognitive strategies. • Men reported higher use of metacognitive strategies than women.
Pichette, F. (2005)	Time on task and L2 reading comprehension	81 adult, college-level ESL learners; proficiency levels from high beginner to early advanced; 4 texts	L1: French L2: English	• Few significant links between time spent reading in the L2 and L2 reading comprehension for beginning learners of ESL. • With advanced students, there is a moderately significant relationship between time spent reading in the L2 and the level of reading comprehension in the L2.
Pichette, F., Segalowitz, N., & Connors, K. (2003)	Relationship between L1 & L2 reading skills	52 Bosnians (17–47 years old) learning L2 French over 1-year period; 4 cloze tests	L1: Serbo-Croatian L2: French	• Evidence of a threshold level of L2 knowledge for effective interlingual transfer of reading skills. • Active reading skills in L1 are necessary for effective L2 reading only partially supported by experiment. • Retention of L1 reading in L2 environment supports acquisition of effective L2 reading skills.
Pigada, M., & Schmitt, N. (2006)	Vocabulary acquisition; extensive reading	1 university-level native speaker of Greek	L1: Greek L2: French	• One month of extensive reading experience enhanced the acquisition of more than 100 target words.

Reference	Theme	Subjects & Texts	Language	Findings
				• Correlation between extensive reading and vocabulary acquisition.
Prichard, C. (2008)	Vocabulary acquisition and dictionary use	34 Japanese women studying ESL at college level	L1: Japanese L2: English	• Dictionary use while reading in the L2 may speed up students' improvements in comprehension and vocabulary acquisition. • Certain L2 learners may profit from learning how to look up words in a targeted manner. • Others need instruction in other basic reading strategies before benefiting from dictionary use or instruction.
Pulido, D. (2003)	Vocabulary	99 adult university students of Spanish as L2; beginning, intermediate, advanced levels; 2 familiar, 2 less-familiar passages	L1: English L2: Spanish	• Correlation between increasing L2 reading proficiency and increasing incidental vocabulary gain and retention. • Correlation independent of topic familiarity. • Sight vocabulary showed some influence on L2 incidental vocabulary gain.
Pulido, D. (2004a)	Prior knowledge and cultural familiarity	23 university students of L2 Spanish at intermediate-high level; 4 passages	L1: English L2: Spanish	• Prior knowledge of the target culture resulted in higher levels of reading comprehension as well as greater vocabulary gains. • Sight vocabulary demonstrated an inconsistent relationship to incidental vocabulary acquisition.

Study	Focus	Participants	Languages	Findings
Pulido, D. (2004b)	Vocabulary	99 adult university students of Spanish as L2; beginning, intermediate, advanced levels; 4 passages	L1: English L2: Spanish	• Text comprehension was generally consistent with lexical gain and retention. • Relationship between comprehension and intake was variable as a result of pre-existing familiarity with the subject of the text.
Pulido, D. (2007)	Vocabulary	99 adult learners of L2 Spanish, L1 English at beginning, intermediate and advanced levels; 4 narrative texts	L1: English L2: Spanish	• Background knowledge does not facilitate the relationship between textual comprehension and retention of meaning.
Pulido, D., & Hambrick, D. (2008)	Comprehension & vocabulary development	99 university-level subjects; 4 texts	L1: English L2: Spanish	• Level and depth of language experience improves L2 vocabulary learning. • L2 vocabulary learning improves reading comprehension. • L2 comprehension improves overall L2 vocabulary development.
Renandya, W. A., Rajan, B. R. S., & Jacobs, G. M. (1999)	Extensive reading	49 adult Vietnamese government officials attending an intensive ESL course in Singapore for 2 months; proficiency range: low to intermediate high	L1: Vietnamese L2: English	• Extensive reading is a viable strategy for older learners. • Quantity of extensive reading related to subjects' proficiency gains in L2.

Reference	Theme	Subjects & Texts	Language	Findings
Riley, G., & Lee, J. F. (1996)	Tests	80 college students studying French, first and second years and native English speakers; 1 text	L1: English L2: French	• Significant differences between summaries and recalls. • Summaries contain more main ideas. • Recall protocols produce a higher percentage of passage details.
Rott, S. (1999)	Vocabulary	95 4th-semester students of German as a foreign language (28 subjects excluded from final analysis); 6 paragraphs	L1: English L2: German	• Even two encounters with unfamiliar vocabulary positively increased readers' vocabulary growth. • Six encounters led to significantly more vocabulary knowledge. • Most participants retained vocabulary over four weeks.
Rott, S. (2004)	Vocabulary	35 learners of German in fourth-semester language classes; 3 texts	L1: English L2: German	• Cycles of input and output were no more successful than unenhanced reading condition in heightening form and meaning connections. • Unenhanced reading leads to the most successful L2 text comprehension.
Rott, S. (2005)	Vocabulary acquisition; glossing	10 university students, all English native speakers	L1: English L2: German	• Comprehension of main ideas was the same using both multiple-choice and single-choice glosses. • Multiple-choice glosses fostered better

Author	Topic	Sample	Language	Findings
Rott, S. (2007)	Input-enchancement and text comprehension	54 learners of German with L1 English in 4th semester language classes; 2 expository, one narrative text	L1: English L2: German	understanding of details and supporting ideas. • Gloss-retrieval and words glossed four times yielded more productive word gain than gloss-bolding and words repeated only once. • Highest comprehension was found when words were glossed four times and followed by gloss-bolding and gloss-retrieval tasks.
Rott, S., & Williams, J. (2003)	Vocabulary	English-speaking university students	L1: English L2: German	• A no-gloss condition led to lesser engagement. • Glossing helps readers develop connections in text comprehension.
Rusciolelli, J. (1995)	Reading strategies	College students, 4th and 5th semester college Spanish; 10 magazine articles	L1: English L2: Spanish	• Instruction in skimming and word guessing was found to be helpful.
Saiegh-Haddad, E. (2003)	Oral reading; L1/L2 relationship	50 university students in Israel taking intermediate-level EFL classes; 3 texts	L1: Arabic, Hebrew L2: English	• No significant links between oral reading fluency and reading comprehension in the subjects' L1. • Strong link between oral reading fluency and reading comprehension in the L2. • Oral reading fluency was lower for the L1 Arabic group than for the L1 Hebrew group,

Reference	Theme	Subjects & Texts	Language	Findings
				while reading comprehension scores were comparable.
Saito, Y., Garza, T. J., & Horwitz, E. K. (1999)	Anxiety	383 students enrolled in 1st-semester university French, Japanese, Russian courses	L1: English L2: French, Japanese, Russian	• Reading in a foreign language can be anxiety-provoking. • Levels of anxiety were variable according to L2 and may be related to complexity of writing system. • Subjects with higher reading anxiety and general L2 anxiety had lower grades in L2 courses.
Sakar, A., & Ercetin, G. (2005)	Technology	44 adult ESL students of Academic English; 1 text	L1: Various L2: English	• Participants preferred visual annotations rather than textual or audio annotations • Inverse relationship between use of annotations and reading comprehension. • Subjects' perception of annotations and hypermedia reading was favorable.
Salataci, R., & Akyel, A. (2002)	Strategies and L1/L2 relationship; 4 texts in Turkish and English	8 Turkish-speaking university students; 4 texts in Turkish and English	L1: Turkish L2: English	• Strategy instruction through the use of reciprocal teaching positively influenced both L2 reading comprehension scores and reading strategies in the L1 and L2.

Study	Focus	Participants	Language	Findings
Salmani-Nodoushan, M. A. (2003)	Text familiarity, task type	541 advanced undergraduate students in Iran majoring in electronics; four proficiency groups (according to IELTS): proficient (93), fairly proficient (164), semi-proficient (186), non-proficient (98); 5 texts	L1: Farsi L2: English	• L2 language proficiency was more important than text familiarity on performance in assessment testing. • Task type was more important than text familiarity to task performance. • No need for language for specific purposes tests.
Saricoban, A. (2002)	Three-phase approach to L2 reading	110 preparatory students (upper-intermediate level) for English department at a Turkish university	L1: Turkish L2: English	• Strategy differences obvious in reading and post-reading stages, but not pre-reading.
Scott, V., & Huntington, J. (2007)	Literary text	48 university students (ages 18–25) at novice level of French; 1 poem	L1: English L2: French	• Novice learners can understand and successfully interpret challenging text in a teacher-moderated group. • First language is helpful for encouraging interpretation of texts in the teacher moderated classroom. • L1 not helpful in small group situations.

Reference	Theme	Subjects & Texts	Language	Findings
Seng, G. H., & Hashim, F. (2006)	L1/L2 relationship	4 native speakers of Bahasa Melayu	L1: Melayu L2: English	• Subjects used their first language in over 30% of strategy-based situations.
Sengupta, S. (1999)	Rhetorical structure	15 Chinese undergraduate learners of ESL; 14 articles and chapters	L1: Chinese L2: English	• Subjects unable to integrate their subjective opinions about what qualified a text as reader-friendly into their own L2 writing. • With time, subjects became more effective L2 readers and pinpointed their own individual problems in L2 reading comprehension and L2 writing.
Sengupta, S. (2002)	Process-oriented L2 reading instruction and L2 reading strategies	25 first-year university students of intermediate L2 proficiency finishing degrees in "Contemporary English Language" in Hong Kong; 14 articles and chapters	L1: Cantonese L2: English	• Process-oriented reading strategy instruction on L2 reading strategies helps students view reading as an active process and as an interactive relationship among the writers, readers, and material. • Process-oriented reading instruction is difficult to implement in a decontextualized setting and therefore challenging to sustain outside the classroom.
Shang, H.-F. (2005)	Technology	40 university freshmen in Taiwan enrolled in intermediate reading class; 3 articles	L1: Chinese L2: English	• Multidirectional electronic discussion format may be more beneficial than simple email applications to increasing L2 reading proficiency. • Technology itself was less important than the subjects' positive attitudes about how

Reference	Focus	Participants	Languages	Findings
				the electronic discussions might benefit their L2 reading performance.
Stavans, A., & Oded, B. (1993)	Strategies	10 Ethiopian college students	L1: Amharic L2: Hebrew	• Unsuccessful participants tended to apply and use strategies in a more perfunctory manner than the more successful learners.
Stevenson, M., Schoonen, R., & de Glopper, K. (2007)	Reading strategies and compensation	22 Dutch high school students tested in L1 Dutch and L2 English	L1: Dutch L2: English	• Readers compensate for language difficulties by treating them with greater attention but without detracting from the global reading process.
Stott, N. (2004)	Cultural content & background knowledge	20 (18 female, 2 male) Japanese EFL students at teacher-training college in Japan (studied L2 for at least 6 years); 1 text	L1: Japanese L2: English	• Subjects not informed that a text was from own cultural context performed much better on reading recall protocol than those who were told the passage was a translation of a Japanese novel.
Suh, J.-S. (1999)	Prior instruction, L2 attitude and process	2 Korean students of ESL at an American university; advanced proficiency; 2 texts	L1: Korean L2: English	• Prior reading instruction was the dominant determining factor in subjects' current attitude toward L2 reading. • Prior instruction was less clearly associated with the reading process and strategies employed.
Taguchi, E., & Gorsuch, G. (2002)	Fluency and word recognition	18 Japanese university-level students	L1: Japanese L2: English	• No significant differences between the control and experimental groups with repeated reading.

Reference	Theme	Subjects & Texts	Language	Findings
Taguchi, E., Takayasu-Maass, M., & Gorsuch, G. (2004)	Fluency and reading rate; repeated reading; extensive reading	29 Japanese post-secondary students; 2 texts and graded readers	L1: Japanese L2: English	• Repeated reading and extensive reading are equally efficacious in improving fluency/reading rate, though no differences in comprehension were noted. • Enhanced fluency promotes a positive attitude toward L2 reading.
Taillefer, G., & Pugh, T. (1998)	L1/L2 relationship	39 2nd-year university students of economics, law, and public administration	L1: French L2: English	• Good readers in L1 and L2 had a strategic approach to reading. • Problem-solving strategies proved most difficult in L2.
Takase, A. (2007)	Extensive reading and motivation	219 secondary school students	L1: Japanese L2: English	• Students enthusiastic about reading in one language or the other. • Enthusiasm for one did not imply enthusiasm for the reading of the other.
Tang, G. (1992)	Processing the literal and conventional meanings of indirect requests by native and non-native speakers	Study 1: 59 native English speakers, 23 Japanese learners of English Study 2: 36 Japanese learners of English, 36 native speakers of English	L1/L2: Japanese, English	• Stories were effectively judged as request or literal stories. • English speakers read target sentences faster than the Japanese learners of English. • Reading speeds were higher for conventional request target sentences than the literal target sentences.

Author (Year)	Focus	Participants	Languages	Findings
Tian, G. S. (1991)	L1/L2 relationship	8 native Chinese graduate students; 3 texts	L1: Mandarin L2: English	• Interdependence between L1 and L2 comprehension strategies is influenced by cognitive universals.
Upton, T. A., & Lee-Thompson, L.-C. (2001)	L1/L2 relationship	20 L1 Chinese & Japanese speakers at 3 levels of L2 English proficiency at US university; 1 text	L1: Chinese, Japanese L2: English	• Readers do not only translate directly from L1 into L2 when reading L2 text.
Uso-Juan, E. (2006)	Content-based academic reading	380 L1 Spanish undergraduates from varying academic disciplines; test booklets	L1: Spanish L2: English	• Language proficiency contributed to comprehension (58% to 68%). • Discipline-related knowledge contributed 21% to 31%.
van Gelderen, A., Schoonen, R., de Glopper, K., Hulstijn, J., Simis, A., Snellings, P., & Stevenson, M. (2003)	Prior knoeledge, speed, metacognitive knowledge, L1/L2 relationship	281 8th-grade native Dutch-speaking students (13–14 years old) of EFL with average of 1.5 years of prior study in English; 4 Dutch and 6 English texts	L1: Dutch L2: English	• Reading comprehension in the L1 significantly contributes to reading comprehension in the L2. • Prior linguistic knowledge (especially vocabulary in the L2) is significant. • Metacognition also provides some explanation.
van Gelderen, A., Schoonen, R., de Glopper, K., Hulstijn, J.,	Reading comprehension in L1, L2, and L3; prior knowledge;	338 8th-grade students (13–14 years old) in the Netherlands learning	L1: Various e.g., Dutch, Turkish, Arabic	• Participants for whom English was the L3 had weaker reading comprehension scores in EFL than did the students for whom English was the L2.

Reference	Theme	Subjects & Texts	Language	Findings
Snellings, P., Simis, A., & Stevenson, M. (2004)	speed; metacognition	EFL (281 were monolingual Dutch (MD), so English was their L2; 57 were bilingual Dutch (BD), for whom Dutch was L2 and English the L3); 4 Dutch and 6 English texts	L2: English, Dutch L3: English	• No significant differences between groups in patterns of reliance on speed, prior knowledge, and metacognition.
van Wijnendaele, I., & Brysbaert, M. (2002)	Word recognition, phonological priming	59 university students (39 L1 French, L2 Dutch; 20 L1 Dutch, L2 French)	L1: Dutch, French L2: Dutch, French	• Cross-lingual phonological priming can be bi-directional. • Visual word recognition is strongly rooted in the phonological.
Wade-Woolley, L. (1999)	L1–L2 skill transfer and L2 word reading	16 participants from each language group, all intermediate low ESL learners in a university department	L1: Russian, Japanese L2: English	• The two groups showed differences in skill with certain kinds of processing, but both groups were equally successful in non-word reading tasks. • L1 Japanese speakers were more skilled on orthographic choice tasks; L1 Russian speakers better at phonemic awareness. • Both groups performed equally well on L2 word reading tasks.

Study	Focus	Participants	Languages	Findings
Wade-Woolley, L., & Geva, E. (1999)	Morphological processing	54 adults, mostly university students (18 Russians; 15 L1 English Canadians; 21 native Israelis)	L1: Russian, English, Hebrew L2: Hebrew	• L1 Russian speakers were better L2 Hebrew text readers than L1 English readers. • L1 Russian speakers were less accurate and slower word namers than L1 English subjects.
Walter, C. (2004)	L1/L2 transfer, proficiency level, working memory	41 French middle & upper school students; 16 French texts	L1: French L2: English	• A low-intermediate group of readers was unable to successfully transfer L1 skills of generating well-structured mental representations of texts into the L2. • An intermediate high group was able to successfully do this.
Waring, R., & Takaki, M. (2003)	Vocabulary acquisition and retention	15 Japanese university students	L1: Japanese L2: English	• Frequency of word occurrence influences vocabulary retention three months after reading. • Most new vocabulary encountered will not be retained without repeated reading.
Wesche, M. B., & Paribakht, T. S. (2000)	Advantages of text-based vocabulary exercises	10 intermediate ESL students at Canadian university; 1 text	L1: French, French Creole, Chinese, Arabic L2: English	• Various vocabulary tasks offer repeated and distinct opportunities for students to learn about various features of words and their definitions. • Text-based vocabulary exercises should accompany reading texts.
Wolf, D. F. (1993)	Assessing L2 reading comprehension	Level 1: 72 US college students enrolled in 4th-semester	L1: English L2: Spanish	• Scores on multiple-choice tests were higher than open-ended questions and cloze task scores.

Reference	Theme	Subjects & Texts	Language	Findings
		Spanish (beginners) Level 2: 72 US college students in advanced-level Spanish; 1 text		• Participants tested in their native language did better than those tested in the target language. • Advanced-level learners scored higher than lower proficiency participants.
Wong, W. (2003)	Textual enhancement, simplified input, L2 reading comprehension, acquisition of target grammatical form	81 university students of 2nd-semester L2 French; 4 versions of 3 texts	L1: English L2: French	• Textual enhancement does not affect acquisition of targeted grammatical form. • An enhancement did not affect free recall of total idea units. • Enhancement did benefit the recall of enhanced idea units. • Simplified input did not affect acquisition of targeted grammatical form, but did result in increased free recall scores.
Yamashita, J. (2002a)	L1/L2 relationship	241 Japanese university students of ESL; three groups formed (high, middle, low) based on L1 reading ability & L2 language proficiency; 5 expository texts	L1: Japanese L2: English	• The combination of high L1 reading skills and high L2 proficiency acts in direct proportion to a high level of L2 reading comprehension among subjects. • L2 language proficiency is a much stronger predictor than L1 reading skills for a high level of L2 reading comprehension. • There is a mutual compensation between L2 language proficiency and L1 reading ability.

Yamashita, J. (2002b)	Reading strategies in L1 and L2	12 Japanese university students of English (4 in each group, based on reading ability)	L1: Japanese L2: English	• The linguistic threshold hypothesis insufficiently explains links between L1 & L2 reading processes and that L1 & L2 reading processes are more closely linked. • Transfer of language-independent strategies from L1 to L2 is more frequent than transfer of language-dependent strategies. • Higher levels of L1 reading skills can compensate for lower L2 reading skills, but only up to a certain level. • L2 proficiency is more indicative of L2 reading strategies and proficiency than L1 reading ability.
Yamashita, J. (2004)	Affect and extensive reading; L1/L2 relationship	59 Japanese post-secondary students; approximately 14 graded readers	L1: Japanese L2: English	• Attitudes toward reading, particularly the value of reading, appear to be L1/L2 interrelated. • Attitudes and proficiency in the L2 are not related. • Positive attitudes toward reading in both L1 and L2 correlate with enhanced L2 extensive reading results.
Yang, Y.-F. (2002)	Metacognition	12 speakers of Chinese, university level; 2 texts	L1: Chinese L2: English	• Comprehension monitoring was found to be a hallmark of highly proficient readers. • Comprehension monitoring can be at least as effective as developing reading strategies.

Reference	Theme	Subjects & Texts	Language	Findings
Yano, Y., Long, M., & Ross, S. (1994)	Linguistic simplification	483 university students; studied for 8 years	L1: Japanese L2: English	• No difference between simplified and enhanced text. • Method of assessment interacted with text type.
Yigiter, K., Saricoban, A., & Gürses, T. (2005)	L2 reading strategies	123 L1 Turkish university students of English language studies at advanced level	L1: Turkish L2: English	• Individuals' L2 needs and interests affect which reading strategies they turn to at which stage when reading L2 texts. • Good readers use more predicting, reasoning about author's aim, and question-previewing strategies in pre-reading. • During reading, good readers use more annotating, analyzing, interpreting, and guessing strategies. • Good readers more frequently summarize, comment on, and reflect on what they've read in a post-reading phase.
Ying, H. G. (2004)	Comprehension of grammatical forms in L2	40 adult Chinese NSs learning ESL; 20 native American English speakers	L1: Chinese, English L2: English	• Subjects are more likely to read a that-clause as complement with fewer syntactic nodes and reduced processing effort. • Subjects demonstrated a preference for interpretation as a relative clause.

Author (Year)	Focus	Participants	Language	Findings
Young, D. N. (1999)	Linguistic simplification	127 university students of intensive 2nd-year Spanish; 4 texts	L1: English L2: Spanish	• Subjects did not have lower recall scores for simplified vs. authentic L2 texts.
Zimmerman, C. (1997)	Reading and interactive vocabulary instruction	35 total ESL college students. All tested in the advanced-intermediate level.	L1 majority: Japanese, Korean Mandarin (rest of the languages not specified) L2: English	• Gains in vocabulary knowledge were attributed to interactive vocabulary instruction coupled with opportunities for self-selected and course-relevant reading.
Zyzik, E., & Polio, C. (2008)	Use of form-focused instruction in L2 literature courses	3 university advanced Spanish literature classes, 65 students total	L1: English L2: Spanish	• A pre-emptive focus on form was limited to vocabulary. • Instructors preferred recasts for giving feedback.

Works Cited

Abu-Rabia, S. (1996). The influence of culture and attitudes on reading comprehension in SL: The case of Jews learning English and Arabs learning Hebrew. *Reading Psychology, 17*(3), 253–271.

Abu-Rabia, S. (1998a). The learning of Hebrew by Israeli Arab students in Israel. *The Journal of Social Psychology, 138*(3), 331–341.

Abu-Rabia, S. (1998b). Social and cognitive factors influencing the reading comprehension of Arab students learning Hebrew as a second language in Israel. *Journal of Research in Reading, 21*(3), 201–212.

Abu-Rabia, S. (2003). The influence of working memory on reading and creative writing processes in a second language. *Educational Psychology, 23*(2), 209–222.

Akamatsu, N. (2003). The effects of first language orthographic features on second language reading in text. *Language Learning, 53*(2), 207–231.

Al-Othman, N. M. A. (2003). The relationship between online reading rates and performance on proficiency tests. *The Reading Matrix: An International Online Journal, 3*(3), 120–136.

Al-Seghayer, K. (2005). ESL readers' perceptions of reading in well structured and less structured hypertext environment. *CALICO Journal, 22*(2), 191–211.

Alderson, J. C. (2000). *Assessing reading.* Cambridge: Cambridge University Press.

Alderson, J. C., & Urquhart, A. H. (Eds.). (1984). *Reading in a foreign language.* London: Longman.

Alessi, S., & Dwyer, A. (2008). Vocabulary assistance before and during reading. *Reading in a Foreign Language, 20*(2), 246–263.

Allan, A. (1992). Development and validation of a scale to measure test-wiseness in EFL-ESL reading test takers. *Language Testing, 9*(2), 101–122.

Anderson, N. J. (2003). Scrolling, clicking, and reading English: Online reading strategies in a second/foreign language. *The Reading Matrix: An International Online Journal, 3*(3), 1–33.

Anderson, N., Bachmann, L., Perkins, K., & Cohen, A. (1991). An exploratory study into the construct validity of a reading comprehension test: Triangulation of data sources. *Language Testing, 8*(1), 41–66.

Associated Press. (2009, January 20). Obama urges unity against "raging storms": First black president takes office, facing an array of problems. Retrieved from http://www.msnbc.msn.com/id/28745226/ns/politics-inauguration/

Auerbach, E. R., & Paxton, D. (1997). "It's not the English thing": Bringing reading research into the ESL classroom. *TESOL Quarterly, 31*(2), 237–261.

August, D., & Shanahan, T. (Eds.). (2006). *Developing literacy in second-language learn-ers: Report of the National Literacy Panel on Language Minority Children and Youth.* Mahwah, NJ: Erlbaum.

Banks, J., & Banks, C. (Eds.). (2001). *The handbook of research on multicultural education.* San Francisco, CA: Jossey-Bass.

Barack Obama als Präsident vereidigt. (2009, January 21). *Frankfurter Allgemeine Zeitung.* Retrieved from http://www.faz.net/s/Rub0A1169E18C724B0980CCD7215BCFAE4F/ Doc~EE46913E826D5457783BF8941779AB02D~ATpl~Ecommon~Sspezial.html

Barnett, M. A. (1991). Language and literature: False dichotomies, real allies. *ADFL Bulletin, 22*(3), 7–11.

Barr, R., Kamil, M. L., Mosenthal, P., & Pearson, P. D. (Eds.). (1991). *Handbook of reading research* (Vol. 2). New York: Longman.

Barry, S., & Lazarte, A. A. (1998). Evidence for mental models: How do prior knowledge, syntactic complexity, and reading topic affect inference generation in a recall task for nonnative readers of Spanish? *The Modern Language Journal, 82*(2), 176–193.

Bell, F. L., & LeBlanc, L. B. (2000). The language of glosses in L2 reading on computer: Learners' preferences. *Hispania, 83*(2), 274–285.

Bell, T. (2001). Extensive reading: Speed and comprehension. *The Reading Matrix: An International Online Journal, 1*(1).

Bengeleil, N. F., & Paribakht, T. S. (2004). L2 reading proficiency and lexical inferencing by university EFL learners. *The Canadian Modern Language Review, 61*(2), 225–249.

Benseler, D. P. (1991). The upper-division curriculum in foreign languages and litera-tures: Obstacles to the realization of the promise. In E. S. Silber (Ed.), *Critical issues in foreign language instruction* (pp. 186–199). New York: Garland.

Bergethon, K. R., & Braun, F. X. (1963). *Grammar for reading German.* Boston, MA: Houghton Mifflin.

Berkemeyer, V. (1994). Anaphoric resolution and text comprehension for readers of German. *Die Unterrichtspraxis, 27*(2), 15–22.

Bernhardt, E. B. (1983). Three approaches to reading comprehension in intermediate German. *Modern Language Journal, 67*(2), 111–115.

Bernhardt, E. B. (1986). Reading in a foreign language. In B. H. Wing (Ed.), *Listening, reading, and writing: Analysis and application* (pp. 93–115). Middlebury, VT: Northeast Conference on the Teaching of Foreign Languages.

Bernhardt, E. B. (1987). Cognitive processes in L2: An examination of reading behaviors. In J. Lantolf & A. LaBarca (Eds.), *Delaware symposium on language studies: Research on second language acquisition in the classroom setting* (pp. 35–50). Norwood, NJ: Ablex.

Bernhardt, E. B. (1991). *Reading development in a second language: Theoretical, research, and classroom perspectives.* Norwood, NJ: Ablex.

Bernhardt, E. B. (1994a). A content analysis of reading methods texts: What are we told about the nonnative speaker of English? *Journal of Reading Behavior, 26*(2), 159–189.

Bernhardt, E. B. (1994b). Teaching literature or teaching students? *ADFL Bulletin, 26*(2), 5–6.

Bernhardt, E. B. (1998). Sociohistorical perspectives on language teaching in the modern United States. In H. Byrnes (Ed.), *Learning foreign and second languages: Perspectives in research and scholarship* (pp. 39–57). New York: Modern Language Association.

Bernhardt, E. B. (2000). Second language reading as a case study of reading scholarship in the twentieth century. In M. Kamil, P. Mosenthal, D. Pearson, & R. Barr (Eds.), *Handbook of Reading Research Volume III* (pp. 793–811). Hillsdale, NJ: Erlbaum.

Bernhardt, E. B. (2003). Challenges to reading research from a multilingual world. *Reading Research Quarterly, 38*(1), 112–117.

Bernhardt, E. B. (2004). From the guest editor: Introduction to the special issue on research methodology. *Reading in a Foreign Language, 16*(2), i–iii.

Bernhardt, E. B. (2005). Progress and procrastination in second language reading. In M. E. McGroarty (Ed.), *A survey of applied linguistics* (Vol. 25.1, pp. 133–150). West Nyack, NY: Cambridge University Press.

Bernhardt, E. B., & Berman, R. A. (1999). From German 1 to German Studies 001: A chronicle of curricular reform. *Die Unterrichtspraxis, 32*(1), 22–31.

Bernhardt, E. B., & Kamil, M. L. (1995). Interpreting relationships between L1 and L2 reading: Consolidating the linguistic threshold and the linguistic interdependence hypotheses. *Applied Linguistics, 16*(1), 15–34.

Birch, B. M. (2002). *English L2 reading: Getting to the bottom.* Mahwah, NJ: Erlbaum.

Birckbichler, D. E., & Muyskens, J. A. (1980). A personalized approach to the teaching of literature at the elementary and intermediate levels of instruction. *Foreign Language Annals, 13*(1), 23–27.

Blackbourn, D. (2006). *The conquest of nature: Water, landscape, and the making of modern Germany.* New York: Norton.

Block, E. (1992). See how they read: Comprehension monitoring of L1 and L2 readers. *TESOL Quarterly, 26,* 319–343.

Böll, H. (1977). Mein teures Bein. In *Werke: Romane und Erzählungen* (Vol. 1: 1947–1951). Cologne: Middelhauve.

Borbein, V. (Ed.). (1995). *Menschen in Deutschland: Ein Lesebuch für Deutsch als Fremdsprache.* Berlin: Langenscheidt.

Borchert, W. (1949). Nachts schlafen die Ratten doch. In *Das Gesamtwerk* (pp. 216–219). Hamburg: Rowohlt.

Bossers, B. (1991). On thresholds, ceilings, and short circuits: The relation between L1 reading, L2 reading, and L1 knowledge. *AILA Review, 8,* 45–60.

Brantmeier, C. (2003a). Beyond linguistic knowledge: Individual differences in second language reading. *Foreign Language Annals, 36*(1), 33–43.

Brantmeier, C. (2003b). Does gender make a difference? Passage content and comprehension in second language reading. *Reading in a Foreign Language, 15*(1), 1–27.

Brantmeier, C. (2003c). Language skills or passage content? A comparison of native and non-native male and female readers of Spanish. *Applied Language Learning, 13*(2), 183–205.

Brantmeier, C. (2003d). The role of gender and strategy use in processing authentic written input at the intermediate level. *Hispania, 86*(4), 844–856.

Brantmeier, C. (2004a). Gender, violence-oriented passage content and second language reading. *The Reading Matrix: An International Online Journal, 4*(2), 1–19.

Brantmeier, C. (2004b). Statistical procedures for research on L2 reading comprehension: An examination of ANOVA and regression models. *Reading in a Foreign Language, 16*(4), 51–69.

Brantmeier, C. (2005a). Anxiety about L2 reading or L2 reading tasks? A study with advanced language learners. *The Reading Matrix: An International Online Journal, 5*(2), 67–85.

Brantmeier, C. (2005b). Effects of reader's knowledge, text type, and test type on L1 and L2 reading comprehension in Spanish. *The Modern Language Journal, 89*(1), 37–53.

Brantmeier, C. (2006). Toward a multicomponent model of interest and L2 reading: Sources of interest, perceived situational interest, and comprehension. *Reading in a Foreign Language, 18*(2), 89–115.

Bretz, M. L. (1990). Reaction: Literature and communicative competence: A springboard for the development of critical thinking and aesthetic appreciation. *Foreign Language Annals, 23*(4), 335–338.

Brisbois, J. E. (1995). Connections between first- and second-language reading. *Journal of Reading Behavior, 27*(4), 565–584.

Brown, F. (1976). *Principles of educational and psychological testing.* New York: Holt, Rinehardt and Winston.

Cadierno, T. (1995). Formal instruction from a processing perspective: An investigation into the Spanish past tense. *Modern Language Journal, 79*(2), 179–193.

Camiciottoli, B. C. (2003). Metadiscourse and ESP reading comprehension: An exploratory study. *Reading in a Foreign Language, 15*(1), 28–44.

Caño, A. (2009, January 21). Obama propone reinventar América. *El Pais.* Retrieved from http://www.elpais.com/articulo/internacional/Obama/propone/reinventar/America/elpepuint/20090121elpepiint_1/Tes

Carpenter, P. A., & Just, M. A. (1977). Reading comprehension as eyes see it. In M. A. Just & P. A. Carpenter (Eds.), *Cognitive processes in comprehension* (pp. 109–139). Hillsdale, NJ: Erlbaum.

Carrell, P. L. (1983). Three components of background knowledge in reading comprehension. *Language Learning, 33*(2), 183–207.

Carrell, P. L. (1984). Evidence of a formal schema in second language comprehension. *Language Learning, 34*(2), 87–112.

Carrell, P. L. (1987). Content and formal schemata in ESL reading. *TESOL Quarterly, 12*(3), 461–481.

Carrell, P. L. (1991). Second language reading: Reading ability or language proficiency? *Applied Linguistics, 12*(2), 159–179.

Carrell, P. L., & Connor, U. (1991). Reading and writing persuasive texts. *The Modern Language Journal, 75*(3), 314–324.

Carrell, P. L., & Wallace, B. (1983). Background knowledge: Context and familiarity in reading comprehension. In M. A. Clarke & J. Handscombe (Eds.), *On TESOL '82: Pacific perspectives on language learning and teaching* (pp. 245–308). Washington, DC: TESOL.

Carrell, P. L., & Wise, T. E. (1998). The relationship between prior knowledge and topic interest in second language reading. *Studies in Second Language Acquisition, 20*(3), 285–309.

Cattell, J. M. (1885). The inertia of the eye and the brain. *The Brain, 8,* 295–312.

Chan, C. Y. H. (2003). Cultural content and reading proficiency: A comparison of mainland Chinese and Hong Kong learners of English. *Language, Culture, and Curriculum, 16*(1), 60–69.

Chi, F.-M. (1995). EFL readers and a focus on intertextuality. *Journal of Reading, 38*(8), 638–644.

Chikamatsu, N. (1996). The effects of L1 orthography on L2 word recognition: A study of American and Chinese learners of Japanese. *Studies in Second Language Acquisition, 18*(4), 403–432.

Choi, I.-C., & Bachman, L. F. (1992). An investigation into the adequacy of three IRT models for data from two EFL reading tests. *Language Testing, 9*(1), 51–78.

Chu, H.-C. J., Swaffar, J., & Charney, D. H. (2002). Cultural representations of rhetorical conventions: The effects on reading recall. *TESOL Quarterly, 36*(4), 511–541.

Chun, D. M. (2001). L2 reading on the Web: Strategies for accessing information in hypermedia. *Computer Assisted Language Learning, 14*(5), 367–403.

Chun, D. M., & Payne, J. S. (2004). What makes students click: Working memory and look-up behavior. *System, 32*(4), 481–503.

Chun, D. M., & Plass, J. L. (1996). Facilitating reading comprehension with multimedia. *System, 24*(4), 503–519.

Clarke, M. A. (1980). The short circuit hypothesis of ESL reading—or when language competence interferes with reading performance. *Modern Language Journal, 64*(2), 203–209.

Coady, J. (1979). A psycholinguistic model of the ESL reader. In R. Mackay, B. Barkman, & R. R. Jordan (Eds.), *Reading in a second language* (pp. 5–12). Rowley, MA: Newbury House.

Cohen, A., Glasman, H., Rosenbaum-Cohen, P., Ferrara, J., & Fine, J. (1979). Reading English for specialized purposes: Discourse analysis and the use of student informants. *TESOL Quarterly, 13*(4), 551–564.

Coleman, A., & Fife, R. H. (1949). *An analytical bibliography of modern language teaching*. New York: King's Crown.

Connor, U. (1984). Recall of text: Differences between first and second language readers. *TESOL Quarterly, 18*(2), 239–255.

Cummins, J. (1979). Linguistic interdependence and the educational development of bilingual children. *Review of Educational Research, 49*(2), 222–251.

Cummins, J. (1991). Conversational and academic language proficiency in bilingual contexts. *AILA Review, 8*, 75–89.

Currie, P. M. (2006). *The shrine and cult of Muʿīn al-Dīn Chishtī of Ajmer*. New York: Oxford University Press.

Davis, J. N. (1989). "The act of reading" in the foreign language: Pedagogical implications of Iser's reader-response theory. *Modern Language Journal, 73*(4), 420–428.

Davis, J. N. (1992). Reading literature in the foreign language: The comprehension/response connection. *The French Review, 65*(3), 359–370.

Davis, J. N., Gorell, L. C., Kline, R. R., & Hsieh, G. (1992). Readers and foreign languages: A survey of undergraduate attitudes toward the study of literature. *The Modern Language Journal, 76*(3), 320–332.

Day, R. R., & Bamford, J. (1998). *Extensive reading in the second language classroom*. Cambridge: Cambridge University Press.

de Bot, K., Paribakht, T. S., & Wesche, M. B. (1997). Toward a lexical processing model for the study of second language vocabulary acquisition. *Studies in Second Language Acquisition, 19*(3), 309–329.

Degand, L., & Sanders, T. (2002). The impact of relational markers on expository text comprehension in L1 and L2. *Reading and Writing, 15*(7–8), 739–757.

Deville, C., & Chalhoub-Deville, M. (1993). Modified scoring, traditional item analysis and Sato's caution index used to investigate the reading recall protocol. *Language Testing, 10*(2), 117–132.

DiDonato, R., Clyde, M., & Vansant, J. (1995). *Deutsch na klar*. New York: McGraw-Hill.

Donin, J., Graves, B., & Goyette, E. (2004). Second language text comprehension: Processing within a multilayered system. *The Canadian Modern Language Review, 61*(1), 53–76.

Doughty, C., & Long, M. (Eds.). (2003). *The handbook of second language acquisition.* Malden, MA: Blackwell.

DuBravac, S., & Dalle, M. (2002). Reader question formation as a tool for measuring comprehension: Narrative and expository textual inferences in a second language. *Journal of Research in Reading, 25*(2), 217–231.

Dussias, P. E. (2003). Syntactic ambiguity resolution in L2 learners: Some effects of bilinguality on L1 and L2 processing strategies. *Studies in Second Language Acquisition, 25*(4), 529–557.

Dykstra-Pruim, P. (1998). Independent reading for beginners: Using children's books in a reading lab. *Die Unterrichtspraxis, 31*(2), 101.

Ercetin, G. (2003). Exploring ESL learners' use of hypermedia reading glosses. *CALICO Journal, 20*(2), 261–284.

Erlanger, S. (2002, July 2). Dear Euro, they sigh (not fondly). *The New York Times.* Retrieved from http://www.nytimes.com/2002/07/02/world/berlin-journal-dear-euro-they-sigh-not-fondly.html

Esplugas, C., & Landwehr, M. (1996). The use of critical thinking skills in literary analysis. *Foreign Language Annals, 29*(3), 449–461.

Euro ist kein Teuro. (2002, June 4). *Süddeutsche Zeitung.* Retrieved from http://www.sueddeutsche.de/

Everson, M. E. (1998). Word recognition among learners of Chinese as a foreign language: Investigating the relationship between naming and knowing. *The Modern Language Journal, 82*(2), 194–204.

Everson, M. E., & Ke, C. (1997). An inquiry into the reading strategies of intermediate and advanced learners of Chinese as a foreign language. *Journal of the Chinese Language Teachers Association, 32*, 1–20.

Fecteau, M. L. (1999). First- and second-language reading comprehension of literary texts. *Modern Language Journal, 83*(4), 475–493.

Felser, C., Roberts, L., Marinis, T., & Gross, R. (2003). The processing of ambiguous sentences by first and second language learners of English. *Applied Psycholinguistics, 24*, 453–489.

Fender, M. (2008). Spelling knowledge and reading development: Insights from Arab ESL learners. *Reading in a Foreign Language, 20*(1), 19–42.

Flaherty, M. (1998). Success in reading Kanji in second language learners. *Psychological Studies, 43*(1), 5–11.

Frantz, D., & Butler, D. (2002, July 11). The 9/11 inquest: Did Germans bungle? *The New York Times.* Retrieved from http://www.nytimes.com/2002/07/11/international/europe/11GERM.html

Fraser, C. (1999). Lexical processing strategy use and vocabulary learning through reading. *Studies in Second Language Acquisition, 21*(2), 225–241.

Fraser, C. (2000). Linking form and meaning in reading: An example of action research. In J. Lee & A. Valdman (Eds.), *Form and meaning: Multiple perspectives* (pp. 283–303). Boston, MA: Heinle and Heinle.

Fraser, C. (2007). Reading rate in L1 Mandarin Chinese and L2 English across five reading tasks. *The Modern Language Journal, 91*(3), 372–394.

Fukkink, R. G., Hulstijn, J. A. N., & Simis, A. (2005). Does training in second-language word recognition skills affect reading comprehension? An experimental study. *The Modern Language Journal, 89*(1), 54–75.

García, G. E., Montes, J., Janisch, C., Bouchereau, E., & Consalvi, J. (1993). Literacy needs of limited-English students: What information is available to mainstream teachers? In D. J. Leu & C. K. Kinzer (Eds.), *Examining central issues in literacy research, theory, and practice. Forty-second yearbook of the National Reading Conference* (pp. 171–177). Chicago, IL: National Reading Conference.

Gardner, R. C., & Lambert, W. E. (1972). *Attitudes and motivation in second-language learning.* Rowley, MA: Newbury House.

Gascoigne, C. (2002). Documenting the initial second language reading experience: The readers speak. *Foreign Language Annals, 35*(5), 554–560.

Gascoigne, C. (2005). Toward an understanding of the relationship between L2 reading comprehension and grammatical competence. *The Reading Matrix: An International Online Journal, 5*(2), 1–14.

Gersten, R., Baker, S. K., Shanahan, T., Linan-Thompson, S., Collins, P., & Scarcella, R. (2007). *Effective literacy and English language instruction for English learners in the elementary grades: A practice guide (NCEE 2007–4011).* Washington, DC: National Center for Education Evaluation and Regional Assistance, Institute of Education Sciences, U.S. Department of Education.

Ghaith, G. (2003). Effects of the learning together model of cooperative learning on English as a foreign language reading achievement, academic self-esteem, and feelings of school alienation. *Bilingual Research Journal, 27*(3), 451–474.

Ghahraki, S., & Sharifian, F. (2005). The relationship between overall reading comprehension and determination of fact/opinion in L2. *The Reading Matrix: An International Online Journal, 5*(1), 36–46.

Godev, C. B., Martinez-Gibson, E. A., & Toris, C. C. M. (2002). Foreign language reading comprehension test: L1 versus L2 in open-ended questions. *Foreign Language Annals, 35*(2), 202–221.

González, R. (2009, January 21). Barack Obama pide "una nueva era de responsabilidad." *El Mundo.* Retrieved from http://www.elmundo.es/elmundo/2009/01/20/internacional/1232471019.html

Goodman, K. (Ed.). (1968). *The psycholinguistic nature of the reading process.* Detroit, MI: Wayne State University Press.

Gordon, C. M., & Hanauer, D. (1995). The interaction between task and meaning construction in EFL reading comprehension tests. *TESOL Quarterly, 29*(2), 299–324.

Grabe, W. (2009). *Reading in a second language: Moving from theory to practice.* New York: Cambridge University Press.

Grabe, W., & Stoller, F. L. (2002). *Teaching and researching reading.* Harlow, UK: Pearson Education.

Graden, E. C. (1996). How language teachers' beliefs about reading instruction are mediated by their beliefs about students. *Foreign Language Annals, 29*(3), 387–395.

Hacquebord, H. (1999). A Dutch comprehension test for identifying reading problems in L1 and L2 students (Research Note). *Journal of Research in Reading, 22*(3), 299–303.

Haggstrom, M. A. (1992). A performative approach to the study of theater: Bridging the gap between language and literature courses. *The French Review, 66*(1), 7–19.

Hammadou, J. (2000). The impact of analogy and content knowledge on reading comprehension: What helps, what hurts. *The Modern Language Journal, 84*(1), 38–50.

Han, Z., & Anderson, N. J. (Eds.). (2009). *Second language reading research and instruction: Crossing the boundaries.* Ann Arbor: University of Michigan Press.

Han, Z., & D'Angelo, A. (2009). Balancing between comprehension and acquisition: Proposing a dual approach. In Z. Han & N. J. Anderson (Eds.), *Second language reading research and instruction: Crossing the boundaries* (pp. 173–191). Ann Arbor: University of Michigan Press.

Hanauer, D. I. (2001). The task of poetry reading and second language learning. *Applied Linguistics, 22*(3), 295–323.

Hare, V. C. (1982). Preassessment of topical knowledge: A validation and extension. *Journal of Reading Behavior, 14*(1), 77–85.

Harper, S. N. (1988). Strategies for teaching literature at the undergraduate level. *Modern Language Journal, 72*(4), 402–408.

Harrington, M., & Sawyer, M. (1992). L2 working memory capacity and L2 reading skill. *Studies in Second Language Acquisition, 14*, 25–38.

Hawkins, R. (2001). *Second language syntax: A generative introduction.* Walden, MA: Blackwell.

Hayashi, K. (1999). Reading strategies and extensive reading in EFL classes. *RELC Journal, 30*(2), 114–132.

Hayati, A. M., & Pour-Mohammadi, M. (2005). A comparative study of using bilingual and monolingual dictionaries in reading comprehension of intermediate EFL students. *The Reading Matrix: An International Online Journal, 5*(2), 61–66.

Hedgcock, J. S., & Ferris, D. R. (2009). *Teaching readers of English: Students, texts, and contexts.* New York: Routledge.

Heinz, P. (1992). *Toward computerized scoring of reading recalls.* Paper presented at the American Council on the Teaching of Foreign Languages Annual Meeting, Washington, DC.

Heinz, P. (2004). Towards enhanced second language reading comprehension assessment: Computerized versus manual scoring of written recall protocols. *Reading in a Foreign Language, 16*(4), 97–124.

Henning, S. D. (1992). Assessing literary interpretation skills. *Foreign Language Annals, 25*(4), 339–355.

Hirai, A. (1999). The relationship between listening and reading rates of Japanese EFL learners. *The Modern Language Journal, 83*(3), 367–384.

Hirvela, A. (2005). Computer-based reading and writing across the curriculum: Two case studies of L2 writers. *Computers and Composition, 22*(3), 337–356.

Hitosugi, C. I., & Day, R. R. (2004). Extensive reading in Japanese. *Reading in a Foreign Language, 16*(1), 20–39.

Hoffmann, E. F., & James, D. (1986). Toward the integration of foreign language and literature teaching at all levels of the college curriculum. *ADFL Bulletin, 18*(1), 29–33.

Hoover, M. L., & Dwivedi, V. D. (1998). Syntactic processing by skilled bilinguals. *Language Learning, 48*(1), 1–29.

Horiba, Y. (1996). Comprehension processes in L2 reading: Language competence, textual coherence, and inferences. *Studies in Second Language Acquisition, 18*(4), 433–473.

Horst, M. (2005). Learning L2 vocabulary through extensive reading: A measurement study. *The Canadian Modern Language Review, 61*(3), 355–382.

Howatt, A. P. R. (1991). *A history of English language teaching.* Oxford: Oxford University Press.

Hudelson, S. (Ed.). (1981). *Learning to read in different languages.* Washington, DC: Center for Applied Linguistics.

Hudson, T. (1991). A content comprehension approach to reading English for science and technology. *TESOL Quarterly, 25*, 77–104.

Hudson, T. (2007). *Teaching second language reading.* Oxford: Oxford University Press.

Huey, E. B. (1908). *The psychology and pedagogy of reading.* New York: Macmillan.

Huggins, A. W. F., & Adams, M. J. (1980). Syntactic aspects of reading comprehension. In R. Spiro, B. Bruce, & W. Brewer (Eds.), *Theoretical issues in reading comprehension* (pp. 87–112). Hillsdale, NJ: Erlbaum.

Hui-Tzu, M. (2008). EFL vocabulary acquisition and retention: Reading plus vocabulary enhancement activities and narrow reading. *Language Learning, 58*(1), 73–115.

Hulstijn, J. H. (1993). When do foreign-language readers look up the meaning of unfamiliar words? The influence of task and learner variables. *The Modern Language Journal, 77*(2), 139–147.

Iwahori, Y. (2008). Developing reading fluency: A study of extensive reading in EFL. *Reading in a Foreign Language, 20*(1), 70–91.

James, D. (1989). Re-shaping the "college-level" curriculum: Problems and possibilities. In H. S. Lepke (Ed.), *Shaping the future: Challenges and opportunities* (pp. 79–110). Middlebury, VT: Northeast Conference on the Teaching of Foreign Languages.

Javal, E. (1879). Essai sur la physiologie de la lecture. *Annaels d'oculistique, 82,* 242–253.

Jiménez, R. T. (1997). The strategic reading abilities and potential of five low-literacy Latina/o readers in middle school. *Reading Research Quarterly, 32*(3), 224–243.

Jiménez, R. T., García, G. E., & Pearson, P. D. (1995). Three children, two languages, and strategic reading: Case studies in bilingual monolingual reading. *American Educational Research Journal, 32*(1), 31–61.

Jiménez, R. T., Garcia, G. E., & Pearson, P. D. (1996). The reading strategies of bilingual Latina/o students who are successful English readers: Opportunities and obstacles. *Reading Research Quarterly, 31*(1), 90–112.

Johnson, K. E. (1992). The relationship between teachers' beliefs and practices during literacy instruction for nonnative speakers of English. *Journal of Reading Behavior, 24,* 83–108.

Johnson, P. (1981). Effects on reading comprehension of language complexity and cultural background of a text. *TESOL Quarterly, 15*(2), 169–181.

Johnson, P. (1982). Effects on comprehension of building background knowledge. *TESOL Quarterly, 16*(4), 503–516.

Juffs, A. (1998). Main verb versus reduced relative clause ambiguity resolution in L2 sentence processing. *Language Learning, 48*(1), 107–147.

Kafka, F. (1970). Vor dem Gesetz [1915]. In P. Raabe (Ed.), *Sämtliche Erzählungen.* Frankfurt am Main: Fischer.

Kamhi-Stein, L. D. (2003). Reading in two languages: How attitudes toward home language and beliefs about reading affect the behaviors of "underprepared" L2 college readers. *TESOL Quarterly, 37*(1), 37–71.

Kamil, M. L., Mosenthal, P., Pearson, D., & Barr, R. (Eds.). (2000). *Handbook of reading research* (Vol. 3). Mahwah, NJ: Erlbaum.

Kasper, L. F. (2003). Interactive hypertext and the development of ESL students' reading skills. *The Reading Matrix: An International Online Journal, 3*(3).

Keeves, J., & Watanabe, Y. (Eds.). (2003). *The international handbook of educational research.* New York: Kluwer.

Kellerman, E. (1985). If at first you do succeed... In S. Gass & C. Madden (Eds.), *Input in second-language acquisition* (pp. 345–353). Rowley, MA: Newbury House.

Kern, R. G. (1994). The role of mental translation in second language reading. *Studies in Second Language Acquisition, 16,* 441–461.

Kern, R. G. (2000). *Literacy and language teaching.* Oxford: Oxford University Press.

Keshavarz, M. H., Atai, M. R., & Ahmadi, H. (2007). Content schemata, linguistic simplification, and EFL readers' comprehension and recall. *Reading in a Foreign Language, 19*(1), 19–33.

Khaldieh, S. A. (2001). The relationship between knowledge of Icraab, lexical knowledge, and reading comprehension of nonnative readers of Arabic. *The Modern Language Journal, 85*(3), 416–431.

Khitab al-tansib: Inaugural address. (2009, January 21). Retrieved from http://aljazeera. net/news/archive/archive?ArchiveId=1167292

Kim, M. (2004). Literature discussions in adult L2 learning. *Language, Culture, and Curriculum, 18*(2), 145–166.

Kim, S.-A. (1995). Types and sources of problems in L2 reading: A qualitative analysis of the recall protocols by Korean high school EFL students. *Foreign Language Annals, 28*(1), 49–70.

Kintsch, W. (1974). *The representation of meaning in memory.* Hillsdale, NJ: Erlbaum.

Kitajima, R. (1997). Referential strategy training for second language reading comprehension of Japanese texts. *Foreign Language Annals, 30*(1), 84–97.

Knight, S. (1994). Dictionary: The tool of last resort in foreign language reading? A new perspective. *The Modern Language Journal, 78*(3), 285–299.

Knutson, E. M. (1993). Teaching whole texts: Literature and foreign language reading instruction. *The French Review, 67*(1), 12–26.

Knutson, E. M. (1997). Reading with a purpose: Communicative reading tasks for the foreign language classroom. *Foreign Language Annals, 30*(1), 49–57.

Ko, M. H. (2005). Glosses, comprehension, and strategy use. *Reading in a Foreign Language, 17*(2), 125–143.

Koda, K. (1993). Transferred L1 strategies and L2 syntactic structure in L2 sentence comprehension. *The Modern Language Journal, 77*(4), 490–499.

Koda, K. (1998). The role of phonemic awareness in second language reading. *Second Language Research, 14*(2), 194–215.

Koda, K. (1999). Development of L2 intraword orthographic sensitivity and decoding skills. *Modern Language Journal, 83*(1), 51–64.

Koda, K. (2005). *Insights into second language reading: A cross-linguistic approach.* Cambridge, UK: Cambridge University Press.

Kol, S., & Schcolnik, M. (2000). Enhancing screen reading strategies. *CALICO Journal, 18*(1), 67–80.

Kondo-Brown, K. (2006a). Affective variables and Japanese L2 reading ability. *Reading in a Foreign Language, 18*(1), 55–71.

Kondo-Brown, K. (2006b). How do English L1 learners of advanced Japanese infer unknown *kanji* words in authentic texts? *Language Learning, 56*(1), 109–153.

Kramsch, C. (1985). Literary texts in the classroom: A discourse perspective. *Modern Language Journal, 69*(4), 356–366.

Kramsch, C. (1998). Constructing second language acquisition research in foreign language departments. In H. Byrnes (Ed.), *Learning foreign and second languages: Perspectives in research and scholarship* (pp. 23–38). New York: Modern Language Association.

Kramsch, C., & Kramsch, O. (2000). The avatars of literature in language study. *Modern Language Journal, 84*(4), 553–573.

Kramsch, C., & Nolden, T. (1994). Redefining literacy in a foreign language. *Die Unterrichtspraxis, 27*, 28–35.

Kroll, J. F., Michael, E., Tokowicz, N., & Dufour, R. (2002). The development of lexical fluency in a second language. *Second Language Research, 18*(2), 137–171.

Kweon, S.-O., & Kim, H.-R. (2008). Beyond raw frequency: Incidental vocabulary acquisition in extensive reading. *Reading in a Foreign Language, 20*(2), 191–215.

LaBerge, D., & Samuels, S. J. (1974). Toward a theory of automatic information processing in reading. *Cognitive Psychology, 6*, 293–323.

La capa de ozono: Chile en el ojo del huracán. (2000, December 6). *Cronica.* Retrieved from http://www.cronica.cl

Lai, F.-K. (1993). The effect of a summer reading course on reading and writing skills. *System, 21*(1), 87–100.

Laufer, B., & Hadar, L. (1997). Assessing the effectiveness of monolingual, bilingual, and "bilingualised" dictionaries in the comprehension and production of new words. *The Modern Language Journal, 81*(2), 189–196.

Lazarte, A., & Barry, S. (2008). Syntactic complexity and L2 academic immersion effects on readers' recall and pausing strategies. *Language Learning, 58*(4), 785–834.

Lee, J. F. (1986). Background knowledge and L2 reading. *Modern Language Journal, 70*(4), 350–354.

Lee, J. F. (2002). The incidental acquisition of Spanish future tense morphology through reading in a second language. *Studies in Second Language Acquisition, 24*(1), 55–80.

Lee, J. W., & Schallert, D. L. (1997). The relative contribution of L2 language proficiency and L1 reading ability to L2 reading performance: A test of the threshold hypothesis in an EFL context. *TESOL Quarterly, 31*(4), 713–739.

Lee, S.-K. (2007). Effects of textual enhancement and topic familiarity on Korean EFL students' reading comprehension and learning of passive form. *Language Learning, 57*(1), 87–118.

Leeser, M. J. (2007). Learner-based factors in L2 reading comprehension and processing grammatical form: Topic familiarity and working memory. *Language Learning, 57*(2), 229–270.

Leffa, V. J. (1992). Making foreign language texts comprehensible for beginners: An experiment with an electronic glossary. *System, 20*(1), 63–74.

Lemke, J. (1990). *Talking science: Language, learning, and values.* Norwood, NJ: Ablex.

Leow, R. P. (2001). Two departments—applied linguistics—do learners notice enhanced forms while interacting with the L2?: An online and offline study of the role of written input enhancement in L2 reading. *Hispania, 84*(3), 496–509.

Leow, R. P., Ego, T., Nuevo, A. M., & Tsai, Y.-C. (2003). The roles of textual enhancement and type of linguistic item in adult L2 learners' comprehension and intake. *Applied Language Learning, 13*(2), 1–16.

Leung, C. Y. (2002). Extensive reading and language learning: A diary study of a beginning learner of Japanese. *Reading in a Foreign Language, 14*(1), 66–81.

Lide, F. (1990). Literature and the foreign language enterprise: A problematic relationship. *Polylingua, 1*(2), 103–123.

Light, R. J. (2001). *Making the most of college.* Cambridge, MA: Harvard University Press.

Liu, J. (2004). Effects of comic strips on L2 learners' reading comprehension. *TESOL Quarterly, 38*(2), 225–243.

Lumley, T. (1993). The notion of subskills in reading comprehension tests: An EAP example. *Language Testing, 10*, 211–234.

Lund, R. (1991). A comparison of second language listening and reading comprehension. *The Modern Language Journal, 75*(2), 196–204.

Luppescu, S., & Day, R. R. (1993). Reading, dictionaries, and vocabulary learning. *Language Learning, 43*(2), 263–287.

MacKay, R., Barkman, B., & Jordan, R. R. (Eds.). (1979). *Reading in a second language.* Rowley, MA: Newbury House.

Maeng, U. (2005). A comparative study of reading strategies in L1 and L2: Case study of five Korean graduate students. *Language Research (Ohak yon'gu), 41*(2), 457–486.

Mann, T. (1999). *Death in Venice, Tonio Kröger, and other writings.* New York: Continuum.

Marinis, T., Roberts, L., Felser, C., & Clahsen, H. (2005). Gaps in second language sentence processing. *Studies in Second Language Acquisition, 27*(1), 53–78.

Mason, B., & Krashen, S. (1997). Extensive reading in English as a foreign language. *System, 25*(1), 91–102.

Maxim II, H. H. (2002). A study into the feasibility and effects of reading extended authentic discourse in the beginning German language classroom. *The Modern Language Journal, 86*(1), 20–35.

McConkie, G., & Rayner, K. (1975). The span of the effective stimulus during a fixation in reading. *Perception and Psychophysics, 17,* 578–586.

McKinley Jr., J. C. (2006, March 3). With 65 still entombed at Mexican mine, ache deepens. *The New York Times.* Retrieved from http://www.nytimes.com/2006/03/03/international/americas/03mexico.html?fta=y

Mills, N. (2006). A reevaluation of the role of anxiety: Self-efficacy, anxiety, and their relation to reading and listening proficiency. *Foreign Language Annals, 39*(2), 276–295.

Mohammed, M. A. H., & Swales, J. M. (1984). Factors affecting the successful reading of technical instructions. *Reading in a Foreign Language, 2*(2), 206–217.

Mokhtari, K., & Reichard, C. (2004). Investigating the strategic reading processes of first and second language readers in two different cultural contexts. *System, 32*(3), 379–394.

Mori, S. (2002). Redefining motivation to read in a foreign language. *Reading in a Foreign Language, 14*(2), 91–110.

Mori, Y., & Nagy, W. (1999). Integration of information from context and word elements in interpreting novel Kanji compounds. *Reading Research Quarterly, 34*(1), 80–101.

Morrison, L. (2004). Comprehension monitoring in first and second language reading. *The Canadian Modern Language Review, 61*(1), 77–106.

Mosenthal, P., & Kamil, M. (1991). Understanding progress in reading research. In R. Barr, M. Kamil, P. Mosenthal, & P. D. Pearson (Eds.), *Handbook of reading research* (Vol. 2, pp. 1013–1046). New York: Longman.

Muyskens, J. A. (1983). Teaching second-language literatures: Past, present, and future. *Modern Language Journal, 67*(4), 413–423.

Nakada, T., Fujii, Y., & Kwee, I. L. (2001). Brain strategies for reading in the second language are determined by the first language. *Neuroscience Research, 40*(4), 351–358.

Nassaji, H. (2003). Higher-level and lower-level text processing skills in advanced ESL reading comprehension. *The Modern Language Journal, 87*(2), 261–276.

Nassaji, H. (2004). The relationship between depth of vocabulary knowledge and L2 learners' lexical inferencing strategy use and success. *The Canadian Modern Language Review, 61*(1), 107–134.

National Institute of Child Health and Human Development (NICHD). (2000). *Teaching children to read: An evidence-based assessment of the scientific research literature on reading and its implications for reading instruction: Reports of the subgroups.* Washington, DC: National Institute of Child Health and Human Development.

Nishino, T. (2007). Beginning to read extensively: A case study with Mako and Fumi. *Reading in a Foreign Language, 19*(2), 76–105.

Oded, B., & Walters, J. (2001). Deeper processing for better EFL reading comprehension. *System, 29*(3), 357–370.

Odlin, T. (1989). *Language transfer: Cross-linguistic influence in language learning.* Cambridge: Cambridge University Press.

Odlin, T. (2003). Cross-linguistic influence. In C. Doughty & M. Long (Eds.), *The handbook of second-language acquisition* (pp. 436–486). Malden, MA: Blackwell.

Oh, S.-Y. (2001). Two types of input modification and EFL reading comprehension: Simplification versus elaboration. *TESOL Quarterly, 35*(1), 69–96.

Organisation for Economic Co-operation and Development (OECD). (2006). *Assessing scientific, reading and mathematical literacy: A framework for PISA 2006.* Paris: OECD.

Ozono, S., & Harumi, I. (2003). Logical connectives as catalysts for interactive L2 reading. *System, 31*(2), 283–297.

Parel, R. (2004). The impact of lexical inferencing strategies on second language reading proficiency. *Reading and Writing, 17*(6), 847–873.

Paribakht, T. S. (2005). The influence of first language lexicalization on second language lexical inferencing: A study of Farsi-speaking learners of English as a foreign language. *Language Learning, 55*(4), 701–748.

Paribakht, T. S., & Wesche, M. (1999). Reading and "incidental" vocabulary acquisition: An introspective study of lexical inferencing. *Studies in Second Language Acquisition, 21*(2), 195–224.

Park, G.-P. (2004). Developing the interpretive mode of communication—comparison of L2 listening and reading comprehension by university students learning English in Korea. *Foreign Language Annals, 37*(3), 448–458.

Parry, K. (1991). Building vocabulary through academic reading. *TESOL Quarterly, 25,* 629–653.

Parry, K. (1996). Culture, literacy, and reading. *TESOL Quarterly, 30*(4), 665–692.

Peace, security isusulong ni Obama. (2009, January 22). *Abante.* Retrieved from http://www.abante.com.ph/issue/jan2209/abroad01.htm

Pearson, P. D., Barr, R., Kamil, M., & Mosenthal, P. (Eds.). (1984). *Handbook of reading research* (Vol. 1). New York: Longman.

Peck, J. M. (1992). Toward a cultural hermeneutics of the "foreign" language classroom: Notes for a critical and political pedagogy. *ADFL Bulletin, 23*(3), 11–17.

Perkins, K., Gupta, L., & Tammana, R. (1995). Predicting item difficulty in a reading comprehension test with an artificial neural network. *Language Testing, 12*(1), 34–53.

Phakiti, A. (2003). A closer look at gender and strategy use in L2 reading. *Language Learning, 53*(4), 649–702.

Pichette, F. (2005). Time spent on reading and reading comprehension in second language learning. *The Canadian Modern Language Review, 62*(2), 243–262.

Pichette, F., Segalowitz, N., & Connors, K. (2003). Impact of maintaining L1 reading skills on L2 reading skill development in adults: Evidence from speakers of Serbo-Croatian learning French. *The Modern Language Journal, 87*(3), 391–403.

Pigada, M., & Schmitt, N. (2006). Vocabulary acquisition from extensive reading: A case study. *Reading in a Foreign Language, 18*(1), 1–28.

Prichard, C. (2008). Evaluating L2 readers' vocabulary strategies and dictionary use. *Reading in a Foreign Language, 20*(2), 216–231.

Pulido, D. (2003). Modeling the role of second language proficiency and topic familiarity in second language incidental vocabulary acquisition through reading. *Language Learning, 53*(2), 233–284.

Pulido, D. (2004a). The effect of cultural familiarity on incidental vocabulary acquisition through reading. *The Reading Matrix: An International Online Journal, 4*(2), 20–53.

Pulido, D. (2004b). The relationship between text comprehension and second language incidental vocabulary acquisition: A matter of topic familiarity? *Language Learning, 54*(3), 469–523.

Pulido, D. (2007). The relationship between text comprehension and second language incidental vocabulary acquisition: A matter of topic familiarity? *Language Learning, 57*(Supplement 1), 155–199.

Pulido, D., & Hambrick, D. (2008). The *virtuous* circle: Modeling individual differences in L2 reading and vocabulary development. *Reading in a Foreign Language, 20*(2), 164–190.

Purcell, J. M. (1988). Cultural appreciation through literature. *Foreign Language Annals, 21*(1), 19–24.

RAND Reading Study Group. (2002). *Reading for understanding: Toward a R&D program in reading comprehension.* Santa Monica, CA: RAND Corporation.

Ratych, J. (1985). Zwei Jahrzehnte literarische Lehrbücher. In M. Heid (Ed.), *New Yorker Werkstattgespräch 1984: Literarische Texte im Fremdsprachenunterricht.* (pp. 68–84). Munich: Kemmler & Hoch.

Renandya, W. A., Rajan, B. R. S., & Jacobs, G. M. (1999). Extensive reading with adult learners of English as a second language. *RELC Journal, 30*(1), 39–51.

Rice, D. B. (1991). Language proficiency and textual theory: How the twain might meet. *ADFL Bulletin, 22*(3), 12–15.

Richardson, V. (Ed.). (2001). *The handbook of research on teaching.* Washington, DC: American Educational Research Association.

Riley, G. L. (1993). A story approach to narrative text comprehension. *The Modern Language Journal, 77*(4), 417–430.

Riley, G. L., & Lee, J. F. (1996). A comparison of recall and summary protocols as measures of second language reading comprehension. *Language Testing, 13*(2), 173–187.

Rohter, L. (2002, December 27). In an upside-down world, sunshine is shunned. *The New York Times.* Retrieved from http://www.nytimes.com/2002/12/27/international/americas/27CHIL.html

Rott, S. (1999). The effect of exposure frequency on intermediate language learners' incidental vocabulary acquisition and retention through reading. *Studies in Second Language Acquisition, 21*(4), 589–619.

Rott, S. (2004). A comparison of output interventions and un-enhanced reading conditions on vocabulary acquisition and text comprehension. *The Canadian Modern Language Review, 61*(2), 169–202.

Rott, S. (2005). Processing glosses: A qualitative exploration of how form-meaning connections are established. *Reading in a Foreign Language, 17*(2), 95–124.

Rott, S. (2007). The effect of frequency of input-enhancements on word learning and text comprehension. *Language Learning, 57*(2), 165–199.

Rott, S., & Williams, J. (2003). Making form-meaning connections while reading: A qualitative analysis of word processing. *Reading in a Foreign Language, 15*(1), 45–75.

Rumelhart, D. (1977). Toward an interactive model of reading. In S. Dornic (Ed.), *Attention and Performance 6* (pp. 573–603). Hillsdale, NJ: Erlbaum.

Rusciolelli, J. (1995). Student responses to reading strategies instruction. *Foreign Language Annals, 28*(2), 262–273.

Safire, W. (2009, January 20). "The Speech": The Experts' Critique. *The New York Times.* Retrieved from http://roomfordebate.blogs.nytimes.com/2009/01/20/the-speech-the-experts-critique/

Saiegh-Haddad, E. (2003). Bilingual oral reading fluency and reading comprehension: The case of Arabic/Hebrew (L1)-English (L2) readers. *Reading and Writing, 16*(8), 717–736.

Saito, Y., Garza, T. J., & Horwitz, E. K. (1999). Foreign language reading anxiety. *The Modern Language Journal, 83*(2), 202–218.

Sakar, A., & Ercetin, G. (2005). Effectiveness of hypermedia annotations for foreign language reading. *Journal of Computer Assisted Language Learning, 21*(1), 28–38.

Salataci, R., & Akyel, A. (2002). Possible effects of strategy instruction on L1 and L2 reading. *Reading in a Foreign Language, 14*(1), 1–17.

Salmani-Nodoushan, M. A. (2003). Text familiarity, reading tasks, and ESP test performance: A study on Iranian LEP and non-LEP university students. *The Reading Matrix: An International Online Journal, 3*(1), 1–14.

Saricoban, A. (2002). Reading strategies of successful readers through the three phase approach. *The Reading Matrix: An International Online Journal, 2*(3), 1–16.

Scarcella, R. (2002). Some key factors affecting English learners' development of advanced literacy. In M. J. Schleppegrell & M. C. Colombi (Eds.), *Developing advanced literacy in first and second languages: Meaning with power* (pp. 209–226). Mahwah, NJ: Erlbaum.

Schleppegrell, M. J., & Colombi, M. C. (2002). *Developing advanced literacy in first and second languages: Meaning with power.* Mahwah, NJ: Erlbaum.

Schlink, B. (1995). *Der Vorleser.* Zurich: Diogenes.

Schulz, R. A. (1981). Literature and readability: Bridging the gap in foreign language reading. *Modern Language Journal, 65*(1), 43–53.

Scott, V., & Huntington, J. (2007). Literature, the interpretative mode, and novice learners. *The Modern Language Journal, 91*(1), 3–14.

Seng, G. H., & Hashim, F. (2006). Use of L1 in L2 reading comprehension among tertiary ESL learners. *Reading in a Foreign Language, 18*(1), 29–54.

Sengupta, S. (1999). Rhetorical consciousness raising in the L2 reading classroom. *Journal of Second Language Writing, 8*(3), 291–319.

Sengupta, S. (2002). Developing academic reading at tertiary level: A longitudinal study tracing conceptual change. *The Reading Matrix: An International Online Journal, 2*(1), 1–37.

Shanahan, D. (1997). Articulating the relationship between language, literature, and culture: Toward a new agenda for foreign language teaching and research. *Modern Language Journal, 81*(2), 164–174.

Shanahan, T., Kamil, M., & Tobin, A. (1982). Cloze as a measure of intersentential comprehension. *Reading Research Quarterly, 17*(2), 229–255.

Shang, H.-F. (2005). Email dialogue journaling: Attitudes and impact on L2 reading performance. *Educational Studies, 31*(2), 197–212.

Shohamy, E. (1984). Does the testing method make a difference? The case of reading comprehension. *Language Testing, 1*, 147–170.

Shook, D. J. (1996). Foreign language literature and the beginning learner-reader. *Language Annals, 29*(2), 201–216.

Shumway, N. (1995). Searching for Averroes: Reflections on why it is desirable and impossible to teach culture in foreign language courses. In C. Kramsch (Ed.), *Redefining the boundaries of language study* (pp. 251–260). Boston, MA: Heinle and Heinle.

Silberstein, S. (1994). *Techniques and resources in teaching reading*. Oxford: Oxford University Press.

Smith, F. (1971). *Understanding reading*. New York: Holt, Rinehart and Winston.

Stanovich, K. E. (1980). Toward an interactive-compensatory model of individual differences in the acquisition of literacy. *Reading Research Quarterly, 16*(1), 32–71.

Stavans, A., & Oded, B. (1993). Assessing EFL reading comprehension: The case of Ethiopian learners. *System, 21*(4), 481–494.

Steffensen, M. S. (1988). Changes in cohesion in the recall of native and foreign texts. In P. L. Carrell, J. Devine, & D. E. Eskey (Eds.), *Interactive approaches to second language reading* (pp. 140–151). Cambridge: Cambridge University Press.

Steffensen, M. S., Joag-Dev, C., & Anderson, R. C. (1979). A cross-cultural perspective on reading comprehension. *Reading Research Quarterly, 15*(1), 10–29.

Stevenson, M., Schoonen, R., & de Glopper, K. (2007). Inhibition or compensation? A multidimensional comparison of reading processes in Dutch and English. *Language Learning, 57*(Supplement 1), 115–154.

Stott, N. (2004). Familiarity breeds contempt: Reading texts from learners' own cultures does not guarantee recall. *TESOL Quarterly, 38*(2), 345–352.

Suh, J.-S. (1999). The effects of reading instruction on reading attitude and reading process by Korean students learning English as a second language. *Applied Language Learning, 10*(1–2), 77–122.

Swaffar, J. (1988). Readers, texts, and second languages: The interactive processes. *Modern Language Journal, 72*(2), 123–149.

Swaffar, J., & Arens, K. (2006). *Remapping the foreign language curriculum: An approach through multiple literacies*. New York: Modern Language Association.

Swaffar, J. K., Arens, K. M., & Byrnes, H. (1991). *Reading for meaning: An integrated approach to language learning*. Englewood Cliffs, NJ: Prentice Hall.

Taguchi, E., & Gorsuch, G. J. (2002). Transfer effects of repeated EFL reading on reading new passages: A preliminary investigation. *Reading in a Foreign Language, 14*(1), 43–65.

Taguchi, E., Takayasu-Maass, M., & Gorsuch, G. J. (2004). Developing reading fluency in EFL: How assisted repeated reading and extensive reading affect fluency development. *Reading in a Foreign Language, 16*(2), 70–96.

Taillefer, G., & Pugh, T. (1998). Strategies for professional reading in L1 and L2. *Journal of Research in Reading, 21*(2), 96–108.

Takase, A. (2007). Japanese high school students' motivation for extensive L2 reading. *Reading in a Foreign Language, 19*(1), 1–18.

Tang, G. (1992). The effect of graphic representations of knowledge structures on ESL reading comprehension. *Studies in Second Language Acquisition, 14*, 177–195.

Tian, G. S. (1991). Higher order reading comprehension skills in literature learning and teaching at the lower secondary school level in Singapore. *RELC Journal, 22*, 29–43.

Une taupe islamiste dans la police du Hambourg. (2002, July 9). *Le Figaro*. Retrieved from http://www.lefigaro.fr

Upton, T. A., & Lee-Thompson, L.-C. (2001). The role of the first language in second language reading. *Studies in Second Language Acquisition, 23*(4), 469–495.

Uso-Juan, E. (2006). The compensatory nature of discipline-related knowledge in English-language proficiency in reading English for academic purposes. *The Modern Language Journal, 90*(1), 210–227.

Van Dijk, T. A. (1979). Recalling and summarizing complex discourse. In W. Burghardt & K. Hoelker (Eds.), *Text processing: Papers in text analysis and description* (pp. 49–118). Berlin: de Gruyter.

Van Gelderen, A., Schoonen, R., De Glopper, K., Hulstijn, J., Snellings, P., Simis, A., et al. (2003). Roles of linguistic knowledge, metacognitive knowledge and processing speed in L3, L2 and L1 reading comprehension: A structural equation modeling approach. *The International Journal of Bilingualism, 7*(1), 7–25.

Van Gelderen, A., Schoonen, R., De Glopper, K., Hulstijn, J., Simis, A., Snellings, P., et al. (2004). Linguistic knowledge, processing speed, and metacognitive knowledge in first- and second-language reading comprehension: A componential analysis. *Journal of Educational Psychology, 96*(1), 19–30.

VanPatten, B. (1996). *Input processing and grammar instruction*. Norwood, NJ: Ablex.

VanPatten, B., & Cadierno, T. (1993). Input processing and second language acquisition: A role for instruction. *Modern Language Journal, 77*(1), 45–57.

Van Wijnendaele, I., & Brysbaert, M. (2002). Visual word recognition in bilinguals: Phonological priming from the second to the first language. *Journal of Experimental Psychology: Human Perception and Performance, 28*(3), 616–627.

Wade-Woolley, L. (1999). First language influences on second language word reading: All roads lead to Rome. *Language Learning, 49*(3), 447–471.

Wade-Woolley, L., & Geva, E. (1999). Processing of inflected morphology in second language word recognition: Russian-speakers and English-speakers read Hebrew. *Reading and Writing, 11*(4), 321–343.

Wallace, C. (1986). *Learning to read in a multicultural society: The context of second language literacy*. Oxford: Pergamon Press.

Wallace, C. (1992). *Reading*. Oxford: Oxford University Press.

Wallraff, G. (1990). *Ganz unten*. New York: Taylor & Francis.

Walter, C. (2004). Transfer of reading comprehension skills to L2 is linked to mental representations of text and to L2 working memory. *Applied Linguistics, 25*(3), 315–339.

Waring, R., & Takaki, M. (2003). At what rate do learners learn and retain new vocabulary from reading a graded reader? *Reading in a Foreign Language, 15*(2), 130–163.

Weber, R. N. (1991). Linguistic diversity and reading in American society. In R. Barr, M. L. Kamil, P. Mosenthal, & P. D. Pearson (Eds.), *The handbook of reading research* (Vol. 2, pp. 97–119). New York: Longman.

Wesche, M. B., & Paribakht, T. S. (2000). Reading-based exercises in second language vocabulary learning: An introspective study. *The Modern Language Journal, 84*(2), 196–213.

Wolf, D. F. (1993). A comparison of assessment tasks used to measure FL reading comprehension. *The Modern Language Journal, 77*(4), 473–489.

Wong, W. (2003). Textual enhancement and simplified input effects on L2 comprehension and acquisition of non-meaningful grammatical form. *Applied Language Learning, 13*(2), 17–45.

Yamashita, J. (2002a). Mutual compensation between L1 reading ability and L2 language proficiency in L2 reading comprehension. *Journal of Research in Reading, 25*(1), 81–95.

Yamashita, J. (2002b). Reading strategies in L1 and L2: Comparison of four groups of readers with different reading ability in L1 and L2. *ITL: Review of Applied Linguistics, 135–136,* 1–35.

Yamashita, J. (2004). Reading attitudes in L1 and L2, and their influence on L2 extensive reading. *Reading in a Foreign Language, 16*(1), 1–19.

Yang, Y.-F. (2002). Reassessing readers' comprehension monitoring. *Reading in a Foreign Language, 14*(1), 18–42.

Yano, Y., Long, M. H., & Ross, S. (1994). The effects of simplified and elaborated texts on foreign language reading comprehension. *Language Learning, 44*(2), 189–219.

Yigiter, K., Saricoban, A., & Gürses, T. (2005). Reading strategies employed by ELT learners at the advanced level. *The Reading Matrix: An International Online Journal, 5*(1), 124–139.

Ying, H. G. (2004). Relevance mapping: A study of second language learners' processing of syntactically ambiguous sentences in English. *Second Language Research, 20*(3), 232–255.

Young, D. N. (1999). Linguistic simplification of SL reading material: Effective instructional practice? *The Modern Language Journal, 83*(3), 350–366.

Zimmerman, C. B. (1997). Do reading and interactive vocabulary instruction make a difference? An empirical study. *TESOL Quarterly, 31*(1), 121–140.

Zuck, L. V., & Zuck, I. G. (1984). The main idea: Specialist and nonspecialist judgments. In A. K. Pugh & I. M. Ulijn (Eds.), *Reading for professional purposes: Studies and practices in native and foreign languages* (pp. 130–135). London: Heinemann.

Zyzik, E., & Polio, C. (2008). Incidental focus on form in university Spanish literature courses. *The Modern Language Journal, 92*(1), 53–70.

Index